TOUCHED
BY
SUICIDE

TOUCHED

BY

SUICIDE

HOPE AND HEALING AFTER LOSS

Michael F. Myers, M.D.,
and Carla Fine

GOTHAM BOOKS

GOTHAM BOOKS
Published by Penguin Group (USA) Inc.
375 Hudson Street, New York, New York 10014, U.S.A.
Penguin Group (Canada), 90 Eglinton East, Toronto, Ontario M4P 2Y3, Canada (a division of Pearson
Penguin Canada Inc.); Penguin Books Ltd, 80 Strand, London WC2R 0RL, England; Penguin Ireland,
25 St Stephen's Green, Dublin 2, Ireland (a division of Penguin Books Ltd); Penguin Group
(Australia), 250 Camberwell Road, Camberwell, Victoria 3124, Australia (a division of Pearson
Australia Group Pty Ltd); Penguin Books India Pvt Ltd, 11 Community Centre, Panchsheel Park, New
Delhi - 110 017, India; Penguin Group (NZ), cnr Airborne and Rosedale Roads, Albany, Auckland
1310, New Zealand (a division of Pearson New Zealand Ltd); Penguin Books (South Africa) (Pty)
Ltd, 24 Sturdee Avenue, Rosebank, Johannesburg 2196, South Africa

Penguin Books Ltd, Registered Offices: 80 Strand, London WC2R 0RL, England

Published by Gotham Books, a member of Penguin Group (USA) Inc.

First printing, September 2006
10 9 8 7 6 5 4 3 2 1

LIBRARY OF CONGRESS CATALOGING-IN-PUBLICATION DATA

Myers, Michael F.
Touched by suicide : hope and healing after loss /
by Michael F. Myers and Carla Fine.
p. cm.
Includes bibliographical references.
ISBN 1-592-40228-3 (trade pbk.)
1. Suicide—Psychological aspects. 2. Bereavement—Psychological aspects.
3. Suicide victims—Family relationships. I. Fine, Carla. II. Title.
HV6545.M94 2006
362.28'3019—dc22   2005035667

Printed in the United States of America
Set in Palatino
Designed by Ginger Legato

To Joice, Briana, and Zachary,
for your abiding love and wisdom. (MM)

To my dear husband, Allen Oster,
for showing me that the capacity to love and be loved
is never extinguished. (CF)

Contents

PART THREE
HOW CAN I GO ON? FINDING MEANING AFTER SUICIDE

Conclusion

Acknowledgments

We are extremely grateful to the many survivors who shared their intimate stories with us as well as the numerous experts who contributed their most current research and knowledge. Their insights and observations enrich our understanding of suicide and offer hope to the millions of people throughout the world whose lives are touched by suicide every day.

We would especially like to thank Dr. Frank Campbell of the Baton Rouge Crisis Intervention Center for his dedication in making sure that survivors are never overlooked in the study and research of suicide, and to Senator Gordon and Mrs. Sharon Smith for their tremendous courage and public commitment to preventing and understanding suicide. The generosity of the time and wisdom of these three special people pays tribute to the memories of all of our loved ones who have been lost to suicide.

We are indebted to Dr. Kay Redfield Jamison for her kindness in writing the Foreword to our book. Her words of endorsement mean a great deal to us, as we greatly admire her tireless advocacy on behalf of the mentally ill. Dr. Jamison's research, teaching, writing, speaking, and work with the media have significantly lessened the stigma against suicidal individuals and their families, and have helped us all.

In addition, we would like to thank Donna Barnes, Lanny Berman, Iris Bolton, Jim Clemons, Joan and Norman Fine, Robert Gebbia, Sonia Heuer, Emily Holmes, Sue Kenyon, Amole Khadilkar, Gordon Livingston, Elizabeth Maxwell, Sherry Davis Molock, Marsha Norton, Jerry Reed, James Rogers, Kathie Russo, Ted Rynearson, Skip Simpson, Melanie Spritz, and James Werth. Their personal experience and professional expertise helped us to better understand the mystery surrounding suicide and to offer specific steps for healing and understanding after loss.

We are also grateful to the many other people whom we interviewed separately or together, including Jim Barrett, Mike Beamish, Charles Edwards, Fred Fox, Anna Graves, Bertha Hanschke, Doug Spearman, Joan Stogryn, Kathleen Troy, and Eli Zal. Their stories and time with us have been invaluable.

On a personal note, Michael would like to thank Bob Simon for his collegiality, mentorship, and scholarly research on suicide risk assessment; Leah Dickstein for her friendship, warmth of heart, and pedagogical collaboration of two decades; Bill Womack for his embracing spirit, integrity, and tireless outreach to troubled youth; and all of my mental health colleagues in Canada and the United States for their commitment to suicide prevention and caring support to survivor families. I would also like to thank, in every way possible, all of my patients who have entrusted me with their lives, allowing me to help them and to chronicle their anguish, despair, and courage so that others can learn or be benefited. Most important, I want to thank my wife, Joice, whose brilliance, zaniness, and enduring affection sustain me; my daughter, Briana, whose healing journey as a survivor of suicide and career in clinical social work inspire me; and my son, Zachary, whose intellectual curiosity and philosopher's mind humble me.

Carla would like to thank Lola Finkelstein for her constant support and inspiration as an independent and compassionate role model; Deborah Glazer and Rabbi Abraham Eckstein for their wisdom and insights; Alexander Kopelman, Sarah Murdoch, and Dolly Velasco for their unconditional friendship; and Janet, Jill, and Ellen Fine for their courage and determination to honor our parents' values and beliefs. I would also like to pay tribute to the memories of Harry Reiss, my inspiration and muse for this book, and my mother, Lillian Fine, who embraced every minute of her ninety years until her last breath on December 2, 2004. Most important, I am grateful to my kind, funny, and loving husband, Allen Oster, and to our adopted daughter, Aukia Marie Betancourt, who brings constant joy and enlightenment into our life.

This book exists today as the result of an extraordinary combination of brave and intelligent people who believed in us every step of the way. Our agent, Jim Levine, helped shape the message of hope and healing after suicide, and his personal interest in the subject was instrumental in making sure that our book would find its needed audience. We would also like to thank Lindsay Edgecombe at the Levine Greenberg Literary Agency for her gracious help in assisting us with many of the details in the publication of the book.

Every page of this book reflects the influence, intelligence, and guiding hand of our wonderful editor, Erin Moore. Erin's enthusiasm and belief in our mission inspired us, motivated us, and, ultimately, educated us. This book is as much hers as ours, and we are grateful and honored to have worked with her.

Finally, we would like to acknowledge the cherished memories of all of our loved ones who have been lost to suicide, and those of us who remember them and hold them dear. We are all connected, and we are not alone.

by Kay Redfield Jamison, Ph.D.

N o one who has not been there can comprehend the suffering leading up to suicide, nor can they really understand the suffering of those left behind in the wake of suicide. It is devastating to all who are touched by it, whether it is as a parent, spouse, child, colleague, friend, or doctor. Shock mixes with rage, despair with denial, and guilt with bewilderment. Always, there is the sense of a life lost too soon, too painfully, or too alone.

We know a great deal about the causes and prevention of suicide but not enough; we know much about how best to counsel those who survive the suicide of someone they love, but this information did not get to them—until now. Dr. Michael Myers and Carla Fine have written a superb book that fills this gap. *Touched by Suicide* is a deeply compassionate, direct, and immensely practical book. It provides well-informed medical and psychological information in a clear manner; directly addresses the concerns, fears, and misapprehensions of those left behind;

and provides extremely helpful day-to-day suggestions about how to survive the tragedy and nightmare that is suicide. *Touched by Suicide* is invaluable.

> Kay Redfield Jamison, Ph.D.
> Professor of Psychiatry
> The Johns Hopkins School of Medicine

TOUCHED
BY
SUICIDE

TOUCHED
BY
SUICIDE

Introduction

Making Sense of Suicide

How do you explain the inexplicable? Make sense of what seems senseless? Speak about the unspeakable? When someone you know and love dies by suicide, these and many more questions—an avalanche of questions—take over your life.

Suicide is a death like no other. It is deliberate and chosen. Is it rational? Rarely. Desperate? Always. Ignited by internal pain, suffering, and absence of hope? Almost always. And it always leaves behind a legacy of mystery and devastation.

Suicide touches you and you are never the same. We know from experience.

Carla:
Like you and millions of others, I have experienced the devastation and transformation of losing a loved one to suicide. Those of us who have been there are linked by a special connection and understanding. Even though each of our stories of loss is unique, we can take comfort that we are there together, and have found individual paths and ways to emerge and even thrive.

When my husband killed himself 16 years ago, I thought I would never recover. I thought I was the only person in the world whom this had happened to, that no one could ever possibly understand what I was going through. In an instant, I entered a different realm of existence from anything I had ever known before. My life split apart, creating a frozen "before" and a permanent "after." It took me a while to understand that suicide and death are different, that first I had to try to understand Harry's suicide before I could begin to heal from Harry's death. But how?

I didn't know where to turn, what to do, what to expect, what to believe in. I sought out support from other survivors and from individual therapy. I worked to break the silence and stigma surrounding suicide by writing my book *No Time to Say Goodbye: Surviving the Suicide of a Loved One*, which relates my story as well as the experiences of many other survivors. I found great strength in meeting and speaking to thousands of people throughout the United States and in other countries whose lives had also been touched by suicide.

I came to understand that there were probably times during my long marriage when I had said the right words or done the right thing to stop Harry from ending his life, that I had almost certainly saved him on several occasions over the years without even knowing it, as you most likely did with your loved one. As the years went by, I found I could begin to remember Harry for how he lived, not only for how he died. I could forgive him, and, maybe even more important, I could forgive myself.

I also learned from other survivors about the great need for a practical guidebook for surviving suicide, a step-by-step manual for living through the chaos that suicide leaves in its wake. We who have been in the foxholes of the front lines reach out to each other with suggestions, tips, advice, and comfort for making sense of suicide. Yet, we also look for professional advice to help us understand the complexities of the human mind, the causes and treatment of mental illness, and the most recent psychological and biochemical research related to suicide. Survivors want to make sense of suicide, and we want to heal.

Michael:

Like so many others, my interest in suicide is rooted in tragedy. In the fall of 1962, when I was a first-year medical student, one of my roommates, another medical student, killed himself. I was shocked and stunned. But I didn't talk about it. None of us did. I buried myself in my studies. A few years later, when I was doing my residency training in psychiatry, I lost three patients to suicide. There was some cursory discussion, but not much. Since becoming board certified as a psychiatrist in 1973, my work has always included treating the seriously mentally ill; when one labors in this branch of medicine, suicidal thinking and acts and deaths by suicide are ever-present.

I am troubled by the loneliness and desperation of individuals who struggle with thoughts of suicide, as well as the confusion of their families and other loved ones. I am troubled by the anguish, regret, and anger often expressed by those who attempt suicide and live to talk about it. Much of my teaching of medical students and physicians-in-training is about how to assess patients for suicide risk and how to prevent them from harming themselves. I am known as a clinician who is not afraid to delve into the private hell of despairing individuals who feel relieved to speak about their thoughts of self-harm and who welcome the opportunity to talk and receive support and guidance.

This forms much of my daily work in hospital psychiatry and in couples' and family therapy. I listen closely to my patients and their families. In my travels to medical meetings, I speak with people who have lost a loved one to suicide and learn from what they tell me about their experiences. I value their observations and stories, which assist me tremendously in my advocacy work and outreach into the public sector. I try my best to demystify the often confusing language and jargon that accompany the study and theories of suicide.

"Suicide is everyone's business," says former U.S. Surgeon General Dr. David Satcher, "and every member of society has a role to play." I know that it is possible to offer lasting relief to people who lose a loved one to suicide, and I am convinced that the number of people who kill themselves each year can be reduced. I am committed to both of these goals.

In the following pages, we present a specific and detailed road map of relief and comfort for each of you whose life and thoughts are touched by suicide. The practical advice and tools we offer are based on our dual perspectives of survivor and mental health professional, and our extensive work in the area of suicide over the past ten years. Although our initial collaboration focused on physician suicide—a personal concern for Carla and a professional one for Michael—we came to see that by combining our joint experiences and insights, we could help bridge the gap between the survivor and the scientific communities in order to better understand how suicide touches our lives.

The book is organized into three sections: The Aftermath of Suicide, Practical Suggestions for Healing, and Finding Meaning after Suicide. You can read straight through, or you may want to check the index or skim the text for what's most relevant to you at the moment. Throughout the book, you will find many personal and intimate stories from survivors who have graciously agreed to share their experiences with us; in order to preserve their privacy, we have changed their names and identifying characteristics, except when noted.

Suicide is not the end, but often the beginning of finding meaning in your now-transformed life. You will get through this and you are not alone.

FOR IMMEDIATE HELP

IF YOU NEED IMMEDIATE HELP FOR YOURSELF OR A LOVED ONE, CALL THE NATIONAL SUICIDE PREVEN-TION LIFELINE (www.suicidepreventionlifeline.org) AT

1-800-273-TALK (8255).

A TRAINED COUNSELOR IS AVAILABLE TO SPEAK WITH YOU 24 HOURS A DAY, 7 DAYS A WEEK.

PART ONE

WHAT HAPPENED?
THE AFTERMATH OF SUICIDE

ONE

The Devastation of Suicide

Y ou are shattered. You think that you have lost your mind, that you're crazy, that you won't be able to live through the next hour, let alone the rest of your life. You are convinced that you're the only person who has ever felt this way, that no one in the world could ever experience such devastation and be able to survive. You feel alone, surreal, isolated, terrified, and dazed. You think you will feel like this forever. You are heartbroken, and your body physically aches from the pain. You have lost someone dear to you to suicide, and have no idea what to do.

Carla:

I know these feelings well. My husband, Harry Reiss, killed himself on December 16, 1989, after 21 years of marriage. Harry, a successful New York physician in the prime of his career, ended his life at the age of 43. He injected himself with a lethal dose of the anesthetic thiopental, and I found him dead in his medical office when he was late coming home and didn't answer his phone or pager.

At that moment, I was transformed. I didn't know it then, but I would never be the same person again. My sorrow and guilt would define me for years; my search for meaning in my husband's too-short and interrupted life would open up new aspects of my own life and personality that I could never have imagined. As I looked at my husband's body lying on his examining table, with the intravenous needle still attached to the crook of his arm, the world as I knew it changed. If someone had told me at that moment that I would be able to function again or think again or write again or love again, I would have dismissed it as pity or fantasy.

Harry's suicide swallowed and consumed me; the *whys* and *what-ifs* of his death haunted my every thought. Why did he leave me without asking for my help? Why didn't he trust me to extend my hand to him? What could I have done to save him? Did I do anything to bring about his decision to die? How could I not have known the depths of his pain? Why did he choose to die alone? How could he have done this to me? What if I had been able to stop him? What if I had been more aware of what was going on with him? Why did this happen? Why? And, how would I ever survive?

At the beginning—and for survivors, the beginning is at least the first three years—all I could think about was Harry's suicide. It took me time to absorb the fact that I would never see Harry again, that I had lost my husband and partner, that I would not grow old with him as we had promised each other more than two decades before, and that all the dreams we had together for our future ended in a single moment from which I was deliberately excluded.

Suicide is incredibly humbling. It makes you realize that no matter how much you love or care for other people, you cannot be their life-support system, you can't keep them going, you can't will your spirit over to them. A loved one's death by suicide is not our choice, yet we who are left behind must learn to live with its consequences and deal with its aftermath.

Harry and I married during college. He was originally from Cali, Colombia, South America, born to refugees from the Holocaust who had fled Vienna in 1938. Harry was extremely successful in his medical career. He was a board-certified urologist with a private practice that was starting to take off; he had recently been promoted to assistant professor at New York University School of Medicine; and he had already published 12 research papers in leading medical journals.

Then his mother had a stroke, followed by a long and painful decline. Within a year of her death, Harry's father died from colon cancer that had been in remission but recurred after the death of Harry's mother. Four months after his father's funeral, Harry wrote himself a prescription for ten times the regular dosage of thiopental to inject into his veins. The medical examiner told me that Harry was asleep in seconds, dead in minutes.

Harry's dedication to his work blinded me from recognizing the truly despondent state of his mind. I still can't believe that he was able to treat patients up to two hours before executing his own death. The possibility of suicide seemed inconceivable to me at the time, as it does to most survivors. Sure, Harry was sad about the death of his parents. Yes, I could see him withdrawing from me in subtle and not-so-subtle ways. But whenever I said something about his state of mind or suggested that he get help, Harry would reassure me. "I'll get over this," he would say. "Trust me."

Uneasily, I chose to trust him. It was only after his suicide, when I checked his computer, that I discovered Harry had been conducting extensive research on the most efficient drug available to bring about the fastest and least painful death. I also found out that he had purchased the thiopental he used to kill himself two weeks before his suicide.

Harry was a wonderful physician. He loved being a doctor, he devoted himself to his patients and his research, he found great comfort and fulfillment in being a healer and helping to ease the pain of others. Unfortunately, Harry was kinder to others than he was to himself, and ultimately unable to find a solution to his own inconsolable pain—hidden from his friends, his colleagues, his family, and me—he chose to take his life. And at first, it felt as if he had taken my life too.

REAL VOICES:

You can't snap your fingers and make the pain go away. Healing the mind and body is a gradual process. You need to have the intention to survive, and if you don't have the tools, you have to reach out for them. Timing is different for everyone. Eventually, grief leaves you and you leave the grief. I learned that if I could survive my son's suicide, I could survive anything.

—Iris Bolton, executive director of The Link Counseling Center in Atlanta and pioneer of the suicide survivor movement

---

How Can I Deal with the All-Consuming Guilt and the Unspeakable Sorrow and Longing I Feel?

You know you have to *go through* the devastation of losing a loved one to suicide in order to *get through* it. But how?

1. *Seek out other survivors.* Survivors share the same language; when you're able to describe the indescribable out loud, it makes suicide seem more real and less like a dream that you have somehow found yourself in. You can confide your fears and regrets openly and without shame to other people who know what it's like to lose someone dear to you to suicide. You can describe the details of the actual act, no matter how graphic or grisly, and know that you won't be blamed for the death. You can engage in a safe exchange of information that isn't based on prurient curiosity and won't be fuel for future gossip.

Suicide survivors do not judge each other—just the opposite. Survivors tell each other: "You did the best you could." "How could you have known in advance?" "It wasn't your fault." And gradually you begin to see that if other people aren't responsible for their loved one's suicide, maybe you aren't to blame either. That if other people don't have the power of life and death in their hands, neither do you. By feeling genuine compassion and empathy for others, you gradually start to become less judgmental and kinder toward yourself.

2. *Find a support group in your community or a chat room on the Internet where you can connect to others who are now residents in your strange new land.* Share your experience with people who understand that mourning a death by suicide is long and everlasting; who can nod in agreement with your story and not turn away; who know that you will get *through* your pain even if you may never get *over* it.

"Going to a support group for the first year after my daughter's suicide gave me back my life," says a Chicago teacher. "Not my sanity, but at least my life." There is laughter as well as tears when you talk about losing a loved one to suicide with people who have been there. The stories of other survivors can help break the isolation and alienation that make you feel different and strange.

"When I exchange e-mails with other people who know what it's like to be grief-stricken about the death of a sibling whom you have not spoken to in years, I feel comforted and relieved," relates a middle-aged woman about the brother she lost contact with 20 years before. "I was crushed after my nephew called to tell me that his father had shot himself. And yet my brother and I had parted angry, and I thought I didn't care."

3. *Surround yourself with people you feel comfortable with.* Compassion comes from unlikely sources. People whom you least expect may come through for you during your time of need. On the other hand, you may also know the hurt and betrayal of friends or relatives or coworkers turning away from you, unable or unwilling to deal with your grief.

Your life sifts out after the suicide of a loved one. Everything is turned upside down and inside out. You almost have to re-create yourself in order to continue on. Be with people who are not uncomfortable with your pain. People who don't turn away or change the subject. People who don't judge you and can look you in the eye. And maybe even more important, people who are able to accept the new person you have become, through no choice of your own. Recognizing these people may be a matter of trial and error, but trust your instincts to help you along.

4. *Accept that you have changed.* Dr. Edward Rynearson, a psychiatrist whose wife killed herself, writes in his wise and perceptive book *Retelling Violent Death*: "I cannot change the end of Julie's story. The best I can hope for is that I change myself as I retell it. There have only been two stages—who I was before and who I am now: changed by Julie's dying. Instead of recovering, the best I can hope for is an acceptance of how I have changed."

Although you didn't ask for this test of your endurance—and would reverse the circumstances if given the choice—you will discover that you are more resilient, less afraid, more empathetic and understanding as a result of what has happened to you. You are not the same person you were before the suicide and will never be. Your life will be different, your friends will be different, and even your dreams and expectations will be different. Sadness and pining for the "old you" will be offset, hopefully, as you embrace the "new you" and your new reality.

Am I Crazy?

"I feel like a madwoman," says a Miami accountant. "My 82-year-old mother took an overdose of her prescription pills more than a year ago. She left a note telling me that it wasn't my fault. I've been immersed in my grief and even have thoughts of going to a psychic to try to contact my mother and ask her what happened. Am I crazy? I haven't been able to concentrate since my mother's death, and I cry all the time. My husband tells me I'm being overdramatic. I'm terrified that these feelings will never go away. Am I going out of my mind?"

There's an old adage in psychiatry that if you think you're crazy, you're not. Many, if not most, survivors feel crazy at some point, especially in the early days and weeks following the suicide. What you're feeling is totally normal. You are in the midst of a catastrophe. You are experiencing feelings, having thoughts, and behaving in ways that are all new to you. Your infrastructure has been rocked. Your purpose is up for grabs. Your life may have lost its meaning. What was predictable is gone. You think and hope that you're having a bad dream and you'll wake up soon.

Do some survivors actually lose their minds, even temporarily? Perhaps—but a true psychosis, a complete break from reality, a nervous breakdown, is very, very rare. What can happen, though, are

- Memory lapses—"I can't remember anything from the time the police officer knocked on the door until my son's memorial service."
- Sensory disturbances—"One week after my wife died, I heard her call my name. When I turned toward her, there was no one there." "No one believes me, but I still see my son sitting at his desk doing his homework when I go into his room. I'm not imagining this, either."
- Thinking troubles—"I keep losing my train of thought and just stop for what seems like hours." "I can't find common words, like I have Alzheimer's."
- Mood swings—"I think I've become manic-depressive. I'm laughing one minute, sobbing inconsolably the next, and then screaming at the top of my lungs after that."

These responses are temporary and will pass. A word of caution, however. If you are not sleeping, not eating, losing weight, withdrawing from your loved ones, unable to go outdoors, or barely functioning, you probably need some kind of medical help.

REAL VOICES:

I had been a psychiatric nurse specializing in post-traumatic stress disorder for ten years when my husband killed himself. My husband's suicide was different from anything I had ever experienced; it bisected my life.

I was at a friend's house when I received the call that my husband's body had been found asphyxiated in his car from carbon monoxide exhaust. My first thought was that I had to go and stop him, even though I knew he was dead. Then I started screaming, "Oh my God," crawled over to a corner, and crouched down.

It was at that moment that I had the first experience of my clinical self observing my regular self. This voice inside me said that being curled up on the floor was not appropriate behavior. I made myself get up and start functioning, even though it felt as if I were sleepwalking.

Shortly after my husband's funeral, I began to have nightmares and intrusive memories that I thought would never end. I couldn't concentrate. A couple of weeks after my husband killed himself, I saw a ventilator of a kitchen fan that looked like the dryer hose my husband had used in his car. I couldn't stop staring at the fan; I was mesmerized.

It dawned on me that I was having trauma symptoms, and this realization was a great source of relief to me. I wasn't crazy, I was in known territory, and I remembered that there is a difference between losing your mind and having weird feelings. I had worked with patients at the hospital in a trauma recovery program based on the work of the psychiatrist Dr. Judy Herman. Like them, after my husband's suicide I experienced a sense of disempowerment, a feeling that I wasn't in control and that there was nothing I could do about it. I also felt disconnected from myself and other people.

Trauma is an extraordinary event. It's like a physical injury, and it affects every part of your life. In the hospital, we would treat patients in a practical way. First, we would establish a safe and secure environment. Then we would encourage the patients to remember and mourn, and help them reconnect with their feelings.

I decided to use the same therapy on myself. I knew that intrusive thoughts, like panic attacks, eventually go away. Once you name the thought, it takes away a lot of its power. It then belongs to you. You wait it out until it goes away, and let yourself consider that what's going on may be normal. You tell yourself that you'll think of this later, not now. So I would "schedule" a time to become hysterical, which gave me permission to have these thoughts and feelings without panicking. This gave me some sense of control.

What I did from the beginning:

- I let people help me and gave them specific things to do. I asked my brother-in-law to come to the medical examiner's office with me to identify my husband's body; I asked a friend to organize a yard sale so I could get rid of my husband's things.
- I tried to honor my husband's memory in different ways. For example, I followed through on his wish for a specific reading at his funeral service as he had requested in his suicide note, and I spread his ashes in the mountains where he loved to hike.
- I knew my husband wanted people to know who he was and what he was like. So I talked about him to friends and coworkers. I gave away his books to his alma mater with his name stamped in them. I donated some of his tools to a community organization that needed them.
- I started thinking of ways to keep myself safe and not to feel so isolated. I made a concerted effort to reach out to

> *people even though I was afraid of putting myself at risk*
> *for exposure and rejection.*
>
> *Everything that happened in my life prior to my husband's sui-*
> *cide prepared me for that moment, and for this I am grateful.*
>
> —Emily Holmes

Carla:

After Harry's suicide, I also had strange thoughts and feelings I had never experienced before. I imagined that Harry wasn't really dead, that I had made up the entire event. Sometimes, I felt his presence beside me. I found myself standing at the front door with our loyal dog, Cinco, by my side, waiting for Harry to come home from work as if nothing had changed.

When I met other survivors through support groups and went to individual therapy, I realized that my behavior wasn't crazy. What happened to me was crazy, but I was structurally sound and would be okay. It helped to know that other people were having similar experiences, and I could share my darkest thoughts with them without feeling defensive. In turn, I could identify with their fears and anguish, and we could laugh together with a humor shaped by the extreme. Suicide is defined by its isolation and alienation; to know you're not alone is the first and most important step in the long journey ahead.

Why Am I So Angry?

Anger is a healthy and normal emotion, but it can also be powerful and frightening, especially when it's directed at a person who has just died. How can you be angry at a loved one who has killed himself or herself? Why would you be raging at someone who was so gentle in life, who was so kind, so generous? Theories abound, but we know from developmental studies that children lash out at anyone or anything that hurts them. It is a reflex, and just because you grow into an adult doesn't mean that you are completely free of childhood emotions when you're in crisis. Furthermore, when you lose someone to suicide, it hurts, it hurts terribly. As a result, you may regress, either a little or a lot, and find a range of primitive emotions returning.

When you're angry, you at least have some power and control. This anger can serve to protect you if, deep inside, you're feeling powerless and bewildered. Many people who face loss explain that their temper keeps them sane; without it, they say, they'd be locked up in a straightjacket!

Anger at your loved one can also serve another function. It can protect you briefly, or at intervals, from your guilt and rage at yourself. It can protect you for having missed a clue or for not being a "good enough" spouse or parent or friend. Anger can also protect you from your relentless and obsessive churnings, as well as the sorrow and heartache you are suffering.

"You just have to accept that there will be a softening over time," says a St. Louis judge whose 22-year-old son shot himself. "I experienced a rage at my son that frightened me. Why couldn't he have come to me for help? Why did he have to take what he was feeling to the extreme? Why didn't he try to hold on? How could he have done this to his mother and sisters? In killing himself, my son destroyed our family, and none of us will ever be the same again."

Anger can also be directed at the unfairness of life. And who doesn't feel this when your son or daughter, your father or mother, your husband or wife, your sister or brother, is dead and almost no one you know has had this kind of loss?

"I'm angry that the world goes on even though my baby has died," says the mother of a 12-year-old who hanged himself. "Why doesn't it stop? My world has stopped. It doesn't make sense and never will."

Michael:

Anger is also common in the face of bad news—being told you have breast cancer; being laid off because of cutbacks; failing an exam that you studied for much more than your peers. The good news is that anger at the unfairness of life always passes with time. You will regain perspective and grace. You will be able to share the joy of your friends and family members who are celebrating birthdays and graduations, even though these milestones have been wrenched from you by your loved one's suicide. Some of the kindest and most thoughtful individuals are survivors, and they will ride your anger out with you without fear or judgment.

Carla:

My reaction to Harry's suicide was pure rage. I felt betrayed, abandoned, and even foolish. Husbands are supposed to confide in their wives and consult with them about changing jobs or buying a new car or even vacation plans. Didn't Harry consider that his killing himself might have an impact on my life? Did he care?

A husband is also supposed to take care of his wife, to make sure her future is secure if something happens to him. Suicide is a messy death in every respect, and Harry left me with financial and legal problems that took years to sort out. I was furious that my husband, a man whose mission in life was to help others, not only chose to destroy himself and the life we had built together since we were seniors in college, but also left me alone to clean up after him.

Yet, my anger allowed me to function. It protected me from my terror of acknowledging the reality that Harry was dead, that I was a widow, that my life would never be the same. After arranging the funeral, referring Harry's patients to other physicians, closing down his office, giving away his clothes, and taking care of my finances and other day-to-day details, my almost palpable fury finally began to burn off. Now, mixed in with my constantly changing emotions, there was such a profound sorrow and longing that it almost crushed me with its physical force.

Is Denial Ever Healthy?

"Grief is a private emotion," says a Kansas housewife whose father killed himself when she was in high school. "I don't want the world to see my face. I look at Dad's suicide through a lens covered with silk-screen—it's always hazy. My mother and I never talk about him, and I've told my children that he died of cancer. It works for me, and that's the way I want to keep it."

Carla:

My initial reaction was also to cover up Harry's suicide. I told everyone except for a few close friends and my immediate family that Harry had suffered a heart attack. I don't know who I was protecting—Harry or myself. Now I think I was protecting both of us: I didn't want people to think Harry was "disturbed" in any way, nor did I want to be blamed for being a "bad" wife who couldn't even keep her husband alive. It takes a lot of work to keep up a lie, and I found avoiding the truth to be draining and exhausting.

Several weeks after Harry died, a good friend who knew about the suicide warned me that there would be people who would make hurtful comments when they found out that Harry had killed himself. "Turn around and walk away," he advised me.

As I reluctantly began to accept Harry's decision—with heartache and regret—I started telling the truth when and if I cared to. I also began to understand that privacy is different from secrecy, and it's your story to tell or not tell as you see fit.

Michael:

Shame and other unpleasant emotions are attached to the word "secrecy." If you're ashamed that your loved one killed himself or herself, you're keeping a big secret inside because you're afraid that people might judge you—or the person you lost. If you feel that your loved one's suicide is not another person's business—and you feel protective of him or her or yourself—then you have a right to privacy.

If I Don't Talk about What Happened, Will It Still Continue to Bother Me? Can the Pain Ever Go Away on Its Own?

Anything upsetting that you push out of your conscious mind will eventually end up "biting you in the back." Not talking about the suicide or your feelings will not make your pain go away; you may begin to have nightmares, develop migraines, start to drink or do drugs, or even become sick (see Chapter 3).

In the early stages of grief, however, you may prefer not to think about the suicide of your loved one. You may cope better by trying to put your loss out of your mind for a while. You may even feel worse if you talk about it. If you feel a bit better—or get some respite for a few hours—by going back to work or busying yourself with some task, then go right ahead. This may be normal for you. You may be able to speak about what happened later or when you find someone you're comfortable talking to.

"My wife was aghast that I went into work the day after our son's funeral, but I had no choice," says the father of a 17-year-old who shot himself. "I thought I was going to crack up if I didn't grab hold of some piece of my fractured sanity."

Michael:

The pain of losing someone to suicide never really goes away, and it may be years before you're ready to deal with it. I have treated scores of patients who begin their work with me with a statement like: "I've got unfinished business. I'm here because my father killed himself when I was seven years old. That was forty years ago. Now, I'm ready and need to talk about it."

Speaking openly and candidly about your loved one's suicide is the first step in allowing others to acknowledge what you are going through. By talking about something that has been taboo previously—and still is in some communities—you are helping to break new ground, and should consider yourself a pioneer and pacesetter.

Your honesty also helps to diminish the bad emotions attached to suicide—shame, failure, selfishness, sin, and so on—and make it more acceptable for others to use the "s" word. You are giving permission to your family, friends, colleagues, and strangers to be frank and unafraid, honoring those who have taken their own lives. As others begin to use the word "suicide" when talking about your loved one's death, you will not feel so alone, isolated, or self-doubting.

How Can I Tell the Difference between Normal Grieving and Depression?

First, some definitions. **Grief**—also called *normal grief, bereavement,* or *uncomplicated grief*—is a normal and appropriate emotional response to loss. It is usually time-limited and subsides gradually.

Common characteristics of grief include

- Initial shock and disbelief.
- Painful feelings of loss and sadness.
- A sense of emptiness and hopelessness.
- A loss of interest in your usual activities.

It's even considered normal if you have brief experiences of thinking that you hear the voice of your deceased loved one or if you see his or her image at times. This may happen off and on for several weeks or months.

Complicated grief—also called *traumatic grief* or, by the older terms, *pathological* or *abnormal grief*—is defined by both its intensity and length, lasting beyond the first six months after your loved one's death.

Complicated grief includes

- Persistent sadness.
- Continuing bitterness and anger.
- Preoccupation with thoughts about your loved one.
- Longing and yearning feelings.
- An inability to accept the death.

Complicated grief may also include distressing and intrusive thoughts about your loved one's death—especially how he or she died—and avoiding any reminders of your loss, such as situations or people. If you have guilty feelings, they are all about your relationship with your loved one; you will not be struggling with guilt about other aspects of your life.

Depression—also called *major depression, major depressive disorder,* or *clinical depression*—has symptoms similar to complicated grief, but often feels quite different, more severe, more frightening, and very physical. Depression is relentless and protracted, while normal grieving comes and goes.

With depression, you may experience the following:

- A persistent and overwhelming sad mood with no letup.
- A loss of interest in most things and a lack of pleasure or joy in activities or people.
- A feeling of guilt about many or most things, way beyond your relationship with your loved one who died.
- Rumination, churning, or obsessing about the past, espe-

cially anything that you view as your mistake, failure, or shortcoming.

- Low energy, being tired all the time, feeling 100 years old. You may feel like you're dragging around cement blocks on your feet.
- Trouble falling asleep or staying asleep; waking up very early in the morning and not being able to get back to sleep.
- Loss of weight or overeating out of anxiety or loneliness.
- Feeling worthless, useless, ugly, and bad.
- Increased thoughts that life is not worth living.

With depression, you may go from ideas of wishing you were dead to thoughts of how you would kill yourself. In sum, you really are not functioning like you used to and should get to a doctor right away.

Post-traumatic stress disorder—Recent research has shown that roughly a quarter to a half of grieving individuals may have complicated grief plus depression or complicated grief plus post-traumatic stress disorder (PTSD). PTSD bereavement symptoms are connected to a traumatic event, and the suicide of a loved one is almost always traumatic.

If you are experiencing the following, you may have PTSD:

- A continuing feeling of shock and helplessness.
- Frequent images of your loved one intruding into your mind, especially if you found the body and the death was particularly violent or disfiguring.
- Avoiding most people and situations, and becoming almost housebound.
- Startling easily, for example, when the phone rings or someone comes to your door.
- Always feeling afraid, nervous, or tense.
- Nightmares.

Grief, complicated grief, depression, and PTSD can all overlap in some ways with each other. It's worth a visit to your medical doctor or a mental health professional for advice on how to sort out what's going on with you. Your health and survival are too precious to compromise.

Are Suicidal Thoughts Ever Normal?

When you lose someone you love to suicide, thoughts of wishing you were dead are very common. Wishing to die in your sleep or get run over by a bus are sometimes called *passive thoughts of suicide*, but you may also have active thoughts of killing yourself. Most of the time, these thoughts arise from intense mental pain, or what Dr. Edwin Shneidman, the founder of the American Association of Suicidology and a giant and pioneer in the study of suicide, calls *psychache*. The wish to kill yourself and be dead offers you relief from your anguish.

You may also have thoughts of suicide because you want to join the person you've lost. You may find these suicidal thoughts comforting or even calming, especially if you're also feeling depressed. Your thinking may go something like this: "I like to think about suicide as a way out of this hell. If I'm not feeling any better by Christmas, I will kill myself. It's a relief to know that I don't have to go on living my useless life."

Fears that you may not survive the death of your loved one are also common. You hurt so much and miss your loved one with such ferocity that you can't imagine living through this. If it has been several weeks or months and you do not feel any better—or feel worse—this can be very frightening and discouraging. Death seems inevitable, and the old notion of "dying of a broken heart" no longer seems abstract or mythical to you.

If you wish you were dead, have thoughts of killing yourself, or despair that you will not be able to come through your loss, you must share this with someone. Tell a family member, a close and trusted friend, a religious or spiritual counselor, a survivor in a support group or an online chat room. You will feel less alone, less odd, less forlorn. It is also very important to get the perspective of a mental health professional: You may be at serious risk of harming yourself directly or of becoming sick from physical neglect.

If you think you are in a crisis and would like immediate help, you can call the National Suicide Prevention Lifeline—**1-800-273-TALK (8255)**—24 hours a day, seven days a week. Trained counselors will answer any questions or concerns you may have about yourself or someone you care about, as well as identify resources in your area. You can also go online at www.suicidepreventionlifeline.org

---

ARE YOU THINKING ABOUT SUICIDE?

If you experience any of these thoughts or feelings, you may want to get help:

1. Can't stop the pain.
2. Can't think clearly.
3. Can't make decisions.
4. Can't see any way out.
5. Can't sleep, eat, or work.
6. Can't get out of the depression.
7. Can't make the sadness go away.
8. Can't see the possibility of change.
9. Can't see yourself as worthwhile.
10. Can't get someone's attention.
11. Can't seem to get control.

Reprinted with permission from the American Association of Suicidology (2005).

"Just going on living was the challenge," explains Iris Bolton. "I didn't want to kill myself after Mitch died, but I wouldn't have minded if a truck hit me. If I had to live with that kind of pain for the rest of my life, I couldn't do it. It was the closest I ever got to understanding how my son could want to die."

How Long Will I Need to Mourn?

Give yourself as much time as you need to mourn your loved one's death. Don't listen to well-intentioned advice from people who urge you to "get on with your life" or to "let go of your loss." Only you know how long it takes to be able to incorporate the suicide of someone you love into the everyday doings of your life.

Grieving is a very personal and individualistic experience. We are all shaped by our past and the way in which we grew up. Think about how you have handled previous losses in your life. How did you react compared with how you're reacting now? How was the death different? What are some of the similarities? Losing your daughter to suicide today may feel much more wrenching than when your mother died of breast cancer 10 years ago. You had no preparation for your daughter's death, but you did for your mother's. Your daughter died alone; you were holding your mother's hand when she took her last breath. You aren't sure of your daughter's place in an afterlife; you know your mother is at peace. But what helped you to heal after your mother died may also help you now—spending time with your sisters, attending religious services, keeping a diary, assembling a collage of photographs for your extended family, doing volunteer work in your community.

Your religious and cultural background also affects how you mourn a death by suicide. There may be certain prayers, rituals, or traditions that will give you solace and comfort, and help you with your healing. You can even create your own.

"After my fiancé shot himself, I decided to wear black for one year, until the first year anniversary of his death," explains a Montreal advertising executive. "Some of my colleagues and family members thought I was being melodramatic, as if I were living in the Dark Ages. I heard criticism that I was flaunting my fiancé's suicide, that I was wearing black all the time just to be in people's faces about his death. But for me, wearing black felt like a mark of respect for him and our relationship. It also shielded me from any unwanted overtures from other men."

The time you need to mourn can be involuntary and happen automatically: "I slept through the night for the first time since my sister died. I guess that's a good sign that maybe I'm beginning to heal, but there's a part of me that feels guilty about it." Or it can be voluntary and by design: "I've decided to visit my father's grave once a month now, instead of every Sunday. I'm okay with this; it feels right to me." Both are ways of healing as time passes.

You will know if there's something "wrong" with how you grieve or if it's going on too long. This realization will come from within you, not from anyone else. Trust your instincts or that part of you that somehow lets you know you're basically okay and are still functioning in many ways; you're making progress, feeling a bit better today than you did a month ago or two months ago; and you're drawing upon some inner reserve and strength that you never knew you had.

If you begin to doubt yourself, speak to other survivors and see what they think. They may reassure you that what you're still feeling is normal or tell you that something doesn't seem quite right if it worries them.

Most survivors agree that the first year after a suicide, you are in a virtual state of shock. Even though you are functioning, you probably won't remember much of what occurred during this time. In addition, there are usually a lot of details to be taken care of, which can also mask the reality of what is going on and further numb your brain.

Be prepared for the second year to be the most difficult. The shock is starting to wear off, and you're beginning to feel the pain full-force. Also, it may seem that because you survived the first year, you somehow deserve to be rewarded. Specifically, your loved one should come back! The game is over. You did everything right. You played by the rules. You made it through those terrible 12 months. So enough, already.

It's during the second year that the reality of your loved one's absence hits you. It is forever. You will never see your husband or your daughter or your best friend again. You'll never have absolute resolution about his or her reasons for choosing suicide. This is all there is. Although the second year is the most difficult period in the mourning process, there is one silver lining—it takes you to the third year, where the fog seems to lift a bit and you begin to incorporate the loss of your loved one into your life, separate and distinct from the suicide.

Five years is an important milestone for a suicide survivor because it's a testament to your ability to survive more or less intact while beginning to make changes in your life, both big and small. It's also when you start to realize that it's possible for something meaningful to emerge from your loved one's suicide—something that may help you or others. And seven years is almost biblical. It's a cycle in our lives where we have been transformed, as Dr. Rynearson writes, from who we were to who we are now.

Why Is There Still Such Stigma Attached to Suicide? Why Is There So Much Mystery and Misperception?

Suicide breaks all the rules. People we know and hold dear have defied the course of nature and determined when and how they died. Our loved one's act throws our own perceptions to the winds; our way of looking at life and death is sundered. The question "Why do we die?" has always been an unanswerable mystery;

with suicide, the question reshapes into "Why did my loved one choose to die?"

People are afraid of what they don't understand, and stigma exists because of fear. There is also the fear that suicide is somehow contagious—that if it happens to you, it can happen to me, so I'd better stay away. And because suicide was considered a sin not so very long ago, it takes time to extinguish that kind of thinking when someone kills himself or herself.

According to a study conducted by the Centre for Suicide Prevention, many survivors report experiences of stigma after suicide, including being avoided by acquaintances; having people refrain from talking about the deceased or behave as if the deceased has not really died; and, in some cases, being taunted or ridiculed.

Most people's lives have been touched by suicide in one way or another, and talking openly about it reduces its stigma. Whether it's the loss of a loved one or a coworker or a teacher or a friend, suicide is an intrinsic part of the fabric of our existence. As the secrecy of mourning your loved one's death begins to diminish, you will begin to heal. In letting go of the silence and the shame, you will also let many other people out there know they are not alone in their grief and pain.

Can I Ever Restore Some Sense of Balance to My Life?

Michael:

Yes, balance will return to your life—although you may wonder how, given the way you are feeling right now. But the personal stories of survivors are testament to the capacity of human beings to move through this terrible pain. You will do this in your own unique way. My survivor patients describe "baby steps": getting a haircut, taking a walk in the woods, reading light fiction, languishing in a bubble bath, building a bird feeder. You may go back to the gym. You may plant a garden or begin piano lessons. What is key is that you are doing something for yourself once more, and that's okay.

Carla:

I will always disagree with Harry's decision to die. I still think he was wrong, he was selfish, he made a mistake. Even with everything I now know about suicide, depression, mental illness, personality problems, impulsive behavior, and despair, in my heart of hearts I have not fully accepted Harry's decision to end his life. I regret how much he has missed. I mourn for all that he could have accomplished. I ache for the experiences that we didn't share. But mostly I have forgiven him, and much of the time I have also forgiven myself.

I didn't plan to marry again. I was terrified of dating. After all, it's not exactly a turn-on—or so I quickly discovered—to tell a man that your husband killed himself.

But, as you know or will come to know, the road to recovery is filled with unexpected twists and turns. Seven years after Harry died, I met a kind and compassionate man who respected my love for Harry and cherished me as a caring woman who had experienced and survived both the joys and sorrows that life brings. There was no one more amazed than I to discover that my ability—or capacity—to love had not been extinguished by Harry's death. Two years later, Allen and I decided to get married. We both agreed that we wanted to have a big wedding, filled with music and dancing and laughing and eating and lots of fun. We wanted our union to be joyous and we wanted to share it with others.

I was ready for happiness, believe me. But what I was not prepared for was the guilt that flooded through me as the day of the wedding approached. I couldn't get beyond the idea that I was forsaking Harry—or, at the very least, his memory. I was not prepared for the shame of, in my mind, abandoning my husband, and the blame that flooded through me, knowing that I had survived and was moving on while Harry was lying in the cold ground.

When Allen and I went to meet a rabbi to ask him if he would marry us, I worried through all the possibilities. I was nervous the rabbi might turn us down if he found out that Harry had killed himself. In the bottom reaches of my mind, I felt guilty. I still believed that I could have saved Harry and therefore had contributed to his death. I was unworthy, undeserving. All those thoughts I believed I had put to rest came out of the darkness to haunt me once again.

When the rabbi asked if either one of us had been married before, I mumbled "yes." Then I was silent. "He died," I finally blurted out.

"Your husband must have been young," the rabbi said. "Was it an illness?"

I took a deep breath. "No, he killed himself." The rabbi reached across his desk and took my hand. "I am so sorry," he said. "Would you like to talk about it?"

I told the rabbi that Harry's parents had died within a short time of each other, and how he had never seemed to recover completely from their deaths. I told him how Harry had killed himself only four months after his father's funeral.

The rabbi listened carefully. "My parents also died within one year of each other," he said. "I have never known such sorrow. I was thirty-six years old and married to a woman I loved more than the world. We had two wonderful children who were the light of my life. Yet, it didn't seem to matter. All I could feel was the terrible loss of my parents. Even the love of my wife and children couldn't reach me. Ever so slowly, I emerged from my pain and came to cherish the love of my family once again."

I understood what the rabbi was trying to tell me. That I hadn't been a "bad" wife, that Harry's journey was his alone, that despair and grief are private and powerful.

Allen and I celebrated our marriage at a wedding that was joyous and filled with friends and relatives, laughter and song. During the ceremony, the rabbi said: "Everyone here wishes you great happiness. Because you deserve it."

We all deserve happiness. Our scars are part of us, as are the wonderful memories of the person we lost. With time, we come to understand and accept that we can embrace life and still honor and cherish our loved one's memory at the same time. It is a gift we accept without knowing why.

TWO

Searching for Reasons

"I believe that suffering is at the heart of every suicide," says Dr. Edwin Shneidman in an interview with the *Los Angeles Times*. "I still believe it's critical to look at personal stories, emotional circumstances, and private histories in the study of suicide, not just the biology and pharmacology of suicide and depression." After studying and writing about suicide for 50 years, Dr. Shneidman adds, "If I were to do it all over again, I would probably study love."

Carla:
My one-sentence explanation for Harry's suicide changes all the time. "Both his parents died in one year." "He didn't want to live anymore." "He was stupid." "He was overwhelmed." "He was grief-stricken." "He was impulsive." "I really don't know why."

Survivors are consumed by the *why* of suicide. We look for answers, we speculate, we turn the clues over and over again, as if trying to unravel a murder-mystery that we instinctively realize will never be solved. Although we know who the victim is, know who the perpetrator is, and even know the cause and means of death, we don't know what the motive is and we never will. The "real" reason dies with our loved one, and we are left behind—feeling helpless and guilty and ineffective—to try to put the pieces of an unsolvable puzzle back together.

"My brother's suicide was like stepping on a land mine," says a New York writer. "Thirty-six years later, there's not a day that goes by that I don't think of him or try to figure out what happened."

REAL VOICES:

The Canyon of Why begins with this thought or statement: "Why did they do this?" The entrance occurs spontaneously with the knowledge that someone we care about has chosen to die by suicide. The Canyon of Why is as deep as any canyon that can be visited on this planet. It has very difficult and steep sides. Yet even though the Canyon of Why is dangerous and difficult, it can be navigated and traversed with support and knowledge of the emotional geography that makes up this journey.

—Frank Campbell, Ph.D., *The Canyon of Why: Healing Metaphors for Survivors of Suicide*, work in progress

---

Will I Ever Really Know What Happened?

At times, you feel possessed. The incessant search for *why*. The endless questions. The *if only*s and *what if*s, the *could have*s, *should have*s, *would have*s. The obsessive pursuit of signs or reasons to bring some kind of resolution or insight or understanding. The fear that you will never know, that you will be haunted by lost chances and missed opportunities forever.

"I was devastated when my fraternity brother killed himself, even though we weren't that close," says a 36-year-old computer programmer. "He was a good-looking, Tom Selleck–type of guy who got dumped by his beautiful girlfriend. He was always so confident and cool, and the women were always chasing him. We all figured he would just move on, even though he was obviously devastated. How can one thing in your life make you want to kill yourself?"

Is there ever a single cause for suicide? More than 90 percent of people who die by suicide have been living with depression, or some other type of mental illness that is often unrecognized and un-treated. The remaining 10 percent are individuals who kill them-selves after reasoned consideration and with no evidence of mental illness (*rational suicide*), or who may truly be healthy but act on im-pulse. Some deaths may make no sense at all.

For the most part, however, psychological autopsies, or detailed investigations of the factors that can lead to suicide, show that there are usually many reasons why people kill themselves. Often, these clues or signs may be masked or unknown to family members, close friends, and associates; they may not even be visible to the person who ends his life or her life.

To illustrate, let's consider the "Tom Selleck–type of guy" whose suicide so shocked his unsuspecting fraternity brothers. It's possi-ble that he had risk factors no one knew about: a past suicide at-tempt, a history of depression or drug use, a family history of suicide. He may have been living with symptoms of depression that he very cleverly hid from those who knew him even before his girlfriend dumped him, and made wobbly by the depression, he really crashed when she left. It's also possible that his outgoing social personality was a cover-up, and that deep inside he was a rather shy, sensitive, and self-deprecating man. Maybe the thought of being on his own was too overwhelming for him. Maybe he felt terribly injured and abandoned, and despaired of ever meeting someone else again. Had he been drinking the day he killed himself and become acutely hopeless and impulsive? Is it possible that he didn't really want to die but miscalculated and went too far—that he was angry at his girlfriend and wanted to make her feel guilty for leaving him? And finally, unilateral breakups are the most traumatic of separations. They are especially tough for men, and not all men "move on" easily. Maybe he was one of them.

Why Am I Convinced that If I Know the Reason for the Suicide, I Will Feel Better?

"I thought we were the most normal family in town," says a sophomore at UCLA. "My mother and father seemed so happy, my brothers and sisters got along. Then, when I was in junior high school, my mother drove her car off a cliff. She left us a note saying that she couldn't take it anymore. Take what? I thought she loved being a stay-at-home mom. I thought she really liked taking care of the house and being with us all the time. How could we have missed what was going on? I have so many questions to ask her and it tears me up to know that I'll never get a chance."

When you lose someone you love to suicide, not only are you in mourning, but you feel anxious, off balance, and uncertain. One way you can regain your equilibrium is through understanding. By asking questions and searching for answers, you begin to feel some relief. You may feel a degree of mastery and self-control as you move further along with possible answers to those now-familiar questions: Why did they do it? Am I at fault? How can I go on?

Michael:
When I meet with families whose loved one has died by suicide, they often feel soothed by any insights that I might be able to share with them. Respecting doctor-patient confidentiality, I do my best to try to answer questions posed to me:

- "I don't think that your divorce had anything to do with your son's decision to die. As you know, he was very upset when he relapsed and started using cocaine again.

This, coupled with his not being able to practice medicine again, makes me wonder, like you, if he just couldn't forgive himself."

- "Your mother was very kind and thoughtful of others. She spoke often about how much she loved you. I really can't imagine that she was thinking of how her death would break your heart."

- "I'm so sorry for your loss. Your brother was a good man, and I liked him a lot. He worked hard in treatment with me but he had a lot of inner struggles, things that were very private to him and caused him a lot of shame. It was very sad and he suffered a lot."

Carla:

I have mostly accepted that I will never know the *why* of Harry's suicide. But I also wonder, if I had the chance to ask him, if he would even know himself. To me, that's even sadder than living with the hurt and confusion of his leaving me with no time to say goodbye.

Why Do I Think That I or Someone Else Caused the Suicide? Why Is It Easier to Blame Myself or Others than to Blame the Person I Lost?

"My boyfriend jumped from the window of our fourteenth-floor apartment," says a Toronto nurse. "He had been suffering from terrible depression and was seeing a psychiatrist and taking Prozac. He was twenty-eight years old. He told me that he wanted to die and that he would never be committed to a hospital. I got really scared and called his mother. While I was on the phone with her, he went to the window and jumped. I started screaming hysterically and his mother, who heard everything, started yelling at me, 'Stop him, stop him.' I dropped the phone and ran down fourteen flights of stairs.

"There was already a crowd when I got down to the street. His mother lives nearby and she came over right away. When she saw the EMS and cops, she started screaming at me that it was my fault, that I should have taken him to the hospital. Everyone was looking at me. Why is it my fault when I only was with him three years and he grew up and was with his parents for the whole rest of his life? Why is his mother blaming me? Is she right?"

One of the first thoughts you have when you learn that someone you love has killed himself or herself is "This should not have happened; this death was preventable." You search to see who's at fault. Is it your son's girlfriend? Is it your sister's mother-in-law? Is it your father's psychiatrist? Is it you?

Blaming ourselves or others is very common and probably represents another dimension of trying to make sense of something so senseless. It may feel less painful to assume the blame for your loved one's death than to criticize him or her. On the other hand, you may feel very justified faulting others for your loved one's death—he or she was stupid, blind, or negligent—and you think he or she deserves to be blamed. When others agree with you, your perceptions are further validated.

You may also spend time trying to figure out what happened, as if you are a detective investigating a crime. In a sense, you are saying to your loved one, "Don't worry, I'll get to the bottom of this, I'll figure out who's to blame." Or, you may be saying, "Although you killed yourself, you're not responsible; I'm the one at fault here. I have failed you and I'll do everything possible to find out why."

You may also find yourself blaming the person you lost and think: "You coward, why did you kill yourself? I hate you for this—and don't even try to make me feel guilty." This raging and defiance is a way of warding off your guilty feelings, and your self-examination will come later. As time passes and you regain some stability, you may find yourself looking inward. You may be less angry at your loved one for dying this way; you may even start to feel a certain compassion. If you are unable to stop feeling over-whelmingly guilty for the suicide, however, it's probably a good idea to talk to someone. There could be a huge irrational component to your guilt that you can't see, but others can.

Sometimes your blame may be irrational or frenzied, and you may lash out almost reflexively at specific people or society in general. When you act like this, you're probably in the early hours or days of your grief, and still in a state of shock to some degree. With the passage of time, you will regain some perspective and feel more in control. You may also have more of an understanding that suicide is no one's fault, and gradually come to accept that it is possible to live with the uncertainty of never fully knowing the *why*, after all.

What Is the Role of Depression and Other Mental Illnesses in Suicide?

According to the American Association of Suicidology (AAS), approximately two-thirds of all people who die by suicide are depressed, and the risk of suicide in people with major depression is about 20 times that of the general population. Depression, often undiagnosed and untreated, is the major cause of suicide. The National Institute of Mental Health reports that about 60 percent of people who die by suicide have a mood disorder of some type, including major depression, bipolar illness, and low-grade chronic depression (dysthymia). Another significant group suffers from alcoholism, other substance-abuse disorders, or a combination of both. A smaller percentage of individuals who die by suicide have lived with other mental illnesses—schizophrenia, anxiety disorders, eating disorders, attention deficit hyperactivity disorders, and personality disorders, especially borderline and antisocial types. Individuals who have a combination of two or more of these diagnoses, called *comorbidity factors*, are at the highest risk of suicide.

NOTE: You can have one or more of these diagnoses and not be at any risk of suicide. Some people, even when severely ill, have never had a single thought of suicide. The difference between actually feeling suicidal and thinking about how you might kill yourself depends on many factors:

- How symptomatic you are at the moment.
- Whether you have had anything to drink or have taken any drugs.
- Whether you are receiving any treatment.
- Whether you are also struggling with a general medical illness.
- Whether you are alone or isolated.
- Whether you have had a recent loss.

AAS research finds that people who are depressed and exhibit the following symptoms are at a particularly high risk for suicide:

1. Extreme hopelessness.
2. Lack of interest in activities that were previously pleasurable.
3. Heightened anxiety and/or panic attacks.
4. Insomnia.
5. Talking about suicide, or a prior history of attempts.
6. Irritability and agitation.

"My seventy-seven-year-old father shot himself five years ago," says a Cleveland bus driver. "I always thought I was a good son; now, I don't know anything. I saw that my father was sad after my mother died, but now I think he may have been clinically depressed. What are the signs? How can I be a good father to my daughter and a good husband to my wife if I couldn't even have saved my father?"

Michael:

We don't always know whether depression will lead to suicide. It's important to keep in mind, however, that **the majority of people who have depression do not die by suicide.** The risk of suicide depends on how severe the depression is, whether the individual has had suicidal thinking or has attempted suicide in the past, and whether or not the person has ever been admitted to a hospital for psychiatric treatment and care.

And men are different from women. About 7 percent of men with a lifetime history of depression will die by suicide, whereas only 1 percent of women with a lifetime history of depression will die by suicide. Why? Men are less likely to recognize how severely depressed they are, less likely to reach out for help, and less likely to accept treatment. Men also tend to isolate themselves more than women do, have alcohol or other drug use combined with their depression, and be more impulsive than women.

Note: As a survivor, you may find that some of this information helps you to understand why your loved one died by suicide. If you have had depression before yourself and some of these suicide risk factors apply to you, talk to a professional. Losing someone to suicide is extremely stressful, and stress can trigger a repeat depression in any individual.

My response to the Cleveland bus driver who lost his father to suicide is this: Stop beating yourself up. It is very sad that your dad killed himself but it's not your fault. Hindsight is 20/20. Even if your dad was clinically depressed, you didn't know the signs then. Also, is it possible that your dad tried to hide his depression or suicidal plan from you? Perhaps he wanted to join your mother in his idea of an afterlife, and he wouldn't have wanted you to try to save him. My hunch is that if you ask your daughter whether you are a good father or if you ask your wife whether you're a good husband, they would both say "yes."

WHAT ARE SOME OF THE WARNING SIGNS OF A SUICIDAL PERSON?

1. Threatens to hurt or kill him/herself, or talks of wanting to hurt or kill him/herself.
2. Looks for ways to kill him/herself by seeking access to firearms, available pills, or other means.
3. Talks or writes about death, dying, or suicide, when these actions are out of the ordinary for the person.
4. Exhibits any one or more of the following signs:
   a) Hopelessness.
   b) Rage; uncontrolled anger; seeking revenge.
   c) Acting recklessly or engaging in risky activities, seemingly without thinking.
   d) Feeling trapped, like there's no way out.
   e) Increased alcohol or drug use.
   f) Withdrawing from friends, family, and society.
   g) Anxiety; agitation; unable to sleep or sleeping all the time.
   h) Dramatic mood changes.
   i) No reason for living; no sense of purpose in life.

Seek help as soon as possible by contacting a mental health professional or calling 1-800-273-TALK (8255) for a referral should you witness, hear, or see anyone exhibiting any one of the above warning signs. You can also get further information from the American Association of Suicidology at www.suicidology.com.

Reprinted with permission from the American Association of Suicidology (2005).

What Is Depression and What Does It Feel Like?

Depression is an illness; it is not simply feeling down or being in a bad mood. Depression is a *biopsychosocial illness*: *bio* for biological factors; *psycho* for psychological factors; and *social* for social and cultural factors.

- The biological part of depression deals with brain chemistry: When you're depressed, there are lowered levels of serotonin and other neurotransmitters in your brain. These chemicals are essential and regulate your emotions and thoughts. When they are depleted, you feel despondent, sad, or flat, and your thinking is slowed down or disjointed.
- The psychological part of depression is how your mind reacts to what is going on in your life now as well as how it reacts to events from your past such as loss, trauma, abuse, separation, and so on.
- The social part of depression includes additional forces that may be less immediate but are nevertheless significant, like unemployment, isolation from family or friends, discrimination, and so on.

When you're depressed, there is often a mix of all of these forces occurring.

Note: Depression can also occur when your life seems to be fine and there are no triggers you can readily identify. This can be puzzling and makes you feel odd, even self-indulgent, for being depressed. This kind of depression is very much like a medical disorder, coming over you for no discernible reason. It is more common if you have a family history of depression or if you had an episode of depression earlier in life.

What does depression feel like? There is no one picture, but in two words, "not good." If you were to throw out this question to a roomful of people who have experienced depression, some typical responses might be

- "Horrible—a black cloud descended over me and wouldn't go away."
- "I was worried 24/7, as if I were in overdrive. I couldn't turn my anxiety off."
- "I was dead inside, flat, lifeless, shut down, a shell of my old self."
- "Terrifying. I was racked with guilt and shame, and couldn't stop thinking about the most foolproof way to kill myself."
- "I didn't feel depressed, I felt demented. I couldn't add two and two; I was sure that I had some rare virus, some type of disease that was eating away at my brain."

REAL VOICES:

Garrett was well loved and loving. But his problems were deeply internal. At the end, when he was overwhelmed with darkness, the light went out of his eyes. He wrote in his suicide note: "To those I love—when I die, please don't cry. For me, I am in a better place, just where I want to be. No more sorrows, no more pain, just sunshine, no more rain. The one thing I know is my love for you. If I could only love myself the way you love me. The only consolation is that your son will no longer be in pain." Garrett suffered silently, but we deeply believe that he will continue to touch people's lives.

—Oregon Senator Gordon and Sharon Smith, whose 22-year-old son, Garrett, killed himself in 2003. One year later, the U.S. Congress passed the Garrett Lee Smith Memorial Act supported by Senator Smith, authorizing millions of dollars each year for the development of suicide prevention and intervention programs.

- "I couldn't stop crying, I couldn't focus, I couldn't eat, I had no energy, I couldn't even shower. I just stayed in bed and prayed that God would take me away."

The most telling stories are those of sufferers. Many have written eloquent accounts of their illness as well as their recovery. (See Resource Directory, page 275.)

What Is Bipolar Disorder?

Bipolar disorder, formerly called *manic-depressive illness*, is characterized by both manic and depressive episodes. When individuals are manic, they have a persistently elevated or irritable mood as well as heightened self-esteem, rapid speech, racing thoughts, and irrational and high-flying ideas that they are rich, very intelligent, or very important. They are busy, sleep very little, and may run up enormous debts from spending recklessly or investing without restraint. They may also become sexually inappropriate, throwing all caution to the wind. When they are depressed, they act just the opposite, as described above.

If you have bipolar illness, you will need to be on medication and under the care of a psychiatrist or a primary care physician, even if you have a mild form. Why? The illness does not go away. Like most people with bipolar disorder, however, you will be able to live a very full and productive life as long as you take mood stabilizers such as lithium or other drugs, and receive psychotherapy.

NOTE: With bipolar disorder, you are most at risk for feeling suicidal during a bout of depression or if you are having a *mixed episode*—a frightening and confusing combination of manic and depressed symptoms that alternate rapidly over hours or days.

If you are having a difficult time accepting a diagnosis of bipolar illness and are reluctant to agree to treatment, you may find some comfort in the eloquent and wise words of Dr. Kay Redfield Jamison, who lives with bipolar illness. In her book *An Unquiet Mind: A Memoir of Moods and Madness* Dr. Jamison writes

"At this point in my existence, I cannot imagine leading a normal life without both taking lithium and having had the benefits of psychotherapy. Lithium prevents my seductive but disastrous highs, diminishes my depressions, clears out the wool and webbing from my disordered thinking, slows me down, gentles me out, keeps me from ruining my career and relationships, keeps me out of a hospital, alive, and makes psychotherapy possible.

"But, ineffably, psychotherapy heals. It makes some sense of the confusion, reins in the terrifying thoughts and feelings, returns some control, and brings the hope and possibility of learning from it all. Pills cannot, do not, ease one back into reality; they only bring one back headlong, careening, and faster than can be endured at times. Psychotherapy is a sanctuary; it is a battleground; it is a place I have been psychotic, neurotic, elated, confused, and despairing beyond belief. But, always, it is where I have believed or have learned to believe—that I might someday be able to contend with all of this."

Is Suicide Genetic?

Major depressive disorder, bipolar illness, schizophrenia, and substance-abuse disorders tend to run in families, and all of these illnesses have some risk for suicide. According to the American Psychiatric Association treatment guidelines, there is an increased risk of becoming suicidal in individuals with a history of suicide among their relatives, because of both genetic influences (what you inherit from your parents) as well as environmental influences (what you learn growing up in your family). At this time, however, scientific research has not yet confirmed a specific genetic basis for suicide risk.

REAL VOICES:

Spalding's mother killed herself, and her suicide was a very big part of Spalding's life and even his art. But he was depressed and nothing seemed to help. Spalding tried everything, but to no avail. He made four suicide attempts in a two-year period, and killed himself on his fifth try. I think the first attempts weren't really serious— when Spalding finally did it, he meant it. I also believe that he probably regretted it when he jumped into the river from the Staten Island Ferry, because Spalding's life was ruled by regrets.

I'm sad but not ashamed; I just think of suicide as another way of dying. I tell our children that he didn't do this to them, that he wanted to end his feelings of pain. One week after Spalding died, a bird flew into our house. It was a small gray bird and when we opened the door, it left, but flew in again the next day. This went on for three days. I felt as if it was Spalding's way of saying to us that he was okay.

—Kathie Russo, producer and widow of
writer and performance artist Spalding Gray

Note: Even if you have family members who have died by suicide or have experienced suicidal thinking and/or suicide attempts, you are not jinxed. Many people who have lost relatives to suicide, especially more than one family member, feel terrified that they are doomed to suffer the same fate. It's true that you are more vulnerable than someone without this history, but instead of panicking, you should use this information to do whatever you can to reduce your risk. This includes educating yourself and your children about suicide, watching your alcohol intake, paying attention to your lifestyle, and, most important, getting help at the earliest hint of illness in yourself or your loved ones.

What Is the Role of Substance Abuse in Suicide?

1. *What is the connection between alcohol and suicide?* "My father was an alcoholic, so I just think of his suicide as the end of that story," says a Dallas housewife. "He wrote a long, rambling woe-is-me note before he set fire to himself in the backyard. My mother's drinking has become heavier since my father died, and I feel powerless to help her. I just hope my children don't take after my side of the family and will grow up to be happy, healthy adults."

Alcoholism is associated with an increased risk of suicide. If you are an alcoholic, you are six times as likely to kill yourself as someone in the general population. Studies have also found that 50 to 75 percent of alcoholics who die by suicide also have suffered from major depression. Abuse of drugs, including alcohol, is now the second-most common psychiatric reason (after depression) for suicide. And if you are an alcoholic, you are also more likely to attempt suicide than someone who isn't.

Alcohol can make you susceptible to suicide in several ways:

- Alcohol is a depressant chemical itself. Although a drink or two may make you feel happy and relaxed, too many drinks will lower your mood. If you are already fighting depression, alcohol can increase your despondency and color your thinking. You will probably feel even worse than before.
- Alcohol is a disinhibiting agent, meaning that it lowers your inhibitions, your reserve, and your protective defenses. You are more likely to impulsively want to die when you have alcohol in your system.
- Excessive alcohol affects your relationships with others— especially your intimate relationships—in a negative way. People who love you can get fed up and exhausted

when you are drinking, and eventually run out of patience. Losing an important relationship can trigger suicide.

- If you are taking antidepressants for depression and drinking at the same time, you are not going to get much benefit—if any—from the medication. Your depression may worsen, including your thoughts about killing yourself. What's more, it's dangerous. You can get sleepy, pass out, fall, or injure yourself or others if driving.

- Over time, alcoholism affects almost every organ in your body, including your brain. With brain damage, you lose intelligence, memory, mood control, and independence—making you vulnerable to self-destruction.

2. *What is the connection between recreational drugs and suicide?* Most recreational drugs are extremely addictive, and there is a very strong connection between the use of recreational drugs and suicide. In fact, it is suggested that the spread of substance abuse is a factor in the two- to fourfold increase in youth suicide in the United States since 1970.

There are many different recreational drugs—marijuana, crystal methamphetamine, Ecstasy, heroin, and cocaine, to name a few; some are "downers" and some are "uppers." **It is now believed that the greatest risk factor is the amount of drugs you take, as opposed to the type.** Unfortunately, many people living with a mental illness, such as a major depressive disorder, bipolar illness, dysthymic disorder (low-grade chronic depression lasting years), schizophrenia, and so on, use recreational drugs. The combination can be deadly.

3. *What is the connection between prescription medication and suicide?* Medications that are prescribed by physicians for anxiety, depression, insomnia, or pain can also, in rare instances, precipitate suicidal thinking or a suicide attempt. If you feel worse on your medication, you must stop taking the drug immediately, then call your doctor or go to your nearest emergency room.

Prescription medications are also used by some suicidal people to kill themselves (so-called drug overdoses), so you should go through your medicine cabinets regularly and throw out all of these kinds of medications if they're no longer being used.

4. *What is the connection between steroids and suicide?* "I was close to my brother growing up, but then in high school, he started lifting weights and taking steroids," says a Detroit social worker. "His whole personality changed, and he became physically and emotionally abusive to me. It was like when he bulked up, we lost him.

"My brother joined the police force after graduation and I was terrified because now he had a gun. I knew his life would end violently, and it did. I will never forget the look on my father's face when the police came to our house to tell us about my brother's suicide. My father blames himself and my mother just won't talk about it. I'm so worried about my parents that I've put my mourning on hold. What I can't understand, though, is how my brother could work as a hostage negotiator. He once persuaded a suicidal man to put down his gun. How could he help others and not himself? I'm sure it was all the steroids that played games with his head."

Anabolic steroids are hazardous drugs. They can cause depression and they are addictive. Anabolic steroids can make people feel high, euphoric, or irrational, and make them very dangerous to themselves or others. *'Roid rage* describes the violent aggression associated with steroid use. Adolescents who use steroids to enhance muscle mass may be especially susceptible to suicide, given that they are already living through an at-risk stage of the life cycle. Someone who uses anabolic steroids is most vulnerable to suicide or violence toward others if he or she begins to take higher and higher doses, or suddenly stops taking the drug altogether.

5. *How can you tell if substance abuse will lead to suicide? Are there signs to look for?* Substance abuse is a general risk factor for suicide. If you are worried about your sister, watch for changes in her moods and observe whether she seems increasingly depressed. It is considered a serious development if she appears to be drinking more than usual or is using drugs more frequently or without restraint. Also, look for *rapid mood cycling*—that is, she's on top of the world one day and down in the dumps the next. If she is hinting at life not being worth living or talking about harming herself in any way, then it's time to act. **Ask directly whether the person you are concerned about is considering suicide, and if so, get immediate professional help.**

Do Antidepressants Cause or Prevent Suicide?

Carla:

I remember sitting at support group meetings and hearing people say: "I'm convinced it was the antidepressants. One week after my daughter started with her medication, she killed herself. It was like she was revved up on the pills." Or, "I begged the doctor to put my mother on Prozac but he said she was just sad over the death of my father. I know the pills would have saved her."

We are told that antidepressants are the magic bullet against suicide. Then we read that they can cause suicide. This confusion just adds to our pain and disharmony. If the experts have no idea about what prevents—or brings about—suicide, how should we?

Michael:

It can be especially heartbreaking when it seems as if the antidepressant your loved one was taking for comfort and relief may actually have led to despair and suicide. The jury is still out on whether antidepressants can cause people to kill themselves, but fortunately, there is now an increased awareness in the medical community about the potential risks of antidepressants in patients with depression. This includes children as well as adults and adolescents. Physicians who prescribe antidepressants—mostly psychiatrists, family physicians, and pediatricians—are now advised to monitor their patients closely for agitation, worsening of mood, violent thoughts, severe insomnia, development of suicidal thinking, and worsening of symptoms if the person is already suicidal.

Bottom line? Antidepressants save lives and are generally well tolerated by most people. Become and stay informed about the drug prescribed to treat depression if you are a patient yourself or if your loved one is. Report any worsening of depression to your doctor and, if necessary, go to an emergency room for help. If you have any questions or doubts about the effects of the antidepressants, **ask your doctor immediately.**

Can Suicide Ever Be Caused by Reasons Other than a Mental Condition?

Carla:

"Was he depressed?" That is usually the first question I'm asked after I tell someone about Harry's suicide. I would love to answer a definitive "yes." It would make everything easier if I could give a specific name to what he did and why he did it—a neat, contained explanation for his unfathomable action.

But, as I have learned over the years, suicide is a very chaotic death. It's chaotic physically and it's chaotic emotionally; there's nothing neat or tidy about it. Harry was very sad about his parents' deaths but he continued to work and function until his own death. Was he just a good actor or was I in denial? Does it matter if Harry killed himself because he was suffering from inconsolable grief over his double loss, or from undiagnosed depression? The answer will not change the end of his story, but would it have changed the end of mine?

Michael:

One of the challenges of all mental health professionals is to guard against "overdiagnosing." In fact, many in the United States at the moment are questioning whether psychiatrists already have too many diseases in our classification system and are willy-nilly coming up with even more! When it comes to suicide, I think we should consider the possibility of not knowing the *why* as well as searching for a hidden or unrecognized illness. I believe that not every death by suicide is due to a mental illness or due to a rational decision. Sometimes, we just don't know.

What About Chronic Illness and Suicide?

On January 2, 2002, Admiral Chester Nimitz, Jr., 86, the son of the World War II Pacific fleet admiral, and his 89-year-old wife, Joan, both in deteriorating health, each took their lives with what their daughters said was an overdose of sleeping pills. According to an article in *The New York Times*, Admiral Nimitz had made it clear to his family for more than a decade that when the time came, he and his wife intended to take charge of their own deaths.

Admiral Nimitz left a note saying they didn't want to be resuscitated: "Our decision was made over a considerable period of time and was not carried out in acute desperation. Nor is it the expression of a mental illness. We have consciously, rationally, deliberately, and of our own free will taken measures to end our lives today because of the physical limitations on our quality of life placed upon us by age, failing vision, osteoporosis, back pain, and painful orthopedic problems."

It is not uncommon to have thoughts of "ending it all" when living with a chronic physical illness that may be painful or debilitating. It is also normal to have suicidal thoughts if you know you have a terminal condition that will lead to your inevitable death. Although the prospect of more painkillers or chemotherapy or dependence on others can make you question the value of continuing on, the reality is that, in the end, most of us fight to live with every breath we have. There are some people, however, who don't want to face what they know lies ahead. Like Admiral and Mrs. Nimitz, they choose to exert whatever control they have left and end their lives on their own terms.

Suicide deaths like these are very individualistic—as are the reactions of the loved ones who are left behind. Some family members are sympathetic and supportive; for others, the notion of a loved one making a decision to die by suicide is unthinkable. Such deep divisions are reflected by the reaction to the article about the joint suicide of Admiral and Mrs. Nimitz from two readers of *The New York Times*:

- *My elderly parents committed suicide together in 2000; they took narcotics and were found with plastic bags tied over their heads and pillows on their faces. . . . Without exception, I and all the surviving close relatives of their generation remain horrified and deeply wounded by their suicides. . . . Suicide is the ultimate selfish act, no matter whether the person who chooses to die in this way is 18 or 80.*
- *Is the choice of a peaceful death at the end of a long life more selfish than the desire that one's own loved ones cling to a painful and undignified existence?*

"My uncle's suicide is easier to accept intellectually than emotionally," explains Erica, a veterinarian from Virginia. "He was a prominent obstetrician in our small town—he even delivered me—and he killed himself at the age of 40 after being diagnosed with bone cancer. I was very young, but my parents told me that my uncle didn't want to live with the pain he knew he would suffer. Even though it made sense, all I knew was that my father couldn't stop crying. His brother was a beacon in our family, the most successful and accomplished of all his brothers and cousins. My grand-mother was crushed, and never seemed to recover from my uncle's death. Understanding the motivation for a suicide doesn't make you feel any less abandoned or the loss of the person any less painful or sad."

If your loved one is living with a chronic illness and brings up the topic of suicide with you, you may have an opportunity to en-gage, to ask questions, to dissuade. You may seriously question your mother's judgment and wonder if she is depressed. You may ask your father to speak to his doctor or make an appointment for him to see a mental health professional. You may want to make sure your grandmother is getting the best possible medical and nursing care for her physical pain, mental pain, breathing, and loneliness. Whatever happens, you have to feel that you've done your best.

Andrew Solomon, whose mother took an overdose of barbitu-rates in 1999 with the approval of her husband and two sons after a valiant two-year struggle with ovarian cancer, writes about her death in his bestselling book *The Noonday Demon: An Atlas of De-pression.* "As long as there is even a remote chance of my getting well, I'll go on with treatments," she tells Andrew after receiving her diagnosis. "When they say that they are keeping me alive but without any chance of recovery, then I'll stop. When it's time, we'll all know. Don't worry, I won't take them [the barbiturates] before then. Meanwhile, I plan to enjoy whatever time there is left."

Her family supported her decision and was with her throughout her painful dying and peaceful death. "My attachment to my mother was so strong, our sense of family so impermeable, that per-haps I was always being set up to be incompetent to tolerate loss," Andrew Solomon observes. "Assisted suicide is a legitimate way to die; at its best it's full of dignity, but it is still suicide, and suicide is in general the saddest thing in the world."

Can Being Overwhelmed Cause Suicide?

Let's say, for example, a man is out hunting with his young son. He inadvertently shoots and kills his son, who has run ahead of him in the woods. Upon seeing his son's lifeless body, the father turns the gun on himself: One tragedy has turned into two.

Why do some people choose suicide at these times and others don't? Blaming yourself for a loved one's death can make you feel that you also deserve to die, and can cause intense guilt and self-blame that may result in suicidal behavior and thoughts. Fortunately, most people don't act on their impulses. Feeling forgiven for what you have done—or think you have done—is essential for healing, as is rediscovering, usually with great agony and self-inspection, that your life still has meaning and purpose after such a tragedy.

There are also other experiences, both traumatic and everyday events, that can cause you to feel overwhelmed and unable to cope. If you or someone you care about seems suddenly or gradually at loose ends, lost and confused, act immediately by first trying to talk about what's going on, then seeking out professional help and guidance.

What Is the Role of Impulsivity in Suicide, Especially in Young People?

Impulsivity is one of the danger signals for imminent suicide risk. In adolescents, being impulsive is not uncommon. This trait, plus depression and/or use of alcohol or other drugs, can make for a very perilous situation. Emergency room physicians who treat adolescents who impulsively have taken an overdose of aspirin or over-the-counter sleeping aids report that upon awakening, most of the young people describe having felt acutely overwhelmed with stress or anxiety or hopelessness about a relationship breakup, a fight with their parents, a bad report card in school. They may be embarrassed, but most are relieved that they didn't die. That's not to say that they weren't serious about killing themselves; they were at the time of their overdoses.

Another cause of impulsivity in adolescents and adults is attention deficit disorder (ADD), especially the hyperactive type (ADHD). Some individuals have a personality that is impulsive; that is, they act before they think things through. Teens who self-mutilate ("cutters") are impulsive, and cut their wrists, arms, or other parts of their body when upset. They don't necessarily want to kill themselves, but feel better and more alive with the pain or the sight of blood. Stimulant drugs like amphetamines or other street drugs can also make people impulsive. And severe depression, especially when accompanied by a lot of anxiety and physical agitation, causes impulsivity.

NOTE: Firearms, one of the most lethal methods of self-harm, are used in approximately half of all youth suicides. In addition, the risk of suicide is five times greater in households with guns. According to an article in the *Journal of the American Medical Association*, in homes where there are children and teenagers, such practices as keeping a gun locked and unloaded, as well as storing ammunition locked and in a separate location, can have a protective effect and reduce the rate of youth suicide.

What should you do if your adolescent son or daughter says something like, "If you don't get off nagging me about my grades, I'll kill myself"? Your first response must be to back off. You need to calm down and so does your teen. Give her or him a time-out. Research shows that most individuals who are feeling impulsive about harming themselves become less impetuous or restless within 30 minutes. Some people need to be left alone; some will respond to "venting" with a close friend, sibling, or anyone they trust at the moment.

Later, you may want to approach your son or daughter with such words as "I'm sorry about coming on so strongly before about your grades. I'm worried about how you're doing at school. But first, we need to talk about what you mean by killing yourself. Can you tell me?" Watch your tone. Reach out in a kind, concerned, and helpful way. Listen. Don't interrupt or start giving parental guidance until your son or daughter is ready to hear you.

NOTE: If you or a loved one are feeling restless, you can't sit still, you can't sleep, you have to pace or keep moving constantly—and you're feeling quite depressed—get help immediately! If you are not aware of nearby medical help or don't have the resources, call 911 for advice or **1-800-273-TALK (8255)** to connect you to the nearest available suicide prevention and mental health service professional in your area.

Can Suicide Be Motivated by Anger or Revenge?

"My husband killed himself in our bed with me sleeping next to him and our two children in the next room," says a Salt Lake City travel agent. "When is suicide rageful and angry? And how do you mourn under those circumstances? How do you forgive?"

Can suicide ever be motivated by anger or cruelty? Is there such a thing as rageful suicide? The answer is yes, and this scenario is when the term *self-murder* really fits the description of suicide. The individual kills himself or herself instead of killing you. Although this is chilling, it is less frightening than the far-too-common stories in the press: "Man Slays Ex-wife, Then Shoots Self." "Son Found Dead after Stabbing His Parents." "Heartbroken Mother Murders Children She Loved, Then Hangs Herself."

NOTE: You must be very careful not to conclude falsely that your loved one's suicide is directed at you or is an act against you, to punish you, to make you pay, to ruin your life, or to make you suffer. Many people who kill themselves are really not thinking about the implications of the specifics of their deaths, such as the location in which they do it; who might find them; how bloody it might be; how horrific they might appear; who has to clean up the scene; and so forth. They are in a frenzy, and what appears to be the ultimate "fuck you" is not that at all.

People can be very irrational, even psychotic, in the days and weeks before killing themselves. As their worlds become more constricted and isolated, their thinking can become very distorted and they are unable to see beyond themselves and their terrible inner pain. Their degree of self-pity may be huge, and sometimes they can become full of rage and paranoia. Kind and caring loved ones, as well as treating physicians, can be perceived as suspect, unhelpful, disappointing, and not genuine in their concern.

So how do you mourn family members or friends whose suicide is cruel or nefarious and seems directed at you? You need to talk with others about what it feels like to have someone so angry at you. Is it hatred they felt toward you or was it their illness taking over? You need to communicate about the anger that you may feel toward them, not just for killing themselves, but perhaps for almost taking you with them.

What if you experience relief at their death? You may feel guilty

---

REAL VOICES:

I think that too little attention is paid to the anger embedded in nearly every act of suicide. It's easy to discern and sympathize with the hopelessness and pain that those who kill themselves are experiencing. But I think that it's important for families trying to come to terms with these losses to confront the reality that any person contemplating suicide has to weigh the devastation that he or she is about to inflict on loved ones.

—Dr. Gordon Livingston, psychiatrist and author,
whose son Andrew killed himself in 1992 at the age of 22

at feeling safer or calmer now that they are dead. These feelings are normal, given how these people may have hurt you when they were alive. Forgiveness? Maybe, maybe not. But you don't need to forgive to heal, and your insights into their death may be sufficient for you to gradually accept their suicide with less pain and turmoil.

What Is Existential Distress and Can It Be a Factor in Suicide?

Being in an *existential crisis* or in *existential distress* refers to an inner questioning about the meaning of life, especially one's own life. It is not an official psychiatric term or diagnosis, but some examples include

- "My life is up for grabs. I don't know if I still want to keep working as a nurse or change professions."
- "My marriage is a mess—do I want to stay with my wife?"
- "I can't stand this city anymore—should I move to Greece, where I've always wanted to live?"

The philosophy of *existentialism* stresses self-determination and responsibility for one's being and living. Less emphasis is placed on biology, genetics, and culture for determining how you live and function.

Existential distress can be a factor in suicide in at least two ways. One is that you take complete ownership for your life being in the state that it is. Simply put, if your life is a mess, then it's all your fault. It's not because of your mother dying when you were seven, your wife leaving you for another man, your boss berating you, or your being genetically prone to bipolar illness. And second, it's your life and you have the right to end it if you want. No one has the right to stop you, including psychiatrists or family members. It's about autonomy and doing what you want, regardless.

Is the Method by Which a Person Chooses to Die Particularly Significant?

Carla:

Harry was a physician who died a "medical" death. He researched and prescribed the drug he used to poison himself; he set up the intravenous equipment; he inserted the needle into his vein; and he administered a dosage that he knew would be both rapid and lethal.

But not all physicians use drugs to kill themselves, just as not all police officers use guns to end their lives. Survivors often talk to each other about the significance of the *how* our loved one died, not only the *why*.

- "How could my seventy-six-year-old mother have hanged herself? Where did she buy the rope? How did she know how to make the knot? How was she able to stand on a chair?"
- "My daughter was so meticulous. How could she have slit her wrists and gotten blood all over her white bedspread?"
- "My aunt knew nothing about guns. How did she know how to load the bullets?"

The method of death adds another layer of mystery to the seemingly infinite number of unanswered questions about our loved one's suicide. Is there a connection between the *how* and the *why*? Will understanding the method of death give us some kind of insight into our loved one's state of mind? Can it ever help us with our understanding or healing?

Michael:

Do we ever truly know someone? Being a psychiatrist for over 30 years has taught me a lot about privacy and secrets. When a patient confides something in me that they have never told anyone—not their spouse, best friend, no one—I am often awestruck. Not so much about the specifics, but more about why we deem certain things privileged and keep them hidden from trusted others. Certainly, we all have the right to concealment and to holding things inside. And often there is a fierce attachment to private matters—illustrated by patients who will sometimes tell me that they regret sharing such personal information with me. One patient said, "It's not that I don't trust you and your ethics around confidentiality, it's more about letting myself down in some way because I let you in."

When I'm given the opportunity to enter the private worlds of my suicidal patients, and they tell me how they would kill—or plan to kill—themselves, what they say can be very elaborate. They want the suicide to work. They research it, as if they are on a mission. They need to get it right. And I think this goes some distance in explaining how the most gentle of souls can leap from a 35-story building, set himself on fire, or blow her chest open with a shotgun.

Sometimes the method is shocking to those who don't think their loved one has the "courage" to kill himself or herself. This can be very deceptive. Mental health professionals who treat depressed and suicidal people are not placated by the patient who says, "I'd never kill myself; I don't have the guts." Desperate and agitated people who need immediate escape from their pain and anguish can be extremely impulsive. Swallowing corrosives, electrocution, and jumping from a height are examples of methods that are often unplanned.

NOTE: Some bereaved individuals become amateur psychologists in their attempts to understand their loved one's suicide, to unravel the mystery, to find tidbits of information. Others have well-meaning but actually insensitive friends or family members who "volunteer" to be on the case. This can be very hurtful and also disrespectful of your loved one. Although you may be haunted by visions of your loved one's violent death, these will fade in time and eventually become more bearable.

Do Suicide Notes Make You Feel Better or Worse?

Carla:

Harry never left me a note. I searched his office and our apartment. I looked in his books, on his computer, in his filing cabinet, on his clothes. It's been a long time, yet I still steel myself for the time when I may, just may, come across a folded piece of paper or a scribbled message tucked away somewhere. And then I'm afraid of what I may find and what the note will say.

It is estimated that only 15 to 20 percent of people who die by suicide leave some kind of note. Cynthia Hubert writes in *The Sacramento Bee* that suicide notes "can offer consolation to loved ones or can compound their pain. They can give valuable insight into the question of why a person chose to take his or her life, or they can cause further confusion." She quotes Dr. James Rogers, a noted suicidologist from the University of Akron: "Researchers once believed that notes left by people who took their own lives were the golden road to the kingdom of understanding suicide. In fact, suicide notes rarely offer good answers to the ultimate question. They may answer questions as to the triggering event in the death, but the *why* is always much deeper."

Is not leaving a suicide note a further rejection for the survivor? "My mother left a note for my sister but not for me," says a 23-year-old woman who was planning her wedding when her mother drowned herself in a river. "This was almost as painful as her suicide, if not more so."

Why do some people write notes and not others? Researchers

have analyzed suicide deaths according to age, marital status, gender, social class, ethnicity, and race, and cannot find any insights into who leaves notes and who doesn't. What is clear, though, is that there is tremendous interest in suicide notes. Survivors hope that a note will explain why their loved one chose suicide and will contain a goodbye and a few words of comfort. Coroners hope that a note will partly confirm or dispute the cause of death as suicide or something else. Suicide prevention experts hope that studies of notes will assist in the quest for knowledge and efforts to lower the rate of death by suicide.

"If suicide notes are indeed attempts at communication, then they are dismal failures, " writes Marc Etkind in his book . . . *Or Not to Be: A Collection of Suicide Notes*. Survivors tell of notes asking questions that can never be answered, making accusations that can never be addressed, offering references that can never be understood.

- "Why didn't you let me go on the senior class trip?"
- "I didn't want to be a burden on you anymore."
- "How could you have stopped loving me?"
- "I will never forget what you told me last night."

There are notes that go on for pages and others that are only a sentence or phrase. There are loving notes, angry notes, lucid notes, desperate notes.

- "I am in a better place and am finally at peace."
- "You never saw my pain."
- "I have thought this over and it's what I want to do."
- "There's nothing left for me."

According to recent research, there are some common themes and messages in suicide notes: apology and shame, love for those left behind, life being too much to bear, instructions regarding practical affairs, hopelessness and nothing to live for, and advice for those left behind. Suicide notes written by young people tend to be longer, richer in emotions, and often begging for forgiveness. Suicide notes written by the elderly are usually shorter, contain specific instructions, and are less emotional.

If your loved one leaves a note full of pain and suffering, this may corroborate your thinking that your loved one is "now at peace" or "in a better place." Even an upsetting note can be healing: "At least Holly left us a note even though it was pretty ugly, implying that we were dismal failures as parents," says a grieving father. "It means a lot to us that she took the time to write, that we were in her thoughts at the very end. I only wish that we had been able to talk about this while she was alive."

If you were left with an extremely hostile, raging, and hate-filled note, talk with a trusted family member, friend, or therapist to get some kind of a reality check. How much of this venom do you deserve? How much reflects the disturbed state of the person who wrote it?

There are several ways to deal with issues raised in a suicide note:

1. You might simply tell others about the questions raised in the note and ask for their feedback. You may want to be careful with whom you decide to share the note, however, and whether you disclose all or only some of its content. You may be feeling protective of the person you have lost, and regardless of how upsetting you find the note to be, you don't want other people judging your loved one for what he or she has said or done.

2. You may want to address the person who died. Even though it will be a monologue, speaking directly to your mother or best friend can be very therapeutic. You might

do this in the privacy of your home, at the graveside, where the ashes were scattered, at a meaningful or significant location, or in your house of worship.

3. You can write your loved one a letter and answer the questions and issues posed in the suicide note, adding whatever else you might want to say or explain.

4. If you have a friend who is willing, you can also set up a role-play. He or she can be your loved one and ask you the question or questions addressed in the suicide note. This may be very emotional, but can also be healing and curative.

Many survivors are frustrated when a loved one's note is removed by the police or other law enforcement officials. Depending on local procedures, sometimes a note may not be released until a criminal investigation is completed to confirm that the cause of death is suicide, not homicide. For survivors, waiting to read or possess a suicide note is intensely painful. Sometimes you are able to obtain a copy of the original note from the police right away. In other cases, you may have to hire legal representation to get the note back into your possession.

"I had to yell and scream in the sheriff's office of my small town," says the mother of three young children. "I didn't even know that my husband had left a note until the EMS driver, who was a friend of mine, told me that they had found one at the scene. I couldn't believe that they didn't inform me. If they were trying to protect me, they were all wrong. I wanted to read what my husband said, even if it was hurtful. He wrote it to me, so why shouldn't I have it? I threatened to camp out with my kids in the sheriff's office until the note was released. Finally, my lawyer was able to get a copy for me—I still don't have the original. My husband's words were difficult to read, but at least I can share his last moments with him. It's not much, but it's all I have."

Michael:

Dr. Edwin Shneidman writes, "In order to commit suicide, one cannot write a meaningful note; conversely, if one could write a meaningful note, one would not have to commit suicide."

Do suicide notes ever offer insights? Yes, there are insights, but only in the minority of cases, given how few people leave notes and how rarely they are coherent. In addition, you must not read rejection into your loved one's not leaving a note. That is too self-punishing. Most suicidal people are too sick to think about others and too impaired to write.

Many years ago, a patient showed me a note that he had written to me just before he overdosed, expecting to die. I was visiting him in the intensive care unit when he handed me a small, torn fragment of a paper table napkin with one word, "sorry," written in pencil. He berated himself for not being more eloquent—he was a professor of classics—and apologized for "forgetting" to thank me for being his doctor.

"My brain just wasn't working," he told me. "I couldn't find the words. It was as if I had had a stroke." As I gazed at the dismal morsel of paper, I felt very sad. My eyes began to well up, and I was struck by how much this dignified and proud man had been diminished by his illness. I quietly thanked him for thinking of me.

How Can I Live with This Uncertainty for the Rest of My Life?

Michael:

How is it possible to live without resolution? How is it possible to reconcile the present with the past without being able to fully understand what happened? "The unexamined life is not worth living," writes Socrates. You gain knowledge by asking questions, especially the questions that have no concrete answers.

Many scholars end their lectures by saying: "I have endeavored today to leave you with more questions than answers—I hope that I have succeeded." You would be wise to remember that your endless questioning, your quest for understanding, your pursuit of meaning, are acts of love and respect for your loved ones. Their death forces you to examine not only their life, but also your life as well.

REAL VOICES:

It really helps to connect to other survivors and see that there will be stages, that it's not endless uncertainty and suffering. At first, you think you will always feel this way, it will never end, and you won't be able to endure it. "Recovery" doesn't apply to suicide; it's the wrong word. There isn't recovery, but a rebirth or a metamorphosis, a new life marked by this event. It took me awhile to understand that this new life did not mean having to forget my daughter.

Other survivors never gave me hope that I would have a "normal" life. Yes, I would still have a life, but it would be without my daughter, so how could it ever be "normal" again? I could also see that I could have joy at times and wouldn't suffer with such intense pain every moment.

I now have a sense of continuity between my daughter's suicide and my present life. I have incorporated her into the present in a way that's safe, as if she's here. I speak about her to others. I remember special times I spent with her. I look at her photographs. I'm no longer afraid that her death will consume me. At the beginning, each memory of her felt like a new loss and threatened my survival. Now, each memory of my daughter is a new connection to her.

—Sonia Heuer, lawyer and mother,
whose 15-year-old daughter killed herself in 1989

Carla:

Survivors live in the land of uncertainty. We have to learn to adjust our lives to never having definitive answers, to never having permanent resolution, to never having clarity. At the beginning, it feels that it will be impossible or too torturous to live this way. But then we meet other survivors, talk with counselors and mental health professionals, seek out spiritual guidance, open our hearts, and try to find peace in a private way that works best for us. No one is more surprised than we are when we turn out to be more resilient, more courageous, more resourceful than we ever thought possible. This is the light that gets us through.

PART TWO

What Can I Do? Practical Suggestions for Healing

THREE

Protecting Your Health

"Death by suicide is not a gentle deathbed gathering:
It rips apart lives and beliefs, and it sets its survivors on a
prolonged and devastating journey."
—Dr. Kay Redfield Jamison, *Night Falls Fast: Understanding Suicide*

Carla:

It's very scary. Just when you think it can't get any worse, it does. How much can a person take? When does the bad news stop finding its way to your door?

- "Two years after my mother's suicide, I was diagnosed with breast cancer."
- "My younger son killed himself three years after his brother's suicide."
- "My sister stopped talking to me after her husband's suicide and won't even let me see her kids anymore."
- "My wife and I divorced five years after our daughter killed herself."

As a survivor, I worry about what happens to us after the suicide of someone we love. How are we affected physically? What actually happens to our bodies? Are our psyches irreversibly changed?

Have we become damaged goods? Are we being punished? How can we protect ourselves and the people we love?

Michael:

These scenarios are the stories of some survivors, but not all. What follows are some important questions. I hope that the answers can help explain the seriousness of your loss, what could happen to you, and some steps that you can take to get through this.

Is Suicide a Trauma?

Suicide is often a traumatic event, but not always. Some survivors actually feel relief when a loved one dies. For example, if your daughter was living with an intractable mental illness, with little or no break from her suffering, you may feel that she is now at peace and her battle is over. Or, if your father abused or neglected you and continued to wreak havoc on your life or on those whom you love, you may feel at peace with his death—even a certain sense of freedom that he can't hurt you anymore.

According to a recent study, suicide is the most frequent form of violent death in the world, followed by homicide and war-related deaths. As a result of these alarming findings, public health research is now moving beyond how survivors are affected by the immediate impact of a loved one's death to what kind of long-term support, outreach, and intervention might be helpful in their recovery.

It's important to remember that by whatever means your loved one chose to kill himself or herself, the death was still violent. Don't be swayed by people who say, "Aren't you relieved that your mother overdosed on pills? That's so peaceful, as if she just drifted off to sleep." What may feel violent to you is that your mother experienced despair and powerlessness in the final moments of her living, and especially that she died alone. What also feels violent is how the news affects you: unexpectedly, intrusively, and aggressively.

Psychiatrist Edward Rynearson, writing about violent dying, describes the distress of being tormented by the replay of the terror and helplessness you imagine your loved one may have suffered at the time of his or her death. You may feel "haunted," unable to stop obsessively ruminating and recounting every detail of his or her suicide that you can remember or reconstruct. The traumatic nature of suicide is often accentuated by the public nature of such a death: Your privacy is wrenched from you as your family, friends, neighbors, and strangers launch into an uninvited inquest into the *who, what, when, where,* and *why* of your loved one's death. Suddenly, the drinking habits of your brother or the marriage of your daughter is open for public scrutiny, and their lives are savagely and unfairly eclipsed by the violence of their deaths.

The degree of trauma you experience also depends on the closeness of your relationship with the person you lost. You may feel assaulted, injured, wounded, or even amputated by the suddenness of such a death. This can be a terrible and frightening experience because, in an instant, a part of you has been taken away and you no longer feel whole.

Trauma can also result if you are the one who discovered the body of your loved one. Finding your father hanging from a crossbeam, your son dead of a gunshot wound, or your sister asphyxiated in the garage cannot help but leave scars. It is an unexpected and horrific ordeal. Both your mind and body can be affected, with unwanted and recurring images invading your consciousness and affecting your mental as well as physical health.

Can My Immune System Be Affected?

We have known for some time that your immune system—that part of your body that fights all kinds of diseases—is compromised when you are struggling with loss. Although you don't have a lot of control over what has happened when a suicide occurs, there are ways to reduce its traumatic and stressful impact on your well-being:

- You may not feel like it, but you have to eat. This includes a well-balanced diet, as well as taking supplemental vitamins if necessary.
- Light exercise will help. You can also try yoga and meditation.
- Guided imagery, a mind-body intervention aimed at easing stress, has also been found to promote a sense of peace and tranquility. By using your imagination, you learn to relax rather than feel tense and solve problems rather than feel helpless. EMDR (Eye Movement Desensitization and Reprocessing), a type of psychotherapy, is also helpful for dealing with traumatic memories. You learn to feel less anxious when thinking about the specific details of what has occurred, and work to regain a sense of control over your life. These treatments should only be conducted by a licensed health professional.
- Sharing your experiences with other survivors, a mental health professional, a religious or spiritual advisor, or a trusted friend acts to reduce the pressure-cooker feelings of having nowhere to turn at this time.

Note: The most effective therapy to protect your immune system is to keep company with people who are loving and kind and have your best interests at heart.

What Are the Physical Symptoms of Stress?

Almost any part of your body can reflect the immense stress you are undergoing following a suicide. The most common physical manifestations are headaches, neck and lower-back pain, aching joints in your hands (making you think that you have developed arthritis), and jaw and mouth pain, often called TMJ (for the temporomandibular joint where it occurs). You may develop chest pain and breathing difficulties, stomachaches, or changes in your bowel and urinary habits that you find worrisome. The list is long, and can make you feel as if you're falling apart at the seams.

What Are the Emotional Symptoms of Stress?

1. *Dissociation*: When we dissociate, we split off emotions from our thoughts because they are too intense and overwhelming to experience. "I don't remember having any feelings after my daughter's suicide," says a Philadelphia corporate executive. "I was going through the motions of arranging the funeral, greeting my friends and family at the service, even returning business calls, as if I were on automatic pilot."

With dissociation, it may seem as if you are detached from your feelings, that you are almost frozen and numb. You may experience out-of-body episodes where it feels as if you have left your physical being and surroundings. Not knowing what this is can be very alarming.

"When my daughter came over to tell me that her father, my ex-husband, had hanged himself, I reacted in slow motion," explains a Phoenix grandmother. "I sat down on the couch and began asking her all kinds of questions. All of a sudden, I was up above my body, looking down at my daughter and myself speaking. Everything was slowed down, almost as if I were watching a movie but not at the right speed."

As odd or frightening as these states seem, they are almost always temporary. In a way, they are benign and self-protective because the pain you are experiencing is just too much to bear in full force. One of the miraculous aspects of our minds and bodies is how unknown or unexpected mechanisms can come into play and coddle us when we are needy. It's almost as if we have a sixth sense to help us get through the shock, and are able to buy time in order to let the reality of such horrible news slowly sink in.

If you should develop any symptoms of dissociation, you might feel better telling someone else about what you're experiencing. It's possible that a family member or close friend can easily identify with you because they are having similar thoughts and feelings, or have in the past. Even if not, they might be able to understand why you seem so cool or in control as you go through each day. They may be wondering why losing your loved one doesn't seem to be "hitting" you or why it seems as if you don't really care that you have just lost someone so dear to you.

Note: Dissociation as it is described here is not the same as dissociative identity disorder (DID), the current term for multiple personality disorder. DID is a long-standing and very serious condition that requires intensive treatment. The trauma of suicide rarely, if ever, causes DID.

2. *Memory lapses:* The inability to recall important personal information, called *dissociative amnesia*, can occur after a particularly stressful or traumatic event. You may have problems with your memory and forget things you normally remember. Trauma can bring on many new feelings that can be very frightening and disconcerting, and there is probably a good reason for your temporary memory loss: Your memory gaps may be shielding you in some way from the full impact of your loved one's suicide.

You may also experience a memory lapse that lasts for a day or two following the suicide, almost as if you have blacked out. This isn't the same as passing out or becoming unconscious, but you may find that you can't remember big chunks of time, especially in the early days. For example, you may remember everything up to receiving the news of the suicide or finding the body, then remember nothing else from that moment on.

Michael:

Dissociative amnesia is much more than simple forgetting. It is different from not remembering the last name of one of the mourners at your father's funeral, or arriving at the service without your glasses, or forgetting to lock your car door. Here's an example:

A former patient of mine, a respected physician, took a massive overdose of sleeping pills and alcohol. When I learned of his death, I called his wife to express my condolences over the telephone and ask if I could help in any way. Five days later, I attended my patient's funeral, where I introduced myself to his wife and their children at the church reception following the service. We spoke for about 10 minutes.

About six weeks later, my patient's wife made an appointment to come in to see me. She began the visit by telling me that her husband had died, then gave me a copy of the pamphlet that was handed out to the mourners at the church. She went on to "walk me through" the order of the service—the poems, the prayers, the selection of music, the specifics of the eulogies, and how happy she was that so many people attended, given the public nature of her husband's suicide.

"It was a beautiful service," she told me. "I wish that you could have been there. I don't think that my husband ever really knew how many people loved and respected him."

Slowly I pulled out my copy of the pamphlet, which I had kept in her husband's chart, and gently told her that I had been at the funeral. She acted pleased, then added, "It's too bad that you didn't stay afterward and talk to me—I would have liked to introduce you to our children." My face must have given me away at that moment because she said, "Oh my God, don't tell me that we did talk and that you met the kids." I smiled and she smiled. Then she said, "These weird memory things are one of the reasons that I've come to see you." She went on to give me many examples of things told to her by her family and friends that she had no recollection of.

3. *Panic attacks*: "Suddenly I couldn't breathe—I thought I was dying," says Mollie, a 45-year-old accountant. "I remember the exact place and time. My husband and I were in our seats at the theater waiting for the performance to start. It was two minutes to eight P.M. It was the first time that I had really been out to anything social since my sister killed herself. I felt as if I needed to escape the theater before I passed out. We were in the middle of the row, but I bolted. I just stepped over people like I was running from a burning building. My husband didn't know what was going on. Once I got to the lobby, near the open doors and fresh air, I could breathe again. It felt like hours, but it couldn't have been because I remember the lights going dim in the theater at eight o'clock. I saw that from the lobby."

You may find yourself suffering from feelings of panic and paralyzing fears that you never had before. During a panic attack you might feel

- A sudden burst of fear or discomfort.
- A pounding of your heart or an increase in your heart rate.
- Sweating of your palms or brow.
- Shaking or trembling of your hands or legs.
- Trouble taking air into your lungs or tension in your throat muscles.
- Pain or discomfort in your chest.
- Nausea.
- Light-headedness, as if you might faint.
- Detached or unreal, a bit like dissociation.

- A fear of losing control or going crazy.
- Tingling or numbness of your skin.
- Chilled or hot and flushed.

The good news is that these terrifying symptoms only last a few minutes and always go away completely. The bad news is that a few minutes can seem like an hour.

Recognizing that you're having a panic attack greatly reduces its sting and enables you to ride it out. Other tips that may help:

- Slow your breathing down. Concentrate on taking a few deep breaths and conjuring up a relaxing or pleasant scene.
- If you are near a window, breathe in fresh air. If the room feels hot and stuffy, open the window or get to cooler air.
- If you're wearing a tie, loosen it. If your shirt or coat is buttoned up tightly, undo some of the buttons.
- If your hands are clenched, your jaw is tight, or your neck is rigid, relax your muscles.
- Tell yourself that what you're experiencing is a panic attack and it will go away. Tell yourself that you will be fine—and you will.

If your symptoms don't go away quickly or keep coming back and make you afraid to go places or be alone, it may be wise to seek help. An emergency room physician or primary care physician can check you out to make sure that you are physically fine. You may want to consider consulting a psychotherapist or psychiatrist to help you understand what's going on. For example, in *cognitive behavioral therapy* (CBT) you learn about panic and what causes it, how to recognize what triggers you, how to reduce your anxiety, how to change your thoughts from scary ones to acceptable ones, how to reward yourself for gains that you make, and so forth.

Other types of therapy can also help you gain insight into underlying factors—starting with the loss of your loved one—or vulnerabilities from your past that may be contributing to your stress. Marital and family therapy may be beneficial if your panic symptoms are arising as a result of relationship issues. In addition, your doctor can prescribe certain medications to help ease your symptoms.

4. *Self-destructive behavior*:

- "I started smoking again after my coworker died from an intentional overdose. I had stopped for more than ten years and now, two months after her very sad funeral, I'm back to one pack a day. I guess it's the price I have to pay."
- "I'm really getting worried about my drinking. I've always been a 'one drink a day' kind of guy, but since my daughter died, I'm up to two or even three drinks each night, and more on the weekends."
- "Look at me, I'm a blimp. I've put on forty pounds in the last year since my husband killed himself. It's like I have no self-esteem, like I don't care anymore."
- "My doctor put me on a tight leash with my sleeping pills. I was taking more and more of them without even realizing it. I've been so nervous and lonely since my mother died. We were like sisters."

Don't give up on yourself. Many people start smoking or drinking or overeating or abusing prescription drugs again—some for the first time!—when struggling with traumatic events in their lives. When you lose someone to suicide, especially a person you are very fond of and whom you miss terribly, it's very common to enter a "what the hell" or "devil may care" type of state. You're grieving and seeking comfort in any way you can.

Be careful with unhealthy habits, however, and give yourself a date to do something about them. It's never too early to stop smoking, go back to one drink a day, restart your diet, or gradually reduce your sleeping pills. Try to fill the void created by your loved one's suicide with new activities, friends, hobbies, volunteer work, or whatever helps you the most.

How Can I Protect Myself and My Family from Becoming Physically or Emotionally Ill?

"I'm worried about my middle daughter," says a distraught mother. "She's become totally withdrawn since her grandfather's suicide and refuses to talk about it or see a counselor. She stopped eating and is thin as a rail, and she recently broke up with her boyfriend. Now she spends most of her free time in her room. She used to be so outgoing and cheerful. I'm really afraid she's thinking about killing herself. What can I do?"

You have good reason to be worried. Your daughter is having more than a grief reaction to losing her grandfather. She sounds depressed. It is critical that you try to talk to her. Don't hesitate to ask her if she's wondering about her life, if she thinks it may not be worth living, or if she's having thoughts of harming herself. Even if she denies having any of these feelings, you should probably suggest that she makes an appointment to speak to her primary care physician. This may feel less threatening to her than going to a counselor, which she may dismiss with an excuse like, "I'm not crazy, you know." If your daughter refuses to go, make the appointment yourself, and let her know that you have done so. Tell her that you will go with her and just sit in the waiting room. You have every right to be firm with your daughter; your concern is based on authentic worry and love for her.

Although you may not feel like it, it's very important for you and your family to get back into some kind of routine in order to

HOW CAN I HELP SOMEONE WHO IS THREATENING SUICIDE?

1. Be aware. Learn the warning signs.
2. Get involved. Become available. Show interest and support.
3. Ask if he/she is thinking about suicide.
4. Be direct. Talk openly and freely about suicide.
5. Be willing to listen. Allow for expressions of feelings. Accept the feelings.
6. Be nonjudgmental. Don't debate whether suicide is right or wrong, or whether feelings are good or bad.
7. Don't lecture on the value of life.
8. Don't give advice by making decisions for someone else to make them behave differently.
9. Don't ask "Why?" This encourages defensiveness.
10. Offer empathy, not sympathy.
11. Don't act shocked. This creates distance between you.
12. Don't be sworn to secrecy. Seek support.
13. Offer hope that alternatives are available. Don't offer glib reassurances; that only proves you don't understand.
14. Take action. Remove means such as guns or stockpiled pills.
15. Get help from individuals or agencies specializing in crisis intervention and suicide prevention.

Reprinted with permission from the American Association of Suicidology (2005).

maintain—and regain—your health. Draw up a daily schedule to help organize your day and structure your activities. Plan a walk in your neighborhood, a coffee date with a friend, or 15 minutes of gardening to begin your morning. Arrange your meals ahead of time so you aren't tempted to skip eating or snack on junk food. If you live alone, invite a neighbor over to join you for dinner. If thoughtful friends ask you over for a meal, make yourself go. It may be tempting to refuse because you don't feel up to it, but it's better to accept the invitation and keep it brief than not to go at all.

Daily exercise will help keep your muscles and joints supple and give you needed energy. You can work out at home on your own or at a local gym or health club. Walking, either alone or with others, is another good way to keep your body in shape.

It's very important to set aside time each day for your spiritual needs. You may find readings, television programs, DVDs, and CDs of this genre to be helpful. Meditation and yoga may also be healing, and if you are religious, you may benefit from reading, prayer, or attending your house of worship. By recognizing and honoring the spiritual dimension of your being, you may find yourself feeling wiser, less sad, and less self-absorbed.

Seeking out other people who have lost a loved one to suicide, as suggested earlier, is key to your health. Join a support group in your community or go online to a designated and secure chat room. Meeting others in your situation is an excellent way of getting perspective on yourself and charting your future course. It's also a give-and-take: By helping others and being helped by others, you begin to feel better. To quote the famous psychiatrist Dr. Karl Menninger: "Love cures people . . . both the ones who give it and the ones who receive it."

Actively participating in restoring your physical and mental health will help you feel less preoccupied with repeated thoughts of how your daughter spent her final moments or the anguish your partner was in before he took his life. Much of your natural resilience will begin to return.

"People who kill themselves are still surrounded by love at the moment of death," writes Dr. Elisabeth Kübler-Ross, one of the leading experts in death and dying. Take comfort from her wisdom.

How Can I Break Off Unhealthy Relationships?

Research shows that unhealthy relationships can wreak havoc on your immune system. Therefore, it's very important for you to shield yourself from people who shut you down, judge you, behave as if they know best, make you feel as if there's something wrong with you, or are negative or unforgiving. If you're still in the early weeks and months of grieving, your usual defenses may not be working for you; this is not unusual when people are very stressed, heartbroken, or not at their best.

After a suicide, you may be very emotional; your moods may flip-flop easily; and you may feel very thin-skinned. This is normal. Because your usual ability to tune out and defend yourself from people who upset you is lowered, you'll need to take some form of action to protect yourself and your loved ones from potentially harmful remarks and comments. The following scripts may help:

- "As much as I value our friendship, I've decided not to see you for a while. I'm still very sad about losing my wife, and feel that you change the subject whenever I mention her. This really bothers me, and I don't want to deal with it right now."
- "I know that suicide is a tough subject for you. It is for me, too. I think in time, it'll be fine and I'll enjoy seeing you again."
- "The reason I haven't returned your telephone calls is because I get too upset when I talk to you. I feel judged by

you. That I'm somehow not doing this right. That I'm stuck. That I need to be happy. I'll call you in a few months, and we can see where our lives are then."

- "I'm still processing my brother's death and am not ready to 'move on with my life' as fast as you think I should. It's better if we catch up at a later time."

With people who are strangers or acquaintances, simply walk away. You don't need or deserve to hear anything hurtful or painful from them. It may be more difficult, however, to engage with close family members who say: "Are you still going to that support group? When will you straighten up and fly right?" Or, "Stop crying, I'm sick of it. You're becoming a martyr and don't have a monopoly on grief, you know." Or, "We're all very worried about you. The one-year anniversary of Dad's suicide has come and gone and you're still haggard and gloomy. We've decided as a group that if you're not perkier by Christmas we're sending you to a shrink."

Even though your relatives may have good reason to worry, threats and criticisms are not helpful in times of grief. You need to give them a clear message: "Please leave me alone. Your words are hurtful and are making me feel worse, not better. I'm going through this in my own way, the best I know how. Please respect that."

Michael:

What about professional and work relationships? For example, one of my patients noticed that her coworkers seemed to be avoiding her when she returned to the office after her son's suicide. "I hope this doesn't come across as paranoid, but everyone in my department is treating me differently since my son's suicide," she told me. "I see it in lots of small ways. People go on their coffee breaks without asking me to join them like they used to. When we sit around making small talk at lunch, I notice that they don't mention their kids and what's happening with them. I swear that conversation stops when I walk into the photocopying room. And when my coworkers come by my office and see my son's framed photograph on my desk, they look away. His photo has always been there; I haven't moved it. I'm starting to get angry. I'm being treated like a pariah or a criminal. I've always been a straight shooter, so I feel like calling a meeting to confront everyone about how hurtful they're being to me."

After discussing her options, my patient decided to take a different tack. She would simply be herself: If she were having a tough day, she would say so, and if she felt like joining her coworkers for coffee, she would approach them first. She would bring up her son in everyday conversation and ask the other people in the office about their children. And if she felt as if others were talking about her or ignoring her, she would try to see it as their problem, realizing that they felt awkward and didn't know what to say to her.

This story has three messages: (1) You have the right to grieve any way you want to. (2) You are not responsible for the feelings of others. (3) If there's a problem, you can be part of the solution. My patient's proactive approach to a painful workplace situation helped her feel much better; she could protect herself and end her terrible sense of isolation at the same time.

Carla:

I was stunned at the different reactions of friends, family, neighbors, and colleagues to Harry's suicide. A close friend, a social worker with a successful private practice, suddenly stopped calling me. When I phoned her several months later to find out why, she said, "I'm in denial about Harry's death. It's the only way I can handle it." Some neighbors crossed the street when they saw me rather than acknowledge what had happened. There are members of my family who still can't mention Harry's name.

I always say that if my editors had allowed it, I would have also included an "antiacknowledgments" page in *No Time to Say Good-*

bye! Yes, there will always be friends and relatives who will pull away or drop us entirely, but there will also be others who come through for us, sometimes totally unexpectedly. These are the friends who continue to telephone, even if we don't return their calls; the coworkers who don't ask about the grisly details; the neighbors who send over casseroles and prepared meals; the cousins who take our children to ballgames; the people who look us in the eye.

Recently, I had a long conversation with a father whose 19-year-old daughter had killed herself less than 24 hours before. The father, who had returned from work to find his daughter hanging from a backyard tree, was stunned, inconsolable, and wracked with guilt.

"You probably won't remember much of our conversation," I told him at the end of our talk. "But I promise you this: One day you will be making the same kind of phone call to someone else. The terrible pain and anguish you feel about your daughter's death will comfort another person, and you will understand why her death was not in vain."

I will never forget those who reached out to me as I now reach out to others.

Are My Feelings Specifically Related to Suicide? Will They Be Permanent?

Your feelings and reactions are similar to those of other people who are trying to cope with death of any sort, but in particular a sudden and unexpected death such as a homicide or an accident. Individuals whose loved ones are seriously injured or permanently disabled also tell of experiencing similar episodes of dissociation and panic attacks in the first day and months following such an unexpected and catastrophic event.

Where suicide differs from other traumatic losses is in the *intentionality* of the act: Your loved one makes a decision to die and does so. Even when you can accept that your mother was desperate or your boyfriend was frantic or your uncle couldn't see a way to go on fighting, the finality and deliberate nature of their action changes the way you view their death.

After a suicide you may experience

- Rage at your loved one.
- Feelings of betrayal, self-blame, and guilt.
- Concern about your loved one in "God's eyes."
- Shame about suicide.

Are these feelings ever permanent? No. Will you have residual symptoms? Sometimes.

- "It's been five years since I found my mother hanging in our garage. I still have occasional flashbacks of what I saw when I entered that building. But they're not as frequent now, and certainly less graphic."
- "I still get very sad and want to be alone each year on the anniversary of my brother's death. I dread the day before, the day of, and the day after, and then I'm fine. I know that twenty-three years seems like a long time, but it isn't really. I loved him so much and I still miss him like it was yesterday."
- "It's been over three years since my son jumped from a bridge outside of our town. I haven't been able to make myself walk over it yet. I used to get a panic attack just thinking about him jumping and flying through the air. Now, I only get panicky when I approach the bridge. My goal is to be able to walk onto the bridge and bear witness. I want to be with him. I owe him that. I don't want him to be alone—I'm his mother and still want to protect him."

Michael:

Losing someone to suicide is distinct from other deaths. Although you may find your thoughts racing as if you're going mad and your heart pounding as if you're on a roller coaster, you will eventually regain your equilibrium. It takes time and reflection.

Carla:

Suicide and death are two separate experiences. First, you must go through the suicide; then you can mourn the death. Losing a loved one to suicide is different and so are we. Our shared grief makes our losses easier to bear even though we are acutely aware that we are changed forever.

Will My Life Ever Return to Normal?

Carla:

No. Plain and simple. After suicide, you get used to a "new" normal. Life without your husband or mother or aunt. Questions that will never be answered, issues that will never be resolved, loose ends that will continue to unravel.

The word "normal" is permanently erased from a survivor's vocabulary. Your loss will never go away and your wounds will never fully heal. Yet gradually, over time—first with minutes, then hours, then days, then actual chunks of time—you find that the burden of your overwhelming and defining pain begins to ease. You come up with reasons to carry on and look for ways to bring about some kind of meaning and purpose to your life. Your loved one's suicide will become incorporated into your daily activities and your everyday thoughts, and you'll find yourself starting to remember his or her life as well as death. You also come to understand that your very survival will stand as a testimony and tribute to your loved one's enduring legacy.

Michael:

My patients have been some of my best teachers. On his final visit to me, William, a 56-year-old attorney whose son, Mark, killed himself one week after graduating from law school, explained his mixed feelings about stopping therapy after two years. "I'll miss these visits, but I'm ready to move on. I was so despondent, so wrecked, so lost when I started here. Remember how much I wanted to die, how I had given up, how suicidal I was? How you hovered, kept monitoring me, and would only give me a week's worth of medication at a time?

"I never thought I would make it, that I would survive this, that I could have a life without Mark. I'm still so sad and I miss him so much. But each day, each week, each month is a bit easier. There's a silver lining to this nightmare. I'm a better person, a more loving husband, a smarter lawyer, and a more thoughtful friend. I have Mark to thank for that. I will never know why he's dead, but what I do know is that he lives on inside me. And that belief keeps me going and gets me through."

FOUR

Keeping Your Family Together

At the very moment when you are looking for comfort from the ones you love, to unite with them in a strong and secure unit, to be together in a safe harbor during a frightening storm, you may find yourself more alone with your feelings and fears than ever before in your life. Although this is normal, and most often temporary, it is always unexpected and difficult.

"Suicide hits like a meteorite," says psychologist Dr. Edward Dunne, past president of the American Association of Suicidology and survivor of his 16-year-old brother's suicide. "It crashes into a family, leaving each person to circle in his or her own orbit of grief." Often, the people closest to you, those who have experienced the same loss, will experience the suicide of a loved one in completely different ways, and it can be very confusing:

- "Why does my mother continue to insist that my brother was playing Russian roulette instead of accepting the fact that he deliberately shot himself in the head?"

- "How could my husband have gone back to work so soon after our daughter hanged herself? How can he even concentrate on what's going on in his office?"
- "My father is a shell of himself since my mother took pills and suffocated herself with a plastic bag. It's been two years, and he's getting worse, not better. He's just fading away and refuses to talk about it or get help."
- "My sixteen-year-old son has started acting out in school since he found his sister dead of carbon monoxide poisoning in our garage. I don't know how to control him anymore. I think he hates me and blames me for my daughter's death."

Michael:

As a clinician, I see a lot of family pain after a suicide—both in the early weeks and months when you would most expect it, and way down the road, too. This deep hurt and heartache is also present in family members who may appear fine on the surface but are unable to recognize or acknowledge how suicide is affecting them.

Like any family coping with loss or trauma, your family may seem to tear apart or splinter. Hopefully your disagreements will be short-lived, if they occur at all. The good news is there is much that can be done to ease the tensions brought about by a family member's suicide. Many families who have lost a loved one to suicide pass through stages of pain, hurtful misunderstandings, and even estrangement, only to be strengthened and united over the long term.

"We're hardly the Waltons, but after a shaky start we've become a much closer and caring family since Dad killed himself three years ago," says Victor, a law student from Boston. "Suicide rocks your family foundation. Now, we're all like stonemasons, rebuilding brick by brick."

Carla:

"How did this become our lives?" Suicide redefines our concept of our family as well as ourselves. It reconfigures our relationships and makes us act in different ways than we did in the past. Some of us retreat within; others reach out for even more intimacy. We are each shaken to the core, yet continue to look for ways to keep our family, our marriage, our close relationships—and our own sanity—intact.

Survivors ache for continuity, for our family to stay the same even though we're stunned and bereft and have seemingly lost our way. Only by talking to each other as best we can and getting our problems out in the open—a frustrating and sometimes seemingly impossible task—can we begin to restore the fragile balance of our permanently reshaped family relations.

How Does Suicide Affect Family Relationships?

When you lose a loved one to suicide, not only is your personal health at risk, as discussed in Chapter 3, but also your family's health. If you are a widow or widower of suicide, you must contend with your private grief at the same time as you're helping your children cope with the death of their parent. If you are an adult who has lost a parent to suicide, you may still have ongoing relationships to work out with your siblings or a surviving parent. If you are a parent who loses a child to suicide, your spouse and other children will need your attention and care even as you are trying to absorb your own traumatic and tragic loss.

It's estimated that for every death by suicide, seven people are closely or directly affected. Many will struggle with some form of temporary depression, post-traumatic stress, guilt, or shame, as well as a myriad of physical symptoms after the suicide; some may even feel suicidal or attempt suicide themselves. Each person grieves in a very personal way, and your individual response will have a direct impact on your family relationships. What's more, now you are all on the alert, even hypervigilant, to make sure that no one else you love will die by suicide; if you suspect that your mother or grandson is suicidal, you may become overly focused about their every movement and exacerbate an already stressful situation.

Very little is known, unfortunately, about how suicide affects family functioning and stability over the long term. According to 2003 joint findings by the American Foundation for Suicide Prevention (AFSP) and the National Institute of Mental Health (NIMH), this area is now being targeted as an important area for future research, a welcome and much-needed development.

"It's almost impossible to understand the unremitting impact that suicide has on a family," says a San Francisco editor. "My brother's ghost ripples out across space and across generations. My mother never recovered after my younger brother shot himself at the age of twenty-one. His death smashed her soul and spirit, almost like a bad car accident, and she was devastated and defeated for the rest of her life. My father went about his regular routine as if he were an automaton. He just shut down and didn't want to talk about it. I see now that this was his way of coping, but it made it more difficult for my mother.

"After my brother killed himself, I felt as if my life was suspended, that I was drowning and could barely tread water. My world exploded and stood still at the same time, and I was afraid my brother's suicide would consume the rest of my life. I had trouble concentrating, and it took me a while to resume my studies.

"Luckily, I had a great support system with my wife and her family, who were like my own family. Also, my wife had known my brother for a long time—she and I had been high school sweethearts—and I could share a lot with her. But I was a basket case. I felt guilty for what I did and what I didn't do. I was also angry at my brother for what he did to my parents. His death defined the rest of their lives. And, in many ways, defined mine as well.

"My wife and I debated whether we should name our son after my brother. In some irrational way, we were afraid of passing on a kind of legacy, maybe even a curse. So we decided to give our son my brother's name for his middle name. I know it sounds strange, but my wife and I breathed a sigh of relief when our son turned twenty-one and was past the age when my brother killed himself. Even though we could understand intellectually that suicide is taking ownership of your actions, there's still something so primal and mysterious and frightening about it.

"I have a deep sadness that my brother didn't get to know my children and grandchildren. I also still wonder after all these years if I could have been a better brother. I was always the responsible one, yet somehow I let him down. Even if he was a lost soul, I should have been there for him."

Suicide never takes place in a vacuum. Even though it is perhaps the loneliest death imaginable, its reverberations touch many people, especially close family members. Your immediate family and your much larger extended family are affected both as individuals and as a unit.

The legacy of loss extends wide after a suicide: "I lost my brother, my son, my father, my partner, my uncle." "I lost my wife, my granddaughter, my best friend, my niece, my stepsister." The chorus of voices goes on and on as the trajectory of the family expands.

Your family unit is now minus one. How will you notice this? Your loved one's absence is all around: an empty chair at the kitchen table, an unoccupied bed, an undisturbed room, a jacket hanging on the coatrack 24 hours a day. There are no more phone calls, letters, e-mails, or greeting cards. There is a quiet that is strange and unwelcome.

You will notice and miss your loved one most acutely when you recall the ways you functioned as a family. Your mother was the meal planner and cook. Your wife, the money manager. Your son shoveled the snow and your grandmother was the voice of wisdom. Your brother was the clown, your father, the breadwinner. Who will fill their shoes?

Unlike families whose loved one died of cancer or in a car accident, it feels as if your loved one left willingly and deliberately, without regard to how his or her aching absence would affect you and those you care for. You say to yourself that those other families are lucky, that all they have to contend with is sorrow and longing. You have questions and uncertainty and heartache, plus much, much more. You also have feelings of rage, relief, guilt, betrayal, hatred, humiliation, and fear about the suicide—feelings that often seem contradictory, confusing, and unsympathetic.

You may also find it difficult to reconcile your own feelings with those of your surviving family members. You would like someone else to feel similar to you, or if they don't, not to judge you or make you feel any more alienated or alone than you already do. Your anger at your deceased husband or father may also intensify; you're not just angry at what they wrenched from your relationship with them, you're also angry about what their suicide did to other family members and the entire family unit.

"Ever since my mother jumped to her death from the roof of a downtown office building, my father, brothers, and I have been walking around in a daze," says Brenda, a 33-year-old architect from Atlanta. "It's been ten months, but the pain seems to get worse, not better. We're now yelling at each other, pointing fingers at the person we think is to blame, and, frankly, growing apart. I know my mother would have wanted us to have stuck together at this time, yet she brought this on herself. My brothers are married, but I have no one. Does this mean that I'm now responsible for my father? How could my mother have loved us and have done this to us?"

Even though it may seem bleak at the beginning, families don't necessary fracture forever. Over time, there is usually some kind of resolution or uneasy peace. But "time" is the key word. Some days pass too slowly, other days fly too quickly. Each of you needs some time to be alone with your thoughts and time to talk with each other. Keeping your family intact is a long, often rocky, but very worthwhile trek.

Why Do People Grieve Differently?

"Respect each other and each person's way of grieving," advises Iris Bolton. "Support each other and don't be critical of how you may be reacting differently to your loved one's suicide. Feelings come and go, but family is forever."

What is so unique about family members is the different ways they manifest their grief. You may be very open about all of your feelings and need to keep talking about your sister's suicide, re-counting the story over and over. Your mother may also want to discuss what happened but doesn't want to listen again to the de-tails about how your sister looked when you found her dead in her bed from an overdose of painkillers. Your father may be con-vinced that your sister's death was an accident and won't toler-ate any reference to a possible suicide; she has become a saint in his eyes who can do no wrong. Your brother may have totally closed off about anything having to do with your sister, despite being very open and expressive in the early days following her suicide.

We all show our grief in different ways:

- Depression
- Withdrawal
- Anger
- Denial

- Isolation
- Silence
- Overworking
- Anxiety
- Overwhelming sadness

Many of your reactions and emotions will change and overlap with each other, sometimes in rapid succession and other times more slowly. Try not to judge yourself and others during this volatile period or make any statements or decisions that you may later regret. The importance of family is paramount, as Iris Bolton so wisely points out, especially at this time.

"My sister continues to deny that her husband deliberately drove his car into a tree," says Russ, a North Carolina real estate agent. "Even though the police and autopsy reports show that it's almost certain that it couldn't have been an accident, Ana believes that Jack would never do this to her, that he would never abandon her and their three small children.

"I can understand why Ana is having a hard time, yet I have to go with the evidence and facts. Lately, I've noticed a rift developing between us. The more I try to convince her that Jack's death was a suicide, the more she insists that it was an accident. We argue, then pull away from each other, then try to change the subject. We're growing apart, and this makes me very sad."

Losing someone you love to suicide transforms your very infrastructure. Ana's denial about the true nature of her husband's death is a psychological defense mechanism that protects her from having to accept something that she cannot fathom. In the face of bad news, denial is one of the most common strategies that we use to ward off feelings of terror and fears of disintegration or death. Over time, with reflection, weighing the facts, and doing our own investigation of the evidence, we may give up our need for denial. Or may not. It is our right.

NOTE: You must never confront people who cannot or will not accept that the cause of death is suicide. Making them face up to the facts or threatening them is more than insensitive and unkind; it is also dangerous. Badgering them at this time can be an assault on their mental stability, so it's best to be patient and compassionate, even if their reasoning seems unhealthy or bizarre to you. Your family member or close friend may eventually begin to consider that the death may have been suicide or accept that it was definitely suicide. But they may also carry their denial to the end of their lives.

Because existing family dynamics are usually strained after a suicide, conflicts can also arise if one person takes over without regard to the other family members' wishes or needs.

"I have no desire to see my mother-in-law ever again," declares Andrew, a Denver businessman. "My wife slit her wrists three years ago, and you would think her death was my mother-in-law's exclusive tragedy. She practically took over the whole funeral, greeting all the mourners one by one, and repeating what happened over and over. She wouldn't let anyone near me and my children—she said she was being protective, but I think she was being controlling. She complained that I didn't help her write thank-you notes to the people who came to the wake and funeral, although that was the farthest thing from my mind.

"My mother-in-law's focus was on what happened to her; my wife's suicide became her story. It only got worse after the funeral. She packed up all of my wife's clothes and gave them away to charity without first asking me what I wanted. She practically moved into our house so she could be with her grandchildren. When I finally told her to ease off, she reacted by cutting off relations entirely. Now my kids are more confused than ever. My wife was the glue that held us all together and now we all seem so lost."

Some people can keep themselves from unraveling only by taking charge. They are terrified of the uncertainty and ambiguity of their feelings and thoughts that are so common after a suicide in the family. Sadly, their overbearing and controlling behavior can often result in upsetting or alienating the family they so desperately want and need.

Being on the receiving end of this kind of behavior is tough, even infuriating. You should confront family members who have become very dominating and insensitive to your feelings. They may be shocked or surprised at how intrusive they've become, how much they may be disturbing others, and how obnoxious or even cruel their actions are. If they don't listen to what you have to say, or worse, don't seem to care, let them know that you find their attitude upsetting and you don't wish to see them for a while. Tell them that you hope that they will think about what you've said, and, perhaps in time, you will be able to reconnect with each other. Some survivors find that writing a letter to the individual can be more productive than a face-to-face meeting.

The following suggestions may help you ease family differences in grieving after a suicide:

1. If you do find yourself blurting out hurtful things to a family member, apologize. If you can't bring yourself to say that you're sorry, try something like, "I want to talk about last night. I was very troubled and really let loose. Can we speak about it?" You may not feel that you owe your brother or wife an apology, but by addressing the situation and opening up a dialogue, you are making a sincere gesture to get your relationship back on track.

2. If you think that some family members are judging you or others, remind them that each of us has a different personality and grieves in our own way.

3. If you find a family member's manner to be harsh and controlling, it's perfectly acceptable to tell him or her to back off.

4. Remember that there is no "right" or "wrong" way to grieve the suicide of a loved one. This may be one of your family's biggest challenges as the weeks and months go by. If you become concerned about a family member, reach out in as calm a way as possible: "Randy, can I ask you something? I understand that we're all trying to come to terms with Mom's death in our own way. Are you doing okay?"

5. If you have found it helpful to talk to other survivors in a support group, you may want to tell other members of your family, and ask them to join you at the next meeting. If they're not interested, try to accept their decision. This type of gathering may not interest them, especially if they are very reserved. Don't pressure them. As time passes, they may decide to join you.

6. Talking to a professional after losing a loved one to suicide can be very helpful, although it's not the route for every survivor. No matter how much you think certain family members could benefit from therapy or counseling, if they do not want to go, you can't force them. In time, they may change their minds but it will be on their terms. (For children, see Chapter 5.)

7. If a family member becomes involved in suicide outreach programs or suicide prevention organizations, try to be understanding and affirming even if these activities may not interest or engage you. Some survivors who are engaged in suicide-related projects are made by other family members to feel that they are becoming involved because they're clinging to their loved one's memory and can't move on or put their loss behind them. This is wrong. Each person must mourn in whatever way gives comfort.

Carla:

Grieving is so individual. I still can't look at pictures of Harry for more than a few seconds. I can't watch him on home videos or listen to his voice on recordings. A reporter who interviewed me for a story about survivors of suicide astutely observed in his article that I had photographs of my late Labrador retriever, Cinco, throughout my apartment, but none of my late husband.

Yet, I know many survivors who get great comfort from reflecting on their loved one's pictures or being surrounded by his or her image. Sharon Smith tells of finding immense consolation from organizing baby photographs of her 22-year-old son, Garrett, after his suicide, compiling each of his first eight years into separate scrapbooks. Some people like to wear their loved one's favorite piece of clothing or jewelry; others carry a photograph of the person they lost in a locket or in their wallet.

I have come to believe that seeking solace in "whatever helps you through the night" is all right—as long as it's not harmful to yourself or others. Each of us heals in the way it feels best; we are our own guides in uncharted territory and must trust that our instincts will lead us back to safety and home.

Do Men and Women Grieve Differently?

"After my son's suicide, my husband immersed himself in work, while I couldn't even get out of bed in the morning," says a retired management consultant from Washington, D.C. "My daughter went back to her own husband and children after a couple of days, understandably, and I felt I was alone to mourn my son. I had no closure—I wasn't even able to see him in the funeral parlor because the director had advised me against it. My son had shot himself in the head and blown it off, but all I wanted was to hold his hand and hug his body. Why couldn't they have put a towel over the part where his head was missing? Yet, I was in no shape to insist, so I was left with just a closed casket. It still bothers me fourteen years later.

"My husband loved our son as much as I did, but our reactions were so different. I couldn't understand how he could go to the office several days after the funeral and continue his business without missing a beat. How come he was still in one piece and I was shattered? We went to a family therapist to help us understand each other as well as our different responses to our son's death. We also joined a support group together. I now run these groups in my community. Both my husband and I are also very involved in suicide prevention work, which keeps us connected to our son and to each other."

Women and men often have different reactions to loss:

- Men may want or need to talk with others, but less frequently than women.
- Men prefer to talk with fewer individuals.
- Men tend to grieve more privately.
- Men return to work more quickly, and seem to need the structure and distraction of their jobs.
- Men are less likely to go for therapy or attend a support group for grieving individuals.
- Men may internalize their anguish more in such ways as withdrawing from others, having temper outbursts, eating more and putting on weight, and drinking more alcohol. They are less likely to visit their primary care physician than women.
- Men who lose their wives to suicide tend to date earlier and remarry faster than women who lose their husbands.

"We had no frame of reference for the death of a child, let alone the suicide of a child," explains Martin, a corporate attorney from Austin, Texas. "We had no suspicions about our daughter; 'suicide' wasn't even in the vocabulary of our family. In a split second, the world changed. After Tory's suicide, my wife and I went for counseling. She perceived the need for counseling before I did, both for the two of us and for our two remaining sons. Tory's death affected how I felt about my family—if it could happen to her, then it could happen to her brothers, to my wife, to me.

"I was very depressed for a year and a half after my daughter died, and would just sit and cry at the kitchen table. I remember driving my car, wondering if I might jump out and throw myself in front of an oncoming truck. I had thoughts of shooting myself, if I had had a gun. I didn't think the pain would go on so long. Intellectually I knew what the consequences of my suicide would be for my family, but I didn't care.

"It's been seven years since Tory's death, and this year has been easier than my sixth, which was easier than my fifth. Fortunately, my experience in that long dark tunnel is beginning to pass."

How Do I Know if My Family Is Coming Off the Rails?

"I'm furious at my brother for keeping his gun at my parents' house," says Helena, the mother of two teenagers. "He didn't want his hunting rifle in his own home because he has a young son, and asked my father to store it for him even though he knew that Dad had suffered from past episodes of depression. Sure enough, last month my parents had a big fight and Dad got the rifle and shot himself in the chest right in front of my mother. I got this hysterical phone call from my mother and drove over there immediately. The living room was covered with blood, which had also splattered over her.

"Now my brother wants my mother to sell her house and move in with him. She doesn't want to, but he's been pressuring her. My brother hasn't taken any responsibility for my father's suicide, and says that Dad would have found another method to kill himself even if the gun hadn't been there. I don't know about that. We have gotten into these almost violent screaming matches, which further upsets my mother. This is all a terrible nightmare."

No family is perfect, but each varies tremendously in its capacity to come to grips with tragedy. In order to help you differentiate between tension and stress that may be temporary and issues that may permanently divide the family, try to keep in mind how your family was before your loved one's suicide. If your family has traditionally handled conflicts and disagreements between each other by talking things through and getting back on track, that is a good sign. It means that all of you respect each other, despite your differences, and value family loyalty and cohesion. After suicide, tensions will inevitably arise, but with your core values in place, you will discuss any misunderstandings, correct them, and apologize for hurtful things that were said.

Watch for the following signs, which may result in permanent damage to your family structure:

1. *Verbal outbursts and blaming.* Although disagreements and arguments are very common in the early days and weeks following a suicide, that doesn't mean that such fighting is healthy. You may need to blame someone just to make sense of a senseless death. But is that person really at fault? For example, Helena's brother may have kept his gun at his parents' house because he never imagined that his father would become suicidal, despite his history of depression. He probably feels extremely guilty already, despite Helena's perception that he's not taking any responsibility for his father's suicide. In fact, one of the reasons that he may want their mother to live with him is because he feels that he's to blame for their father's suicide.

2. *Family coalitions.* If one or more family members are meeting privately and speaking badly about others in the family, rifts and divisions will inevitably follow. Don't do this. Or, if you're not doing this but a sibling and cousin are, talk to them about it. Tell them that this is unhealthy and unkind, and could result in relationships never being repaired or healed.

3. *Worsening of family relationships with the use of alcohol.* Some of the most volatile and damaging arguments and fights occur when people have been drinking. Family members lose restraint and may say terribly hurtful and nasty things to each other. The fallout may last a long time, maybe even forever.

4. *One or more family members cutting themselves off from the family unit.* In the short term, this may not be so serious; you remove yourself from the dynamics of your family because it is self-protective and allows you some degree of healing before reentering family life. But if your estrangement continues for many months or years, it may become permanent and irreversible. Try to monitor yourself, and as you begin to feel better, visit family members who previously upset you. You may be surprised that you no longer find it distressing or uncomfortable to be around them.

5. *Scapegoating.* This is when one family member becomes the object of blame, derision, and rejection from the others in the family. Even if the person is not trouble-free (for example, he or she abuses alcohol or drugs, has a criminal record, or is considered the "black sheep"), the person does not deserve total ostracism from the rest of the family. Often, the scapegoating of one member is the only way a family can maintain its facade that all is well.

If you are the one who is being "locked out" or blamed, speak to your family members about this. Defend yourself, and tell them that what they are doing is not fair. If you think that certain members of your family are avoiding looking inward by focusing on you alone, tell them that also. Talking about these dynamics might correct rifts and identify other reasons why relations in the family have been strained.

In some families, unfortunately, it is the individual who killed himself or herself who becomes the scapegoat: Suicide is considered so unacceptable and shameful that all of the remaining family members band together and never mention the person who died again. Or they all agree to falsify what they tell the world about the true cause of death.

What Can I Do to Help My Family?

"My father doesn't have a clue what I'm going through," say Marcy, a high school senior in rural Wyoming. "He tried to hide my aunt's suicide from me, as if I were stupid and blind. My aunt lived with my grandmother in the next town and I loved spending time with them. I knew my aunt had problems, yet she was always laughing and happy with me. She took an overdose of her antidepressants, but my father told me that she was in the hospital for some kind of flu. She died three days after taking the pills without ever regaining consciousness.

"I could see how devastated my father and grandmother were, and I confronted my father right before my aunt's funeral. He told me that, yes, my aunt had killed herself and left a very angry note. My father also said that my aunt had a previous suicide attempt several months before, but he and my grandmother didn't want me to know.

"Even though I understand that my father and grandmother thought they were protecting me, I'm still angry. I had a right to know that my aunt was having problems. I could have read up on suicide and become educated about the signs. Maybe I could have even helped my aunt before she did it again. I feel betrayed by my father and grandmother for not sharing what was happening with me, and upset at my aunt for not reaching out to me. More than anything, I'm really angry at everyone for not being honest with me. Now, I'll never know who to believe again."

One of the tenets of family function is counting on the people you love. Regaining a sense of trust that may now be shaky or gone is the first step in restoring a sense of family.

Here is some dialogue that might help Marcy and her father and grandmother begin to reestablish their shared trust:

Marcy: *We need to talk. I don't think that the two of you realize how upset I am about Aunt Mary's suicide. Not just her death and how she died, but how you handled it with me. I'm 17 years old. I'm not a child. And yet you've kept things from me as if I were a little kid.*

Father: *I was only trying to protect you. Mental illness and suicide are scary subjects. I didn't want to upset your schoolwork or your social life. You're always so happy and positive. I didn't think you needed Aunt Mary's pile of problems.*

Grandmother: *I'm really the one who discouraged your father from telling you. When I was your age, we didn't talk about mental illness and people trying to kill themselves. It was all hushed up. I thought it would be better if you didn't know what was going on.*

Marcy: *But this is the twenty-first century! I am so angry about this. I loved Aunt Mary very much. If you had told me about her other suicide attempt, I would have gone over to see her right away. They teach us stuff in school about suicide. It doesn't scare me. I could have helped her. She may even have been alive today and getting proper treatment. I feel so betrayed—by both of you and even by Aunt Mary. No one gave me a chance to help. It's a horrible feeling that I'm living with.*

Father: *I am so sorry, Marcy. I understand now. I realize now that my trying to protect you wasn't fair to you.*

Grandmother: *I'm sorry too. The world is different now, but I guess I forget that sometimes. I regret that we didn't tell*

> *you about Aunt Mary's suicide attempt—or even*
> *ask you for some advice. Your father and I were*
> *really lost for a while.*

Marcy: *Thank you. I feel a little better just hearing your*
words.

Father: *This is so hard for all of us. We need to pull together.*
I still can't believe that she's gone.

Marcy: *I just hope that Aunt Mary knew how much we*
loved her.

Grandmother: *I know she did.*

Communication is the first and most important step in keeping your family together after a suicide, no matter how awkward, uncomfortable, or tentative your conversations with other family members may be.

Is it possible that any kind of normalcy or routine will ever return to your home? Old traditions may be too painful, and new rituals and ground rules may have to be put into place. During this period of intense change, your family should consider the following guidelines:

1. *Tolerate differences.* "I believe that the best way to get through this is to do whatever your heart tells you is right," says Lillie, 42, about her husband's suicide. "I keep moving, traveling, learning. If I slow down, I feel as though a nervous breakdown will catch me. I know that I'm one of the walking wounded, and there's no glue or tape I can buy that will mend my broken heart. I also know there's a fine line between being strong and becoming unhinged. I won't let it happen, I'll be okay. I don't care what my family tells me—this is the way I'm doing it."

After the suicide of a loved one, you may want to surround yourself with lots of people and activities. You may find comfort and reassurance in being in the company of your family and extended family, as well as with your close friends and other survivors. On the other hand, like Lillie, you may find that what works best for you is spending time alone. When you're by yourself, you can think about your loved one, reflect on his or her life and death, and reminisce in your mind and heart. This may feel spiritual to you. You should explain your need for aloneness to your family members, though. This will give them relief, since they may be worried about you and interpret your isolation as something being wrong with you.

It may also help to talk about your loved one's suicide with individual family members on a one-on-one basis, then in small groups, and later as an entire family. Although you may find this repetitive, it can be very healing. Remember that some family members will not want to talk or will be unable to talk. Accept them for who they are and keep in mind that what works for you may not necessarily work for them. They may want to speak later on, but only with certain individuals and not others.

Take care and watch out for each other. This will be difficult when you may be feeling utterly overwhelmed yourself, but reaching out to those you hold dear at this time will help you in the long run.

2. *Establish healing rituals.* Sharing ways to honor a person's memory and establishing a framework for family members to mourn together can be very healing. Draw upon your family history and what your family has traditionally done in the past when a loved one has died. This may or may not be helpful, but it is a starting point. Talk with other survivors and survivor groups for ideas. Some suggestions include

- Establish a legacy or annual memorial in your loved one's name. One family whose daughter was the captain of her high school basketball team set up an athletic scholarship given annually in her name. Another family established an invited lectureship in their father's name at the local library.

- Place a memorial notice in your local newspaper each year on the anniversary of your loved one's death.
- Host a coming-together of all family members each year on the day of your loved one's death. Some families do this on the birthday rather than the date of death. You might consider a candle-lighting ceremony, selections of music, or personal readings and reminiscences. Reassure family members who are reluctant to come that this will not be a depressing or morbid time, but a chance to share both sad and happy stories and honor the person who has died. Those who cannot attend in person because of geographical distance can be invited to call at a specific time or to send a letter or e-mail with their thoughts and wishes.

3. *Be flexible about holidays and family occasions.* "I decided to go ahead with our annual Labor Day barbecue, even though my father had killed himself only two months before," explains Mario, the father of two and grandfather of seven. "My mother just sat in the house and wouldn't come outside; my brother gave me some half-baked excuse why he and his family couldn't make it; one of my daughters walked around pretending nothing had happened and the other one talked nonstop about her grandfather's suicide. My wife tried to keep the grandkids from knowing what was going on, and I just kept grilling away.

"I learned that you can't force a family gathering if the time isn't right. There's no sitting around in a big circle with everyone holding hands and singing 'Kumbaya' together. I just have to trust that even though our family is going through a rough patch, it won't be like this forever."

The permanent absence of a family member is most acutely felt at holidays, birthdays, and other celebrations usually defined by joy and happiness. Try to use this time to remember the person you lost in a way that makes sense to you and can be tolerated—and maybe even shared—by other family members: Set a place for your son at the Thanksgiving table; light a special Christmas candle for your mother; tell your children a story about their father on his birthday; take your parents out to dinner on the anniversary of your sister's suicide.

If you are religiously observant, you may have specific rituals and ways of remembering in keeping with your faith. You and your immediate and extended family may be very comforted by the words and prayers of other people, including complete strangers.

GUIDELINES FOR HOLIDAYS AND SPECIAL DAYS

1. Tell your family and friends what you need and what isn't helpful. You may want to be with people, but you also may want to be alone.
2. Change your traditions. Think of taking a trip to be away.
3. Simplify. Stop writing Christmas cards, for example.
4. Do something for someone else in the name of the person who died. Take presents to a children's hospital or volunteer for a soup kitchen.
5. Do something special for yourself. Stay in bed all day and read a good book; go to a movie.
6. Give yourself permission to grieve. Take time out when the wave of grief comes over you.
7. Know it's okay to laugh again.
8. Know that you're not alone.
9. Let your holidays and special days be filled with grace.

Reprinted with permission from Iris M. Bolton, The Link Counseling Center, Atlanta, Georgia.

This type of recognition and love is especially soothing if you feel you have been judged or alienated because your family member died of suicide.

Try to remember that each anniversary, each birthday, each holiday meal gets a bit easier with the passage of time. What you did the first or second year may not work anymore, and you may want to do something different. Always keep in mind that you are remembering and honoring your loved one's life—don't let how they died eclipse the beauty, the richness, and the brave struggles of how they lived.

4. *Become educated about suicide.* Separating myths from realities may help you break the almost paralyzing hold that suicide has on your life and imagination. The vast majority of survivors know very little or nothing about the subject of suicide before their loved one's death. As you talk with other survivors, read articles and books, examine helpful Web sites, and explore other ways of gathering information, you will feel somewhat better. You may begin to understand some of the *whys* of your family member's suicide. Your knowledge will not only help you to get through each day more easily, but also allow you to help other family members, friends and acquaintances, coworkers, and people whom you haven't even met yet.

5. *Consider family counseling if needed.* One of the functions of a family is mutual support. When suicide strikes a family, everyone is hurting, needs help, and is in no condition to support each other. This is when family counseling can be life-saving—or, more accurately, family-saving. Family counselors or therapists help in many ways, including

- Seeing how your family is functioning or not functioning under the circumstances and making simple suggestions that might help or guide you.
- Assessing each of you as individuals and explaining to

other family members, in your presence, your feelings and behavior. This helps to diminish the worry that family members may have about each other.

- Helping "quieter" family members to open up a bit in a family meeting and asking more excitable or hot-tempered family members to speak more clearly and calmly.
- Alerting you to services that you might not know about, ranging from seeing a primary care physician for physical symptoms or consulting with a psychiatrist for a thorough assessment and possible medication, to recommending local resources.

Most important, family therapists offer hope that you will get through this rough time. They help you see that your family is a group of people in crisis who love and care for each other, and that even if you are not able to show your concern right now, you will over time.

Michael:
Don't be discouraged if it seems that only you or one other relative care about your family's welfare and future. Some survivors who seem the most indifferent or who appear to forsake family solidarity really do value it. Don't give up on those you have been close to in the past. Continue to remember them, to phone and e-mail them, to invite them to get-togethers and anniversaries of your loved one's suicide. Many will eventually show up. Your respect for family and your goal of keeping your loved ones in communication with each other are noble. Your hard work and love for your family, with all its problems and complications, will be worth it.

How Can I Keep My Marriage Intact after Suicide?

It has long been known that the death of a child is one of the biggest assaults to marital harmony and stability. When you lose a child to suicide, it only intensifies the strain between husband and wife. One of the bedrocks of marriage is being able to communicate with each other frankly and openly. It's what gets couples through tough times. When you're both grieving your son's or daughter's suicide, it's very hard to lean on each other. And if one of you were going through a difficult phase with your child at the time of his or her death, you may become the target of your spouse's rage and blame.

"My daughter's suicide eventually unraveled my marriage," says Dina, a nurse midwife. "I just stopped caring. After Kelly shot herself in her junior year of high school, any intense emotion that I experienced would immediately turn into one of pain, and I would cut off. It was almost as if my brain couldn't distinguish between suffering and any other emotion. My daughter's death didn't affect my husband the same way. Whereas I withdrew emotionally, he wanted more intimate contact. We cried together but still felt alienated from each other.

"Unfortunately, suicide is tied into family problems that already existed before; the suicide only intensifies those problems. Kelly was our only child, but my husband and I had other family connections that kept us together after her death—our mothers, brothers, nieces, and nephews. As time went on, however, our connection to each other started feeling increasingly diminished.

"For a marriage to survive the suicide of a child, you have to immerse yourselves in forgiveness and love for each other from the start. You can't be judgmental or angry with each other, because you're already so angry at yourself. You also can't let the suicide be a weapon against the other person, either to attack them or to defend yourself.

"I think that my husband eventually used our daughter's suicide to alienate himself from our marriage and punish me for having an argument with her right before she died. Yet, I could forgive my husband for accusing me because I knew that he loved Kelly so much. His devastation and heartbreak was more suffering than anyone should have to endure. Of course, he also blamed himself for her death, and covered his guilt by blaming me.

"When our daughter died, the nucleus of our marriage died. Nothing was really left even though we stayed together for eleven years after Kelly's suicide. Our life became empty. We started having 'angry sex'—we would just do it and get it over with. I started saying to him, 'What about me? Yes, Kelly's gone, but where do I fit in?' I wanted to create a new life together, but my husband wanted to hold on to our daughter. I felt that in my husband's mind, I had died along with her.

"The burden of responsibility makes the suicide of a child different from other deaths. Kelly used my husband's gun to shoot herself in the head, and most kids usually use something of their parents' to kill themselves: a razor, a gun, prescription drugs, a rope in the house. With suicide, there's a direct link between your child and you without the buffer of a doctor or an illness or an accident.

"For years, I tried to find meaning in my daughter's suicide, but I couldn't. I tried to push her death out of my mind, to block it out. I didn't trust anyone or anything anymore. I couldn't believe anything would ever be permanent again. My energy went into stabilizing my husband and getting him back on track. I had to feel I was doing something, helping him when I couldn't help my daughter. After a long time, I started connecting to everyday events, but I was a completely different person.

"After our divorce, my husband remarried and had a child, even though he didn't want another child with me when Kelly died. Our breaking up has allowed me to remember what my daughter and I shared. I don't have to worry about my husband's guilt anymore;

it's now between the two of us, my daughter and me. I have the freedom and faith to connect with my daughter and am feeling much more like a mother. I'm no longer ashamed about what happened, and I've forgiven her and me. At the beginning I never talked about Kelly; now I speak about her all the time, almost as a tribute. My daughter existed and deserves to be remembered."

Like gardens, all marriages require care, patience, and nurturing to flourish. Your marriage will never be more tested than now, and the following suggestions may help to keep it whole:

1. Try to be kind to each other even though it may be almost impossible at times. When you're tempted to blame your spouse, try not to say it. Mention how you feel in conversation with a friend or another survivor. If you do blurt out blaming statements, apologize.

2. Pick your battles. Is there anything to be gained by provoking a fight? Aren't each of you already struggling with enough regrets and *if onlys*? Save your arguments for other issues in daily living that need to be ironed out. And stay on course—if you're fighting about one of you forgetting the other's birthday, for example, don't bring up your son's or daughter's suicide in that argument.

3. It will help if each of you has a personal outlet for talking about your unpleasant—or lack of—feelings for each other. This could be a friend, another family member, your pastor, a support group, or a therapist. By doing this, you gain some perspective. Some of these feelings may be quite serious and will need to be discussed with your husband or wife. Others may be irrational and will go away just through venting about them with others.

   NOTE: You should never discuss marital matters with a third party without telling your spouse that, *in addition to* talking to him or her, you feel the need to speak with someone else about how you are feeling. Trust is a basic covenant in marriage, and in order for your spouse not to feel betrayed, he or she may have concerns about whom you talk to and the parameters of what is being disclosed. The issue is marital privacy, and it is normal to have strong feelings about this. You should never avoid dealing with tough issues at home by talking with others.

4. How and when you talk to your spouse about difficult emotions is key. Don't bring them up when you're already upset. Try not to attack the other person, but raise the issues that are bothering you in the spirit of trying to make your relationship better. Choose a time to speak with your spouse when he or she is rested and open to talking about something difficult and potentially upsetting. And never try to discuss your emotions if either of you has been drinking.

5. If your relationship seems really grim and the two of you can barely talk to each other, don't automatically conclude that your marriage is over until you consult a marriage counselor or therapist. It's quite possible that both of you are so despondent, demoralized, or depressed that you can't see any remaining goodness in your relationship. A seasoned therapist will be more objective, and may recommend that you at least consider a trial of marital therapy that can be as few as four or five visits.

6. If your marriage is truly over, a therapist will help the two of you separate. Remember, your child's suicide is most likely not the sole cause of your divorce—it's a factor. Perhaps your marriage was already shaky before your child's death. If you have other children, you will be in a relationship of coparenting for the rest of your days, so it is important to work toward a cordial outcome. There is a way to separate and divorce with less fury and

sting and more respect and dignity. Your therapist can assist you with this.

Michael:

You will never forget that terrible day when your family suddenly becomes a survivor of suicide. In the early months and years following the death of your mother or father, son or daughter, husband or wife, sister or brother, grandfather or grandmother, you will not only worry about whether you will be able to endure as an individual, but also wonder if you can carry on as a family. You will grieve hard and long, but it does get easier. Although you should try to watch out for the rest of your family, remember that you can do only so much at once. Try not to take it too personally if your efforts to help your loved ones are rebuffed. You simply have to trust that the people you love will be okay, that they are also hurting terribly and need to find their own way.

Carla:

My mother, a teacher of literature, was always puzzled and somewhat exasperated by suicide, whether it was by a character in a book or by her son-in-law in real life. Her New England background shaped her belief in self-reliance; no matter how difficult life was, she maintained, you somehow muddled through.

Over the years, my mother's attitude toward Harry's suicide gradually changed and softened, as did mine. In a strange and unexpected way, his death allowed my mother and me to be more honest with each other. We discussed the meaning of survival and acceptance, of willpower and resignation, of hope and despair. Harry's suicide also helped us talk more openly and freely as my mother faced her own death at the age of 90. We spoke about her fear of dying, her reluctance to have it all end, the immense emptiness her absence would create in my life, and the unfairness and mystery of it all.

Death, by whatever means, ultimately brings us closer to those we love, even if at first we find ourselves orbiting off in different directions, as Dr. Dunne observes. We all remain connected to the person we lost by a mysterious and powerful force that permanently binds us together and continues to define us as family.

FIVE

Telling Your Children

"You know, you always know."
—Sam, 68, whose father killed himself when Sam was six months old.

With children, honesty about suicide is not only the best policy, it is the *only* policy. You must tell your children the truth in an age-appropriate manner from the beginning, *no matter how young they are*. Children can usually sense when something is wrong, and most will eventually find out what happened one way or another. Children are also extremely resilient, especially if you address their issues and concerns as openly and truthfully as possible.

Why Should I Tell My Child about Suicide?

Carla:

I have never met a survivor who didn't suspect that suicide was the true cause of a family member's mysterious or concealed death. It is an agonizing realization to find out that the truth has been withheld from you, even if you believe that your parents and relatives did so with your best interests at heart. You are left out of the process, everyone knows but you, your reality is shaken, and your

REAL VOICES:

Five-year-old Taylor sat in my office, crying about the recent death of her father. I am always honest with the children who come to see me, but Taylor's mother begged me not to tell her daughter the truth about her father's suicide. She had told Taylor that her father had been killed in an automobile accident. Because I thought it so important that Taylor get immediate help, I reluctantly agreed to her request.

I asked Taylor to tell me what was wrong. "My daddy died," she sobbed. "He killed himself." Surprised, I asked her how she knew that. "I heard my aunt talking about how he shot himself in the head," she confided. "But please don't tell my mommy. She thinks my daddy died in a car accident."

This is a very sad story on many levels. First of all, Taylor is put in the position of protecting her mother and is unable to share the "secret" of her father's death with her or maybe even go to her for her comfort. Next, because Taylor knows her mother is not telling her the truth, she is receiving the message that suicide is shameful and bad. Taylor may also think her mother is not being honest with her because Taylor did something wrong to cause her father's death. And last, and most heartbreaking, Taylor and her mother are not able to mourn their mutual loss together, and are needlessly alone with their terrible feelings of fear and loneliness.

Knowing the truth about suicide allows children to begin grieving; not being honest with them can result in their imagining scenarios far worse than what actually happened. Your children must believe they can trust you. And you, in turn, must trust your children by providing them with clarity, support, and love to deal with their tremendous sorrow.

—Frank Campbell, Ph.D., executive director,
Baton Rouge Crisis Intervention Center, Baton Rouge, Louisiana

trust is broken. Your story has been taken away from you, along with the person you lost.

People tell me about the whispering at a mother's funeral. The police coming to the house after a brother's death. The silence about a grandmother's death. The distressed reaction to questions about a deceased cousin. "Do you think?" they ask me. "Yes," I answer without hesitation.

If you suspect suicide, you are usually right. Pursue the true story even if you're afraid it may be painful. Secrecy will force you to live in the shadowlands, surrounded by illusions and questions. The cycle of stigma and shame about suicide that reverberates over generations can be broken only by acknowledging the truth and passing it on to our children and their children to follow.

Michael:

By telling your children the truth about a family member's suicide, you are delivering a sincere and authentic message that you respect and love them. Being honest with them actually protects their mental health. Children who are confused, who are getting mixed messages, who can't make sense of what they've been told become anxious and emotionally upset. They may be afraid to go to sleep, have nightmares, be unable to concentrate in school, withdraw into themselves, or have tantrums. Some may develop physical symptoms such as stomachaches, headaches, or overeating.

If you tell your children the real truth of how Daddy died, will they be sad? Of course, but they're already sad about losing him. Will they have some anxiety? Perhaps. But you can watch for this and help. Won't they have a lot of questions? Of course. But, you can answer their questions about *why* to the best of your ability and in a reassuring way. You may be the parent, but you are all on this new course together. The more you speak with your children, the more you may discover that they are helping you with your own healing as you are helping them.

HARD ISSUES FACED BY CHILD SURVIVORS

1. Why do people kill themselves?
2. Do people who kill themselves go to hell?
3. Is it my fault?
4. Could I have stopped it?
5. I'm embarrassed to say what really happened.
6. I don't like it when people talk about suicide.
7. Whose fault is it?
8. I'm afraid other people I love will die.
9. I'm afraid I will die.
10. I can't get the picture of the suicide out of my head. What can I do?
11. Are there such things as ghosts?
12. I have to take care of things now at my house.
13. My grades are getting bad at school.
14. Sometimes I feel scared or want to cry for no reason.
15. Do only crazy people kill themselves?
16. How do I tell my friends what happened?
17. This hasn't happened to any of my friends.
18. Why doesn't God help people who want to kill themselves?
19. Will my family ever be happy again?
20. What do we do now?

Reprinted with permission from the Baton Rouge Crisis Intervention Center, Baton Rouge, Louisiana.

Children want and need to know. The difficult issues they face about suicide are very similar to the ones that adults must deal with, and most of their questions will not have clear-cut answers. Although sending your children to therapy can be extremely beneficial, professional help doesn't diminish the importance of initiating conversations with them about suicide, no matter how uncomfortable or awkward you may feel.

Speaking about suicide is not easy: Your own grief may be so overwhelming that you find yourself incapable of responding to your children's anguish and confusion. You may start taking shortcuts, telling your children that everything will be okay, dismissing their concerns, or giving quick and easy answers. Don't blame yourself if you make mistakes; you can get it wrong even if you have the best intentions. If your words don't seem to come out right, say it again in another way. When children pick up on inconsistencies, they will let you know.

Your children will have many, many questions about suicide and death, and all you can do is try your best to answer them. Some questions will have no answers—it is not dangerous or wrong for children to struggle with these unknowns as you yourself are struggling. Try to get as much outside help as possible to give you some direction with language and content; there are many good books and Web sites on the subject. (See Resource Directory, page 275.) You can also ask other survivors for their advice or seek professional help.

If you find that your children are uneasy with the truth, that's fine. Like you, they need time to digest this information. They may cut you off or change the subject when you bring up how their mom or dad died. They may choose not to tell their friends or classmates about what happened, perhaps not even mentioning that their parent or relative has died. What is important for both you and your children, however, is your commitment to be honest and available to them as you each absorb this tremendous loss into your lives in your own way.

How Can I Tell My Child about Suicide?

With suicide, you don't have the luxury of a few hours, days, or weeks to come to some measure of emotional stability before telling your children what happened. You don't have a chance to prepare or practice what you will say or how you say it. What you can do is tell your children that this is a terribly tough time for everyone, that you love them, that you will not leave them, that it's normal for your feelings to keep changing, and that all of you will be better over time.

"It's like being on an airplane and putting your oxygen mask on before you assist your child," says Dr. Frank Campbell. "You must be comfortable with your own emotional responses to the suicide

REAL VOICES:

Children are entitled to know the truth. You can't shove what happened under the rug, because the facts will always resurface. A friend described how awful she felt after she found out about her grandmother's suicide from a cousin. When she asked her mother why she had never been told, her mother replied: "Why should you know about your grandmother? Why should my mother hurt you like she hurt me?"

My friend's mother probably thought she was protecting her, but protecting her from what? I tell my children that suicide is an unhealthy state of mind versus a healthy state. That their father's suicide was not done to them, that he killed himself to end his feelings of pain, not to cause pain to them.

There's nothing to hide about suicide. Spalding's death was public, as was his life. Being honest with our children is what he would have wanted—Spalding never made things up.

—Kathie Russo, producer and widow of writer and
performance artist Spalding Gray

before you can help your children. Kids won't talk to you if you're a minefield or if they think their questions will set you off. Children do better if they know what emotion is behind your yelling or crying. If you feel you're out of control, look for professional guidance. Your getting help will send your children a powerful message that it's okay to ask for and accept help from other people when you're feeling sad or mixed up."

Keep in mind these ground rules when talking about suicide with your children:

1. Begin by telling your children the truth; you can always add more details later.
2. Do more listening than speaking.
3. Answer your child's questions to the best of your ability. It's always acceptable to say, "I don't know. Let me think about that." Or, "I'll find out and answer that later."
4. No matter how young children are, they already have an idea that something has happened. **It's almost a relief when children hear that the death is a suicide because the strange situation now makes sense to them.**

Telling children about suicide is never easy. The following suggestions are based on the groundbreaking work of the Baton Rouge Crisis Intervention Center Children's Bereavement Program directed by Sue Kenyon and Marsha Norton. The programs include suicide-specific services for children ages six to twelve who have lost a parent or relative, as well as a Tiny Tears program for children under five years old.

1. *Use age-appropriate language.* To help your children begin the grieving process, it's important to use the words "die" and "suicide" right from the beginning. Children don't understand that death is permanent until they are around five or six years old, and you may not want to burden them with specific descriptions and explanations before this age. Because not all children of the same age have an equivalent level of maturity or ease with language, you as their parent will know what words and emotional tone are best for your child. Let your daily interaction with your child prior to the suicide be your guide.

Sample language:

- *Daddy died. His body stopped working.*
- *Daddy died by suicide. Suicide is ending your life.*
- *Daddy was alone in the room and there was a gun. The gun went off and Daddy died.*
- *Daddy had a sickness called "depression" (or "alcoholism"). But Daddy didn't know what you and I know. That you can always get help. That suicide is never a solution.*
- *Daddy did get help. He tried hard and so did the doctors. But he never got completely better. He got tired and killed himself.*

2. *Be honest from the beginning.* Kids always find out. Tell the truth so that later on you don't have to change your story. Don't be more specific than you have to.

Sample dialogue:

Son: *How did Daddy die?*
You: *He was killed by a gun.*
Son: *Was it his gun?*
You: *Yes.*

Follow your child's lead and give the information asked for at that time. You can provide further details later.

Son: *Why did Daddy use his gun?*
You: *Do you remember how Daddy was tired all the time and was always sleeping? How he stopped eating dinner with us? How he*

> *used to cry and be very sad? He had a disease called "depression" and died from that sickness.*

Son: *Will I get that sickness?*

You: *Probably not, but you know that you can always get help. There will always be someone there for you. Someone in the family or a doctor will help.*

3. *Apologize for lying.* If children find out about the suicide of a parent or close relative in an unplanned or unexpected manner, they will feel betrayed. If you've never told your daughter about her mother's suicide and want to tell her now, pick a quiet and private time for your talk.

Sample dialogue:

> *I was afraid to tell you the truth about Mom. But I think you're old enough to know now. I thought it was best to keep it from you because I wanted to protect you. But I was wrong. You probably noticed that Mom's death didn't make sense. You were right. I'm sorry for lying to you.*

Eat crow and apologize for lying. It may be hard, but you have to do it to regain your child's trust.

4. *Children's grief may seem transitory.* Kids can cry and then go out to play. That doesn't mean that they are no longer sad or are over their loss. Like adults, children's emotions come and go. Look for moments when it seems like your son or daughter may want to talk and make time for discussion. As your children mature, they will pass through stages of their lives when questioning or wondering about the suicide is more in the forefront than it was in other stages.

5. *There are no right answers. Your best is good enough.* Wait until you feel comfortable before you discuss the specific details of the suicide. If you're not ready to talk to your daughter about how her grandfather drowned, you may say something off the top of your head that you'll regret later on. Keep in mind that your children may need to ask the same question or a similar one many times over; they are trying to make sense of the suicide, just like you.

Sample dialogue:

Daughter: *Why did Grandpa jump into the river and die?*
You: *I have to think about that for a while. Can we talk later tonight when I read to you before you fall asleep?*
Daughter: *Can we talk before I go to bed? I don't want to have scary dreams.*
You: *Okay. How about just before dinner?*
Daughter: *You won't forget? I think about Grandpa a lot. I want to talk about him.*
You: *I promise.*

If you can't talk about the suicide in a way that will be helpful, ask another family member to speak to your son or consider taking him to a therapist specializing in children.

If your children clam up and won't talk to you about how they're feeling, try gentle encouragement and patience. They may be afraid of getting sad and crying. Some children don't want to talk about suicide, but that doesn't mean they aren't grieving—they're just showing it differently.

Sample dialogue:

You: *I really miss your brother and know I would feel better if we could talk about him together. When do you think we can speak about him? Or would you like to speak to someone else about how you're feeling?*
Son: *I don't want to talk about him with anyone. And you can't make me, either.*

You: Okay. What about this? Let's draw together. You and I will both draw pictures of our whole family doing something. Like when we played baseball at the big picnic last summer. Or maybe opening up presents last Christmas. What do you think?

Son: Sure, I'll do that.

Begin by asking your son to explain his drawing to you. You can also open up a conversation by telling him what your drawing means, then asking him what he thinks about it. Try to include references to his brother in your discussion. If your son wants to talk only about happy memories for now, that's fine—he'll probably speak about his more painful feelings later.

NOTE: It's very important to share your emotions with your children and let them see that you are also very sad and thinking about the person who died.

Sample dialogue:

You: Sometimes when I remember all the wonderful things about your brother, I start to cry. I miss him a lot.

Son: So do I. If I'm afraid, I look at his photograph and it makes me feel better.

You: Maybe that would make me feel better too.

6. Emphasize that support is always there, that it's never too late to ask for help. A parent's suicide makes a profound statement that ending your life is an option for solving your problems. Make sure your children understand that it doesn't have to be this way, that no matter how awful things may seem, there's always somebody you can talk to about how you are feeling.

Be very concrete and give specific examples about how getting help will make you feel better:

- Suggest that your daughter speaks with her best friend, her older sister or brother, her aunt or cousin, her teacher or coach. Give several options of people she may want to talk with, and listen to how she responds.

- If your daughter tends to be quiet and doesn't open up easily, you may want to consider sending her to a counselor or therapist specializing in children. If she is reluctant to go, or outright refuses, let it go for now and don't push her. If she becomes even more withdrawn or doesn't want to go to school or play with her friends over the next month or two, you must insist on having her talk with someone. Tell her that you've set up an appointment with a counselor, give her the specific day and time, and say that you'll drive her there. This may work more easily with children and preadolescents, but even the most sullen or stubborn of teenagers will often go with a parent if you are insistent enough. If your daughter doesn't want to go back after the first visit, tell her that she needs to go for at least three more visits, at which time you'll discuss it again.

- Remind your daughter of a time when she was very upset about something, and how when she talked about what was going on, she ended up feeling a lot better. Remind her how her bad feelings went away, and that there was a solution to her problem.

- Share a brief example from your own life about asking for help. Make the story as relevant as possible to your daughter's experience so that she will be able to identify with you.

Michael:

These suggestions are a beginning, a basis for talking to your children about suicide. You will have other ideas of your own and perhaps be given suggestions by friends and acquaintances who have personal experience. **Being honest and open with your children is paramount; how you do it is less critical.** You and your children are beginning a journey together that may continue in some form until the day you die. Be comforted by the love in your heart, the sincerity of your efforts, and the knowledge that you will not be burdened by lies and unspeakable secrets in the future.

SUGGESTIONS FOR HELPING YOUR CHILD THROUGH GRIEF

1. As soon as possible after the death, choose a time and familiar place to talk to your children. Explain directly, simply, and truthfully what has happened. Children need an explanation of how a person dies. In an open environment, they will ask for details and other information when they are ready for them. It may be hours, days, or weeks before they will be ready to ask some questions. Be sensitive to the type of information your child is seeking.

2. Use the deceased person's name when referring to him or her.

3. Use basic words like "die" and "dead" to convey the message.

4. Encourage your child to express feelings. Share your own feelings. Cry together and hold each other. Be careful not to lean on your children and rely on them for your strength. Your children could mistakenly see themselves as your caretakers. It is important to share sadness, but always let your children know that you will be there for them.

5. Take your children to the funeral. Let them observe others mourning and participate with them. Allow your children to return to visit the cemetery if they wish.

6. Allow your children to tell others of the death. The subject should be as open as possible, rather than hidden.

7. Gain an understanding of the grieving process, and be aware of how your own grief is affecting your life. Your children are sensitive to any changes in your mood or feelings. Acknowledge your loneliness, fear, anger, and so on. If you verbalize your own feelings, your children will begin to learn that all feelings are acceptable.

8. During the months following the death, talk about the deceased person. Casually mention things the person said or did. Recall funny stories as well as happy and unhappy incidents. Encourage your children to enter into the conversation and share their memories too.

9. Communicate to your children your appreciation of having had the deceased person in your life.

10. Accept your children's feelings when they express them. Avoid the temptation to say, "You shouldn't feel that way," or to try to make your children feel better or cheer them up. Examples of accepting your children's feelings include "You really miss your daddy a lot." "You're really angry that Susie has a daddy and you don't." "It seems that you're afraid that I might die too."

11. Read, or encourage your children to read, age-appropriate books relating to death.

12. Look for groups or opportunities for your children to meet other children who have experienced significant loss through death.

13. Talk about your religious and spiritual beliefs with your children in a manner that is consistent with the beliefs and customs of your family.

14. Plan something, such as a special outing or vacation, that you and your children can look forward to.

15. Watch for changes in your children's eating, sleeping, or behavior as well as performance in school.

16. Seek counseling if your children's grief is unresolved.

17. Remember that children don't show their feelings in the same way that adults do. Your children may not appear to understand or appreciate the seriousness of death. In addition, their words, facial expressions, and behavior may not reflect the way they feel inside. They may be just learning to express their feelings to others. Sometimes, they are confused and can't even figure out how they are feeling themselves.

Reprinted with permission from the Baton Rouge Crisis Intervention Center, Baton Rouge, Louisiana.

How Do I Explain the Suicide of a Friend or Classmate?

"My daughter's best friend, Maya, shot herself in the school parking lot the day after she turned thirteen," says Claudia, a psychologist from Madison, Wisconsin. "I went to her funeral with my daughter and practically all their classmates were there. It was very emotional, with many of the kids crying hysterically; some were even out of control. The next day at school there was an assembly where a grief counselor gave a short speech to the students. My daughter said it was a joke. She's still inconsolable and it's already been two weeks.

"My daughter and her friends continue to talk incessantly about Maya. Rumors are running wild, and the kids are feeding off each other's panic and fear. Yesterday, one of my daughter's teachers told her class that enough was enough, it was time to move on with their lives and get back to work. My daughter came home shaken, so I've decided to take her to a therapist even though she says she doesn't want or need to go. I'm really surprised that the school is not addressing Maya's suicide in some way. After the first day, there has been no outreach to the students, which I find shocking."

The suicide of a classmate, especially if it occurs within the school setting, can be extremely devastating for a young person. According to Karen Dunne-Maxim, past president of the American Association of Suicidology and expert on schools and suicide, few events in the life of a school are more painful or potentially more disruptive that the suicide of a student. "In a very real sense, the school community is itself a survivor requiring the same sensitive support and help that individuals do after such a tragedy," she writes in *Suicide and Its Aftermath: Understanding and Counseling the Survivors*.

The impact of a classmate's or friend's suicide, both immediate and long-term, depends on the degree of connection between the children. The closer the relationship, the greater the repercussions for the survivor. Children are also more deeply affected if the deceased child confided in them about wanting to kill himself or herself and made them promise not to tell anyone else, or if they had discussed a "suicide pact" together and didn't go along with the plan. Young people with a previous history of psychiatric illness, and/or use of alcohol and other drugs, are also more at risk for a severe reaction to a classmate's suicide, including becoming suicidal themselves.

Here are some tips to keep in mind when talking to your children about the suicide of a classmate or friend:

- Make yourself available to speak with your children whenever they are ready to talk.
- Don't be afraid to ask your children how they're feeling about their loss—let them express any and all emotions without judging them.
- Open up a dialogue about their classmate's choosing suicide as a solution to his or her problems, then emphasize that there are other ways of fixing what's wrong, such as talking to other people, getting professional help, and so on.
- **Ask your children if they're thinking about suicide.** When you bring up the subject of suicide with your children, you are **not** planting a seed or giving them ideas about killing themselves. On the contrary, by reaching out to your children in a concerned and thoughtful way, you are allowing them to express any fears or fantasies they may have on the subject. If your children express thoughts about killing themselves, let them expand upon these ideas. Airing their dark fears may be enough of a release for them. If you become alarmed about the seriousness of what they are telling you, however, seek out professional help for them as soon as possible.
- If your child is showing a lot of aggressive behavior, you should consider a meeting with a mental health professional. Suicide in children and adolescents is often linked with hostility, not only toward themselves but also toward others as well.
- Contact your child's school to see if there is a program or protocol in place after the suicide or attempted suicide of a student. Find out if there is a crisis counselor on-site who may be available to speak to your daughter or son.

In many schools, teachers and staff are briefed on delivering an identical message to their students about a classmate's suicide. This serves to reduce rumors and incorrect information. Your child will probably be told about the death but not in a lot of detail; too much description of the actual event can be risky and perceived incorrectly by students almost as a kit or formula for how to kill yourself.

The suicide of a classmate can also become of great symbolic significance to students, and experts discourage a memorial or dedication at a school where a suicide occurs because that can further mystify the event. Instead, a specific project that students and teachers can participate in together, such as fund-raising for a local suicide prevention program or some other worthy cause, is recommended to express the school's collective sorrow.

Current research shows that there is no definite increased risk of suicidal behavior among the friends and acquaintances of a young person who dies by suicide. *Copycat suicides*, or the cluster of suicides that occur after a suicide (also called *the contagion effect*), are much less common among young people now because of the preventative measures that have been put into place by schools and communities immediately following a young person's suicide. Even with these positive developments, however, it's important not to let down your guard with your children after the crisis of a friend's or classmate's suicide is over; continue to be mindful of your children's behavior and moods, especially if there are any significant changes in the ensuing weeks and months.

Karen Dunne-Maxim's guiding principles for the response of schools to a student's suicide are

1. Nothing should be done to glamorize or dramatize a suicide.
2. Not doing anything can be as dangerous as doing too much.
3. Students cannot be helped until the faculty is helped.
4. Crisis counselors should be available for any student, teacher, or staff person who wishes to talk with them.

Talking to your children and educating them about suicide is both preventative and lifesaving. In an editorial entitled "Death and Self-Censorship," William B. Ketter, editor in chief of *The Eagle-Tribune* in Andover, Massachusetts, apologized to readers who were upset at a news article that omitted the cause of death for an 11-year-old boy who killed himself. Readers wrote to the newspaper that if they had known how the boy had died, it would have been more helpful in explaining his death to their own children.

"We didn't include that fact [suicide] in the story out of sensitivity to the boy's family and because of the newspaper's policy of only reporting on a suicide that is committed in public or by a well-known figure," Mr. Ketter replied to his readers, concluding that "an absolutist policy on suicide doesn't work. We need to pick our way with care every time we're confronted with self-inflicted death and, at the same time, stay true to our obligations to be honest brokers of the news."

When young people kill themselves, their deaths affect many people—their families, their friends, their classmates, their teachers, and their communities. It is a time of collective grief. Some children will be more susceptible than others to the suicide of someone close to their age; their sense of loss will be palpable and their journey more difficult. The emotional fallout can be greatly reduced, however, if everyone pulls together and joins resources to get through what is an extremely trying and traumatic time.

The Legacy of Suicide

"My father killed himself, and depression and bipolar illness runs in my mother's family," says Hugh, a high school freshman. "I don't stand a chance!"

If, like Hugh, your children are fearful that suicide is a "curse" they may have inherited, reassure them that it's not suicide itself that is inherited, but the type of mental illness that carries the risk of suicide. Explain to them that even if there's a possibility they may develop the same illness as a relative who died by suicide, no illnesses are exactly alike. They may have a milder form than their father, and a stronger and more resilient personality than their grandmother. Tell them that by talking about suicide now, they will certainly have the awareness, knowledge, and determination to get professional help and cooperate with treatment before anything serious might happen to them.

Make sure that your children understand that nothing in life is inevitable or predestined, and that there is a great deal they can do to learn about and fight the illnesses that can lead to suicide. Talk about precautions they can take to protect their mental and emotional health, similar to how they can take preventative steps if they know that breast cancer or diabetes runs in their family. Explain how excessive alcohol use and/or other drugs make mental illnesses worse, that more than a couple of drinks will make them even more depressed and can spark suicidal thoughts and attempts; point out that marijuana and other drugs can make them paranoid and at risk of hurting themselves or others.

"I was five years old when my mother killed herself with an overdose of sleeping pills," says Patty, a 34-year-old mother of two toddlers. "I know very little about my mother, and up until the birth of my own children, I have managed to close off my feelings about her. But now I suddenly want to be able to deal with my feelings because I'm afraid that her suicide will eventually begin to affect me negatively. I'm also scared that her death will influence my relationship with my children. I've tried to talk to my father and older brothers about my mother, but I don't think they will ever really admit what she did. Next year, I'll be the same age as my mother when she killed herself. In an irrational but very real way, I'm very frightened. Maybe something will just come over me and I'll want to kill myself also."

Children who have lost a parent or grandparent to suicide, or who have a history of multiple suicides in the family, are often fearful that they are destined to die young or not live past certain anniversaries. Like Patty, they may be afraid they will not live past the age when their parent died or that they are destined to pass the legacy of suicide on to the next generation.

It's important to remember that fear of a bad event is not the same as what actually may happen. Many survivors describe thoughts of suicide very similar to Patty's, ideas that are in the backs of their minds, that are frightening or "weird" or out of their control. These are irrational fears—they will **not** suddenly overtake you and drive you to kill yourself.

Try to distract yourself from your fears by concentrating on positive thoughts about what you enjoy about life, your family, your friends, your work, your interests, what makes you happy and calm. This should help you refocus your thoughts for a while. If, despite your efforts, however, your ideas about suicide keep coming back and are still there every day, talk to someone you can trust. You may be stressed about something completely unrelated to your mother's suicide, such as your job, a relationship, or your physical health, and these worries are causing you to have unrealistic thoughts about also killing yourself. Education is power, and as you begin to separate facts about suicide from myths and shadows, you will feel much better and more in charge of your life.

Michael:

By having the will and grit to talk frankly to the next generation about their ancestors, you may stop what seems like a family pattern. Your children and grandchildren deserve to know the stories of family members who killed themselves. There is so much more to the narrative than how they died; their histories also include whether their suicides seemed to come out of the blue or were almost expected given their repeated suicide attempts and mental instability. Allow your children the opportunity to know their loved ones as people who led interesting lives or chaotic lives, people with strengths and shortcomings, people with beauty and blemishes. They were so much more than family members who died shameful deaths.

Carla:

A survivor who lost both her mother and father to suicide before she was 16 years old describes how she just assumed that killing yourself was only another way to solve your problems. Her parents' deaths taught her that when life gets difficult, you bail out, and she had to work hard to convince herself that facing the hardships of life made more sense than giving up.

Forty years later, this woman, who was orphaned by suicide as a teenager, is a wife, mother, and grandmother. She has come to view the suicides of her mother and father not as a lesson in despair but as an inspiration for survival. "I have chosen to remember and pass on the lovely and comforting memories of my childhood," she explains. "I have always been honest with my children and grandchildren about my parents' decisions to die. But they also know it is my decision—and my wish for them—to appreciate and be grateful for every minute we're alive."

The legacy of our loved ones' suicides are not only in the lives they led but also in the deaths they chose. Speaking honestly and without shame about how they lived and died is the first step in removing the burden of fear and pain from our children's and grandchildren's futures.

SIX

Coping with Specific Circumstances

N o two deaths by suicide are alike. But some types of suicides share specific circumstances that link them together and result in a different kind of mourning process for those who are left behind. Grieving these deaths may be even more complicated or bewildering. They include

- Postpartum—A mother killing herself and possibly her newborn baby soon after childbirth.
- Law enforcement—Suicide among police officers.
- Military—Suicide in the armed forces and during wartime.
- High profile—Suicide of a celebrity, prominent professional, or public figure.
- Multiple suicides—Losing more than one person close to you to suicide.
- Murder/Suicide—A person killing someone else, usually a relative, then killing himself or herself.

The general interest in these suicides creates an added level of stress for survivors because you are most likely facing media attention and public scrutiny at the same time that you are trying to absorb and understand your devastating loss. Your personal grief becomes the focus of speculation and conjecture as your loved one's death is examined and judged by people you don't even know. You may feel violated, that a boundary of human decency has been crossed. You also know that your loved one's privacy has been dishonored, and sadly, he or she is now powerless to fight back.

Carla:
Suicide is always a variation on a theme, and if it's considered sensational or newsworthy in any way, we immediately forgo any shred of privacy we may still have left. We are also faced with complex and seemingly unfathomable contradictions: How can I still miss my sister when she also killed my innocent nephew? Was my uncle a courageous police officer or a troubled and sick man? How could my brother risk his life to protect his country, only to kill himself when he came home from the battlefield? Was my niece's death influenced by her favorite star's suicide? Why do so many people I love kill themselves? Why do I continue to care about my father even though he shot my mother before shooting himself?

Suicide echoes throughout our lives in so many different ways, and our mourning and recovery are never clear-cut or smooth. What helps us is knowing that even within the unfamiliar and often frightening landscape of suicide, there are other survivors who can reassure us that we are not alone or crazy or lost forever.

Michael:
You may have feelings of guilt that you have been a voyeur in the past, that you were galvanized by lurid stories about suicide on television or in the newspapers. You may now feel awful that you

couldn't stop watching replays of these public or sensational deaths or reading about them or discussing them with friends. You may think that this is payback, your comeuppance for participating in such an offensive and insensitive activity. You will need to forgive yourself for being normal. Virtually all human beings are drawn to the shocking story, the sensational, the jarring piece of information. None of us ever thinks that the headline could someday be very personal, that the photograph could be of our mother or our sister, that our family could be dissected for all to see.

What Is the Connection between Postpartum Depression and Suicide?

"Woman Suffocates Baby Daughter and Herself." "Mother Throws Children from Building, Then Jumps to Her Death." "Mom Kills Self and Kids, Dad Hospitalized for Shock."

How do we begin to understand something that is so incomprehensible? How can a mother do something so unfathomable to the child or children she loves? You may even understand a beleaguered mother killing herself, but ask why she had to take her kids with her. To make sense of—but not necessarily to forgive—these actions, you must first understand severe mental illness.

Each year in the United States, between 10 and 15 percent of all new mothers—or approximately half a million women—suffer from *postpartum depression* following the births of their children. This depression is **not** the same as the "baby blues" that affect 70 to 80 percent of all new mothers and involve milder symptoms that usually disappear approximately 10 days after delivery.

According to the Office on Women's Health of the U.S. Department of Health and Human Services, new mothers should seek help or be encouraged to seek help if they experience the following signs, especially during the first 90 days after delivery:

- Strong feelings of sadness, anxiety, or irritability.
- Emotional stress that interferes with taking care of self or family.
- Tearfulness.
- Trouble doing normal, everyday tasks.
- Diminished interest in food or compulsive overeating.
- Diminished interest in self-grooming (dressing, bathing, fixing hair).
- Inability to sleep when tired or sleeping too much.
- Trouble concentrating, making decisions, remembering things.
- Loss of pleasure or interest in things that used to be fun or interesting.
- Overly intense worries about the baby.
- Lack of interest in the new baby.
- Fear of harming the baby.
- Thoughts of self-harm or suicide.

If any of these symptoms lasts most of the day, every day, for at least two weeks, immediate medical attention is recommended. Often, new mothers are embarrassed to ask for help because they are ashamed that they aren't feeling the expected joys of motherhood. The good news is that postpartum depression is treatable, the sooner the better.

What happens after a diagnosis of postpartum depression? To begin, your doctor will conduct a very thorough examination and start treatment immediately. Antidepressant medication **plus** supportive counseling will be very effective. You can continue to breastfeed with most of the newer medications. Your physician will also want to interview your husband or partner: Explaining the disease of postpartum depression to people who support you will enable them to understand what you're struggling with.

FOR IMMEDIATE HELP WITH
POSTPARTUM DEPRESSION

Depression After Delivery (www.depressionafterdelivery.com) is a national support group that provides information and volunteer contacts for women with antepartum and postpartum disorders.

Postpartum Support International (www.postpartum.net) is a support group with international connections and postpartum resources for women and families. 1-805-967-7636

Note: Postpartum depression is very different from *postpartum psychosis,* which is extremely rare, affecting only one in 1,000 new mothers. The potential effects of postpartum psychosis are devastating, real, and considered a medical emergency: The risk for suicide is 5 percent and the risk for infanticide is 4 percent.

Postpartum psychosis usually begins within the first month after delivery, but can occur as early as three to four days after giving birth. Symptoms evolve rapidly and include intense restlessness, irritability, sleep disturbances, confusion, and disorganized behavior. There may be rapid mood swings from depression to elation, false and suspicious ideas (delusions), voices (hallucinations), and obsessive thoughts about the infant. Hospitalization is essential and can be lifesaving for the mother and the baby. Treatment includes close observation for safety, nursing assistance with grooming and diet, medications, rest, and supportive counseling. Follow-up care by a psychiatrist, primary care physician, community nurse, or other support person is recommended to help make sure that both the mother and her child are doing well.

"How could this have happened?" asks Brian, whose 28-year-old wife threw herself under a train with their infant son strapped to her chest, killing them both instantly. "I feel as if I'm living someone else's life. My family has been wiped out; people are saying horrible things about my wife; my baby is dead; and I did nothing to stop this nightmare."

There is no formula for mourning two simultaneous and sudden deaths of loved ones and the total annihilation of one's family. What follows are some suggestions:

1. *Attend to your basic needs.* Force yourself to eat, to sleep as best you can, and to avoid isolation. Accept food and other gestures of help from your neighbors and friends.

2. *Remind yourself that you can survive this with support and time.* You may feel suicidal. You may ask yourself, why bother to continue living now that you no longer have your family? You will feel all alone, and may have fantasies of joining your departed family in an afterlife. If you don't want to put your extended family through what you're living right now, hold on to those thoughts. They will protect you from harming yourself.

3. *Educate yourself about mental illness in new mothers.* Women who kill their infants and then themselves are usually psychotic or out of touch with reality. They often believe that this world is evil or dangerous, that by dying with their children they are escaping together to a better place. These women see their children as an extension of themselves, and consider it an altruistic, protective, and caring act to take their children with them when they die.

Try to find out additional information about your wife's condition from her gynecologist, the family physician, or the baby's pediatrician. If she was seeing a psychiatrist or therapist, make an appointment with that individual to get some insight into what she was battling. Trying to understand why she didn't simply kill herself and leave your child for you to raise will be tough. Psychotic individuals are not rational.

If your wife wasn't undergoing treatment, try to get as much information as you can about mental illness at your local library, online, or from the National Alliance on Mental Illness at 1-800-950-NAMI (6264). (See Resource Directory, page 275, for more sources.)

4. *Accept your rage as normal.* You may derive some small comfort from knowing that your wife was very sick and probably frantic before her tragic actions. However, you may still have intense anger at her for her terrible deed. This is both normal and appropriate.

5. *Understand that this horror is not your fault.* Don't use 20/20 hindsight and blame yourself for ignoring warning signs that your wife was desperate. You are human. Who thinks that this nightmare would ever happen to them? No one.

As with so many illnesses, the best treatment is prevention. Research over the past 20 years has shown that you can reduce the risk of developing a postpartum illness if you pay attention to these red flags in new mothers:

- A depressive episode in the past or prior diagnosis of bipolar (manic-depressive) illness.
- A family history of depression or bipolar illness.
- A history of premenstrual depression—not just premenstrual "tension," but major mood swings with menstruation.
- Isolation and lack of friends nearby for support.
- Marital problems.
- Stressful life events such as unemployment, money troubles, physical illness, and so on.
- Unplanned or unwanted pregnancy.
- Increased anxiety and depressed feelings during pregnancy with no treatment.
- Medical problems with the infant.
- Brief bout of the "baby blues."

Increasingly obstetricians, pediatricians, and family physicians are watching for signs of postpartum illness. You can help by openly discussing any of the preceding signals with them regarding yourself or the woman you are concerned about.

HOW CAN I HELP A NEW MOTHER AT RISK FOR POSTPARTUM DEPRESSION?

1. Advise expectant mothers to avoid life changes during pregnancy. A change in career path or a move is stressful by itself, and adding a new baby to the picture could be more than she can handle.

2. Ask her to go to the gym or take a walk with you. Exercise will not only enhance her health and physical well-being, but also serve as a way to get her out of the house.

3. Help her cook nutritious and balanced meals. Prepare them in advance and store them in the freezer. This will save precious time, and maintain or improve her and her baby's overall health.

4. Make an appointment with a doctor or mental health professional for a new mother if you think she is showing signs of postpartum depression. Most women who have postpartum depression are ashamed to seek treatment and unlikely to do so. In most cases, however, treatment is effective.

Reprinted with permission from the National Mental Health Association.

Police Suicide

"My brother was a wonderful police officer, compassionate and strong," explains Althea, a director of an inner-city day-care center. "I knew he was suffering and I begged him to get help. He was stressed out, drinking too much, his girlfriend was fed up with him, and he was getting sloppy with his appearance, which was very unusual for him. My brother wouldn't tell anyone what was going on, although I can't believe that his partner and the other officers in the precinct didn't notice that something was wrong. Three months ago, he shot himself in the head with his service revolver in his girlfriend's bedroom, right in front of her. His death broke my parents' hearts; they became old overnight. His girlfriend is destroyed. We all saw it coming, in a way, and really didn't know where to turn."

According to www.tearsofacop.com, an informational Web site and chat room that deals exclusively with suicide in law enforcement, every 24 hours a police officer dies by suicide. Twice as many police officers kill themselves each year as die in the line of duty. In addition, one-third of active-duty and retired police officers suffer from post-traumatic stress, and most don't even realize it.

"Suicide is the silent killer in law enforcement," says a young widow. "My husband is a forgotten hero, but I have no medals to pass on to our children."

Research has shown that there are significant barriers for officers who are not feeling well and who should seek psychiatric care. They worry that psychiatric evaluation will result in job sanctions, reassignment, restriction of firearm privileges, missed promotions, and stigmatization. Despite men being more and more open in expressing their feelings, as well as an increasing number of women becoming police officers, law enforcement work is still considered a "macho" profession. You must be tough. And even though there is less disgrace now in seeking mental health care, the stigma is still out there. Police officers who become anxious or depressed struggle with feelings of being flawed or weak, or of letting their buddies down. When it's not easy to go for help, your symptoms only get worse.

Doing police work is psychologically unsettling. Officers are exposed to death, abuse, and other forms of violence, including suicide. Work hours are often irregular. In some communities, and at various times, the public is mistrusting. Police actions are often scrutinized negatively by municipal governments. Court decisions can go against extensive police work. These and other stressors may contribute to the heightened level of emotional distress, marital problems, and alcohol abuse among police officers.

Unrecognized and untreated post-traumatic stress disorder in both active and retired police officers is a cause for alarm. When you add this to ready access to and knowledge about firearms, you have a very dangerous situation.

NOTE: If you are a survivor of police suicide, your grief may be eased by getting involved in prevention efforts. In any occupational group with a significant risk of suicide, there is always room for committed people to lead the way in reducing these unnecessary deaths. Some of your thoughts and suggestions may be innovative. Take them to those in charge where your husband or wife worked. Join a committee or task force if there is one. See what mental health services are available, whether they are being used adequately, and how they can be accessed earlier rather than later.

HELP HOTLINE FOR LAW ENFORCEMENT OFFICERS AND THEIR FAMILIES

1-800-COPLINE (1-800-267-5463)

A 24-hour national hotline exclusively for law enforcement officers and their families, staffed by retired police officers and dealing with all aspects of police suicide, including losing a family member to suicide.

Suicide in the Military

Suicide accounts for 17 percent of all deaths among the estimated 2.7 million service members in the U.S. Army, Navy, Air Force, Marines, National Guard, and Reserves. Suicide is the third leading cause of death after accidents and illnesses for active-duty personnel in the U. S. Armed Forces, with the highest numbers occurring among young, white, enlisted men.

"My husband's suicide was a sad and ironic way to die," says Delia, a 26-year-old widow with an infant son born one week after his father was buried. "Teddy was a brave soldier, yet there are no medals or photographs of him defending his country. Because he died by his own hand and not in combat—or at least in a combat that the military will recognize—his death has a permanent stigma attached to it.

"Teddy was a 'poster Marine'—the best soldier and a respected commander. He joined the Marines because he was looking for a world that would keep him on the straight and narrow. My husband was a military man through and through; he liked being where there was discipline, where he knew the rules. I think it was his dream to die as a war hero. He took chances and never feared impending danger or death.

"I enjoyed being a military wife, following my husband from base to base. Even though my husband was considered one of the best drill instructors in his unit, his behavior started becoming erratic. He began drinking more heavily and he lost his temper more frequently. I think the power he had over so many recruits started to go to his head. When I told my husband I was pregnant, instead of being happy, he said he was afraid that he would be passing on his 'demons' to our child, although he didn't tell me what those demons were.

"Two months before Teddy killed himself, I received an anonymous letter telling me that he was out of control. When I confronted him, he broke down and said that he was feeling overwhelmed. I begged him to get professional help. He said, 'No way,' and although I disagreed with him, I understood. In the military, showing weaknesses is not looked on favorably. Admitting that you aren't at your best or, even worse, that you're depressed, is a blot on your record. The code is death before dishonor: You fix your own problems without asking for help from anyone else.

"I knew disaster was coming and I was right. It was as if I were watching a freight train rushing into a brick wall and there was nothing I could do to stop it. Shortly after our last fight, Teddy had some kind of incident on base and they ordered him to see a chaplain. This is the first step in counseling in the military. A couple of weeks later, he got drunk off base and totaled his car. He called me from jail, crying, 'I'm sitting here in an orange jumpsuit. You don't know what that means for a Marine.' He then added, 'I fucked up, but don't worry. I'll take care of it.'

"I thought he was talking about suicide, but I couldn't say the words: 'Are you thinking about killing yourself?' I didn't know who to speak to on his base because I was afraid to meddle in his career and ruin it. I also didn't want his commanding officer to think of me as an interfering wife. They let him out of jail on his own recognizance. The next day, he got an M16 automatic rifle and ammunition, dressed in full uniform, and shot himself in the head in front of his assembled recruits.

"I don't blame the Marine Corps because Teddy came into the military with his own problems. He loved the Marines and died in his brothers' arms. Yet I think it's important for me to speak up on my husband's behalf, as well as all the others in the armed forces who may be afraid to ask for help. My advice to military personnel is to become aware of the signs and symptoms of depression, and to push for more intervention from the people in command. Most of all, be more aggressive about going for help. I was so afraid to push my husband and interfere in the military chain of command. Now it's too late."

Although your loved one has died by suicide, you may want to speak out about some of the stressors of military life and barriers to seeking help in the armed forces. You may have intimate knowledge of some of these because your husband or wife told you:

- Bullying is a factor in some settings and should cease. It is not the same as firm discipline or rigorous training. Bullying damages self-esteem and causes shame in the victim.
- Some studies of military suicide have noted a recent relationship breakup as a triggering event. Ask to have marital counseling available both on and off the base.
- Do whatever you can to fight the stigma of seeking mental health care. Mental health professionals do this on a daily basis. It's part of advocacy. But the voices of the public, and especially survivors, are always welcome.
- You might want to find out whether your loved one's death by suicide is accepted by the military as an honorable death. If you're not convinced, say something.
- Start a group for survivors on the base if there isn't one. You will be helping yourself and others who are grieving. Young colleagues of the person who died should be invited and encouraged to attend. Because they are not family, they may not define themselves as survivors, when they certainly are. Losing a young military peer to suicide can be a devastating and very threatening experience.

High-Profile Suicides

A musician shoots himself in the head. A movie star overdoses. An elected official hangs himself. A famous writer puts her head in the oven. A prominent businessman throws himself off the roof. Such high-profile suicides usually receive a great deal of attention in the media, with much speculation on the "real" story behind the death. Was there some kind of scandal? Drug use? Corruption? Marital problems? Rumors run wild, with most of the blame for the suicide usually landing on surviving family members. This only intensifies the already immense guilt that surrounds every death by suicide.

"My husband was one of the leading surgeons in our small town," says Lucy, a stay-at-home mother from Stamford, Connecticut. "His suicide was in all the newspapers, and everyone was looking at me the whole time to try to figure out what I did—or didn't do—to make him kill himself. The television reporters were all over my lawn, frightening my children and me. 'Why?' they kept asking me. As if I knew. I felt like the entire town was blaming me. Eventually, I sold our house and moved to a city where no one knew who I was."

Most survivors of suicide of a high-profile person want to be left alone. Some will say absolutely nothing to the media. Others will issue a press release or go before the media once and make a terse statement of what they know and don't know. At the same time, they usually ask the public to understand their need for privacy and request that the media leave them alone. Later on, with time for healing, some survivors may contact the media with ideas for public service based on their loved one's death. This is important work, and goes a long way toward educating the general public about mental illness, the downside of being a celebrity or other public figure, and how members of the community can assist in the efforts to fight suicide.

Being a suicide survivor is very exposing, whether your loved one was a high-profile person or an ordinary citizen. Famous people and their survivors hurt like everyone else, and because mental illness spares no group, people of stature also are at risk, sometimes even more at risk.

High-profile suicides are also more likely to promote copycat suicides among people who may identify with the celebrity or public figure who has died. Individuals who are especially vulnerable come to see suicide as a potential solution to their own problems, reasoning that if the corporate executive with all his money or the singer with all her fame couldn't tolerate life's problems, how will they ever stand a chance?

"My son was obsessed with Kurt Cobain's suicide and I just blew it off," explains a distressed father from Alabama. "I figured it was a stage that he would eventually get through. When my son started missing school and staying in his bedroom all day, playing his guitar, I tried to talk to him about what was going on. I even asked him if he was doing drugs; he denied it and I chose to accept his answer. I had no idea how much my son had been affected by Kurt Cobain's death until I searched his bedroom after he shot himself—he was on life support for four days before he died. There were photographs and song lyrics and lurid articles about the details of Kurt Cobain's last days and minutes of his life. How could I have been so blind about my own son?"

If you're worried that your child or sibling or friend could be affected by the suicide of a celebrity or other prominent person, talk with him or her about it. Trust your intuition. You have become concerned for a reason: For example, your son seems obsessed with the celebrity who killed himself and is now dressing like him, listening to his music over and over, decorating his room with his posters and other paraphernalia, joining an Internet fan club and discussion group, seeking out others who share his fascination.

Ask your son directly if he is thinking of suicide; if you don't trust the answer, don't stop there. Tell him that you are worried, that you feel pushed away and shut out. Ask him about drugs. Again, if you think he's lying, say, "Why don't I feel reassured when you say that?" If you find items lying around the house that are making you suspicious of drug use, or desperate, dark writings, confront him again.

If you feel your son is not being honest with you, consider asking another family member or close friend to speak to him. If your son is a student, tell the school counselor about your concerns. Ask your son about talking to a therapist; the first time around he may veto the notion, but you can always revisit it later when he has had time to give the idea some thought.

Keep two factors in mind that might indicate your son may be at risk of harming himself. First, think about whether your son has been going through some sort of identity crisis even before the suicide of this celebrity. Has he started to reject family and friends, saying they don't understand him, that they're too square or conventional? Has he been drawn to a person or group for answers, for identification? Does he seem lonely and alienated from the mainstream? Are his thoughts heavy or dark? If so, your son may be more likely to be experiencing an extreme identification with a popular or cult figure. Inside, he may really want to be this person or at least part of his or her inner circle. These figures are usually idealized and can do no wrong—including killing themselves.

Second, your son may be romanticizing suicide. That it's a way out of this stupid or screwed-up world. Suicide may even be the opportunity for a better life of some sort, beyond this life as he knows it. Your son may be feeling miserable and angry, and is convinced that no one understands him. Suicide becomes an escape from his pain and confusion.

Research shows that the more extensive the coverage of a suicide story by the media, the greater the chances of finding a copycat effect. Concerned with these copycat suicides or *suicide contagions*, the U.S. Surgeon General has released recommendations in his National Strategy for Suicide Prevention regarding the media's report-ing of suicide:

1. Romanticizing suicide or idealizing those who take their own lives by portraying suicide as a heroic or glamorous act may encourage others to identify with the victim.
2. Exposure to the suicide method through media reports can encourage vulnerable individuals to imitate the method the person used to die. There is an even greater danger if there's a detailed description of the suicide method.
3. Presenting suicide as the inexplicable act of an otherwise healthy or high-achieving person may encourage identi-fication with the victim.

"Celebrities seem to have the perfect life," explains Marie, a New York college student. "They have the money to do whatever they want, whenever they want. When they kill themselves, it doesn't make any sense. They have everything and the rest of us are out here struggling."

Most human beings are fascinated by prominent people and what appear to be their perfect or ideal lives—whether they are bil-lionaires, handsome or beautiful, athletic superstars, multitalented, at the top of their game, adored by others, and so on. Our ordinary lives seem much less bland when we feed off their exciting lives. Yes, we may be shocked and stunned if they kill themselves. But we also grieve, even though we've never met them. We may feel disil-lusioned and question our values and aspirations. We may be angry that they chose suicide, that they've walked away from something we may aspire to or even envy.

Popular magazines and gossip columnists offer their own expla-nations for high-profile and celebrity suicides. "He was going through a horrendous divorce." "She never disclosed to the public that she had bipolar illness." "His doctor told him a week ago that he was HIV-positive." Yet, these bits of information usually provide small comfort. We still can't fathom how people who are rich and famous and powerful could give up so much and take their own lives. We are forced to accept those worn-out truisms that "money can't buy happiness" and "beauty is only skin deep" and "you can't judge a book by its cover." Out of the blue, suicide has now become a part of our lives, and we are left shaken and affected by the *why* of the mysterious death of someone we don't even know.

Multiple Suicides

Some survivors have to contend with losing not just one loved one to suicide, but two or more. Mourning this kind of multiple loss can make you feel even more isolated and confused, regardless of whether there is a family history of many relatives with major depressive or bipolar disorders, as described in Chapter 2, or whether the people who died had no biological connection to you.

- "On the first anniversary of our son's suicide, my husband drove to the park where our son had shot himself in the heart, then did the same thing. In his suicide note, my husband begged my forgiveness and wrote to me that he just couldn't go on without our son."
- "Five years ago, our beloved seventeen-year-old twin daughters killed themselves together. My husband and I assume they made a suicide pact. They were identical twins and very close to each other. They did everything as a unit, including this final horrendous act."
- "I lost both my parents to suicide in the same week. My mother hanged herself twenty-four years ago, and five days after her funeral, I returned to college. When I got off the plane, the police were waiting for me with the

news that my father was also dead. He had shot himself in the heart on top of my mother's grave. I don't know how I survived that. I still don't."

- "I'm a survivor three times over. All within nine months. My grandfather killed himself four years ago. He bolted from his nursing home and leaped from a bridge two blocks away. Two months later, my best friend from college asphyxiated herself when she didn't get into medical school. I knew she had attempted suicide twice before, but I still never thought she would really go through with it. Then, seven months later, my brother's wife killed herself. We think she had postpartum depression that wasn't recognized. Her son was three months old. I was a wreck—she was like a sister to me."

Survivors of multiple suicides face unique problems in mourning and understanding their various losses. The following observations and suggestions may help you with your healing:

1. Some people who have been bereaved by more than one suicide describe experiencing separate and distinct circles of grief. By integrating and merging these different circles, you may find it easier to mourn your multiple losses. But accept the distinct characteristics of each loss. You may not be angry at all about your mother's suicide, but have unbridled fury at your wife for killing herself.
2. Revisiting your earlier loss may help you with your more recent one. This will depend on the nature of your relationship with each person who died and the degree of your emotional connection.
3. Some survivors of multiple suicides feel singled out or "freakish" about what happened. It may help to speak to someone else—either in a survivor group or on the Inter-

net—who has also lost more than one person to suicide so that you can compare your experiences.

4. You may be wondering why you are still alive and actually feel a kind of "survivor guilt" after so much loss in your life. Questioning the value and meaning of life is normal following any death, but especially a death by suicide.

5. Some individuals feel shunned by friends or family after multiple suicides in their life. "People treated me as if I was contaminated," says Barry, 66, who lost his wife and granddaughter to suicide. "They acted like I would infect them with some kind of bad spell or curse." If you fear being rejected or judged, you may choose not to disclose information about your losses. This is your right to privacy.

6. Think about joining a support group for survivors if you haven't already done so after your first loss. If you are having feelings of severe grief or are struggling with "why me?" thinking, you might also consider seeing a mental health professional for therapy.

Murder/Suicide

According to the *Journal of the American Medical Association*, there are approximately 1,000 to 1,500 murder/suicide deaths annually in the U.S., with the numbers remaining fairly steady over the past several decades. The principal perpetrators in murder/suicides are young males with intense sexual jealousy, depressed mothers, or elderly men with ailing spouses. Although murder/suicides are relatively uncommon, their effect on the surviving family members is shattering and long lasting.

"At first I thought everything was okay and my parents were just sleeping," explains Rob, a rancher from northern Idaho. "I was calling their house all day and no one was answering, which was very unusual. In my gut, I knew something was wrong. They live a couple of miles down the road from me, and I drove over to check out what was going on. Their car was in the garage so I knew they were home. I checked my mother's bedroom first. She has mild Alzheimer's and I was worried that if something had happened to my father, she would be confused and upset.

"My mother was lying in bed with her eyes closed, and she looked like she was sleeping. She had her hairnet on, as usual. I went to wake her and she was cold as stone. Ever since that moment, I have not been able to touch a marble statue. I then went to look for my father and found him sprawled on the floor in his bedroom, his right arm stretched out, with a gun lying between his head and his hand. My first thought was that my mother had suffered a stroke and my father killed himself because he didn't want to live without her.

"I ran next door to a neighbor's house and called 911. The police came right away, and told me to wait for them. Luckily, the lead police investigating officer was very compassionate. He made an unbearable and unthinkable situation better. He came back to my neighbor's house and told me that when they had drawn back the covers on my mother's bed, they discovered that she had been shot in the abdomen. They then found a suicide note from my father and went to his room. He had shot himself in the chest.

"The weird thing was there was no blood or mess because my father had hit direct arteries, and both he and my mother bled to death internally. It was almost as if he had X-ray vision. After my father shot my mother, he took the spent casings from the gun and threw them in the wastebasket. He also put the clip for his gun on his dresser. My father had the whole thing all thought out.

"One year before this, my father had had a mild stroke. He went into rehab and came home, but he was never the same. He couldn't drive his car, which was a big thing, and he became more and more depressed. Meanwhile, my mother was suffering from severe arthritis and became addicted to painkillers. I tried to spend as much time with them as I could and thought I was a good son.

"I was always closer to my father. A couple of months before this whole thing happened, he started talking about 'ending it all' and would make a gesture like shooting a gun at his head. I would tell him that I didn't want to end up on the eleven o'clock news, which is exactly where I did end up. I knew he had two guns in the house, a .32-caliber in the safe and a .45-caliber from his army days during World War II. I didn't think anything of this, however, because his ammunition was old and the guns hadn't been used in twenty-five years.

"After my father's stroke, I begged him to go for help but he refused. I told him that my family physician said he was probably suffering from geriatric depression and he said, 'I know.' I feel so guilty that I wasn't more forceful about making him see someone. My sister lives in Hawaii, but I wanted my parents nearby so I could take care of them. A lot of good that did. I read and reread the police reports and still can't believe that both my mother and father died on my watch.

"I hated that my parents' lives were all over the news. The local television station got their photographs from the Department of Motor Vehicles, and ran a long segment in which the reporter interviewed their neighbors and anyone else she could find. The program also featured a silver-haired lady 'expert' on the subject of 'senior suicide.' Who was she to be speaking about my parents? She had no idea who they were. The program even included a film clip of Dr. Jack Kevorkian! How could anyone even try to explain the reason for my folks' murder/suicide when I couldn't understand it—and still can't four years later?

"My parents had a will with very detailed requests for their funeral arrangements; they asked to be buried together. My father wanted to be cremated, so at first I thought I would put his ashes in my mother's casket. But then I thought, no, he murdered her. That's a party he wasn't invited to. I buried them separately in two different states, each in their own family plot. Who knows if I made the right decision? They had been married for almost sixty years."

Murder/suicide can sometimes rupture family relationships beyond repair. "I will never see my grandchildren again," says Agnes, 78. "My son stabbed his wife to death, then killed himself with the same knife. They had three little girls, my granddaughters, who are now being raised by their maternal aunt. She will not let me see my babies, and although I can understand her anger at me, I hope she changes her mind one day. Not only did I lose my son, who I still love in spite of the fact that he's a murderer, I now have lost my only grandchildren. How did my life turn out this way? I pray every night for the answer."

Mourning after a murder/suicide is always complex and confusing. "I feel like a freak," says Doug, a high school junior whose parents' deaths were covered extensively in the media. "I was actually glad that my father killed himself after killing my mother. If he hadn't, I would have killed him myself. I went to his funeral, but I hate him—I can't even think of his death as a suicide even though I know it is."

There is no single "type" or known set of circumstances for a murder/suicide. How you grieve may be eased or aggravated by the facts or what you suspect about the possible reasons:

- Your daughter is in an abusive relationship with her husband and, after many years, finally leaves him to be on her own with the children. He cannot handle the separation and begins to stalk her. She obtains a restraining order. He ignores this, breaks into her home, and kills her and their two children, and then himself. You now have to mourn three loved ones, three innocent victims. Your rage at your son-in-law will be boundless. Do not let anyone suggest to you that you have to forgive him in order to heal.

- Your 70-year-old mother told you a month ago, with great difficulty, that your father accused her of having an affair with their next-door neighbor. She is incredulous and embarrassed. You encourage her to keep reassuring him that she isn't doing anything of the sort and that she loves only him. This doesn't work and he keeps badgering her. You think he's having a mental breakdown and you make an appointment for your father to see his family doctor the next day. That evening he shoots your mother, then turns the gun on himself. You begin your mourning and are told that your father probably had *conjugal paranoia*, a type of mental illness characterized by a delusion or false belief that a spouse is being unfaithful. Grieving this terrible loss may be easier for you if you can forgive your father. He was ill and did not know it.

- Your daughter's husband was diagnosed with Lou Gehrig's disease (amyotrophic lateral sclerosis) five years ago. In addition to her work as a pharmacist, your daughter nurses him continuously until he finally has to go into a care facility. Last Christmas, when her husband is home on a pass, she gives him a lethal dose of insulin, then takes an overdose of barbiturates. They have no children. Your daughter leaves a note with estate instructions for you but no details of why. You wonder, was this a murder/suicide or a double suicide? Did they have an agreement to die together? Or was your daughter's husband so disabled by his neurological disorder that he couldn't kill himself and, out of love for him, your daughter agreed to do it? Your mourning may be less difficult if you think of your daughter as a kind and compassionate wife, not a murderer.

There are no easy answers here. Your grieving will be hard. Talking to other survivors may be of some help, but it may be difficult to find other people in your situation who are coping with murder and suicide. If you seek out professional help, be sure to see someone who is comfortable with your kaleidoscope of emotions. This is your journey, and you have the right to chart your course however you need to.

Carla:

It's amazing how so many of us survive the unthinkable and live through the unimaginable. Where do we get the courage, the stamina, the glue that holds us together? I am so fiercely proud to be among survivors who keep going in the face of experiences that change our lives around and knock our foundations out from under us, whatever the specific circumstances of our loved one's suicide may be.

Michael:

At low times in my life I have been inspired by the words of Emily Dickinson: *"Not knowing when the dawn will come, I open every door."* What comforts me is twofold—that a new day will indeed arrive and that I am an active participant in making that happen.

You are in the midst of a storm, a very bad one that feels like it will never cease. But all storms end. The sun will come out again. By opening up your heart to the goodness of others and by reaching out to others in need, you will brighten. Your resilience will return, and you may be even stronger than before your loss.

SEVEN

Reaching Out for Support

"The language of friendship is not words, but meanings."
—Henry David Thoreau

Carla:

I wouldn't take off my coat during the meeting. It was a cold January night in Manhattan, one month after Harry killed himself, and I had just walked around the block several times before I could gather the courage to enter the church where the Samaritans were holding an open support group for people who had lost their loved ones to suicide. It was agonizing—and terrifying—for me to enter into that space and make it official that Harry was dead. Keeping my coat on gave me some kind of protection, allowing me to pretend that I was just passing through, that my husband's absence was not really permanent, and I had not crossed the threshold into a new world that threatened to consume and define me.

Although I was afraid, I also knew I needed help in dealing with Harry's suicide. I didn't want to be alone in this, and had been feeling increasingly alienated and isolated from my family and closest friends. That night, I met other people who offered me a safe place and calm refuge from the chaos and insanity that I was feeling. By my second meeting, I was able to take off my coat; over time, I was able to help others remove their coats as well.

Michael:

After a suicide, you need to take care of yourself in whatever way you can. By doing this, you also help your friends and family: You ease their worry about you and allow them to remain part of your life. Recognizing that you're not feeling very well, however, is one thing; opening up to someone else or a group is another. It's a giant step. Although we all need support at times in our lives, it's never easy to make the phone call, ring the doorbell, or cross the threshold. You really have to muster up what little strength you have, be courageous, and have faith that what you're about to do will help you in some way. And it will.

WHERE TO GET SUPPORT

For a complete listing of avenues of support following the suicide of a relative or friend, see the Resource Directory on page 275. These resources include reading materials, organizations, Web sites, chat rooms, conferences, and so on.

Breaking the Isolation

For survivors, help comes in many forms: family and friends, neighbors and coworkers, members of your religious or spiritual community, other survivors, strangers who may offer you their hands. Although you usually have to reach out for this help, if you're lucky, you may not have to reach too far.

"The outpouring of support from my daughter's friends after her suicide was both unexpected and truly healing," says Emma, a landscaper from San Diego. "Justine was in art school in Rhode Island, studying photography on a full scholarship. She was talented and sensitive, and had her whole future in front of her. Her roommate found her dead in the bathtub with her wrists slit. There was a suicide note on the bathroom sink, and the despair reflected in my daughter's words was profound. How could a nineteen-year-old experience that much pain in such a short life?

"Justine's friends from Rhode Island as well as here gathered at my house after the funeral to celebrate her life. Their creative outpouring helped transform a terrible, difficult event into a time of meaning. One of my daughter's friends created a montage of Justine's most recent photographs, and another friend gave me an oil portrait of Justine that he had recently painted. We all recited some of the poems that my daughter loved, then sat around the piano singing her favorite songs.

"I felt deeply comforted by so much love and young enthusiasm. Like Justine's friends, I will always try to remember the beauty and joy of my daughter's life, and not the terribly lonely way that she died. I am now looking for a suicide survivor group in my area because I know that I will need as much support as possible for a long, long time."

The defining part of losing a loved one to suicide is the isolation and alienation you feel from all that was once familiar. It's impossi-

---

YOU ARE NOT ALONE

- Each suicide intimately affects at least six to seven other people.
- One out of every 64 people in the U.S., or 4.47 million, has lost a family member or friend to suicide.
- Between 6 and 7 million people worldwide, including 190,000 in the U.S., lose someone close to them to suicide each year.

ble to imagine that another person can understand the depth of your pain, grief, confusion, or loss. You can't believe anyone else has ever experienced what you are going through or felt so alone. Finding others who can be there for you—because they are there themselves—is the first step in your healing.

Research shows that you function much better and heal from stress more quickly if you are not isolated. Too much time by yourself can have ill effects:

- If you are all alone with your thoughts, you may find yourself churning through them over and over again. Without the perspective of another person, a so-called reality check, your thinking may become altered, distorted, or magnified. Soon, your recollection of what actually happened or what a person may have said can take on an exaggerated meaning. You can also begin to doubt what you heard. Being isolated can make you suspicious and paranoid, and you may find yourself questioning your loved ones' intentions and distancing yourself from them.

- It's difficult to distract yourself from your pain when you are all alone: You get no reprieve from your sorrow, your longing, your guilt. You may find some temporary success in intentionally shutting out your sad thoughts by reading a book or watching television, but all too often you'll probably find these thoughts are still intruding and are stopping you from concentrating. This can be very frustrating and exhausting.

- Your mood can plummet with isolation. You can get quite depressed and not be able to function. This state of mind will just add to and compound your already low spirits.

- You can become *morbidly egocentric*, i.e., self-centered because of your loss, preoccupied with your general medical health, prone to various physical ailments, and so forth. In addition, if you're rarely with others, and you dominate the time when you're together by telling them how dreadful you feel, people may start to avoid you. This vicious circle will only worsen your feelings of aloneness.

- You can get stuck or paralyzed in your isolation and feel out of sync with others and what's going on in the world. It takes much longer and is more difficult to move through your grief if you are not in communication with other people or participating in their lives in any way.

If you have always been self-sufficient and prided yourself on solving problems on your own, you may find reaching out for support very difficult:

1. Take some reassurance that you are not alone in having trouble asking for help. Many individuals cannot reach out for support as quickly as others, and sometimes it just takes speaking to one other person to get some relief and feel better.

2. If you have always been a private person and been able to get through hard times on your own, acting independently may be okay for you as you deal with this terribly sad loss. If being self-sufficient is not working this time, however, you may want to think seriously about getting some outside support.

3. You may have trouble seeking help because you are feeling absolutely dreadful about yourself. You may be ashamed and embarrassed about the way you're feeling, your appearance, or your lack of emotional control. If you can't reach out because your self-esteem is so low, or what pride you have left is in tatters, remember that we

all need the love and support of others when we're most broken. You're probably judging yourself much more harshly than a friend or relative who is available and willing to help you.

4. If you're not ready to speak to anyone about what you're going through, try to do something on your own. Go to your local library and read whatever you can about losing a loved one to suicide. If you're familiar with the Internet, you can do all kinds of searching on the subject in the privacy of your own home. You can also read people's comments in survivor chat rooms, and watch from the sidelines without having to volunteer anything about yourself. When you're ready to speak about your situation, you can log on and participate in the discussion.

5. You can call your local crisis center hotline without disclosing your actual identity. You might find it soothing to open up anonymously to a trained counselor or volunteer.

6. If you don't want other family members, friends, or work colleagues to know too much about the details of your loved one's suicide, or if you feel judged by them in any way, you might consider professional help. Some people find it easier to talk to and confide in someone who starts off as a complete stranger. And if you want to seek help in a city distinct from where you live, that's fine.

Dr. Frank Campbell of the Baton Rouge Crisis Intervention Center believes that it is important to break the isolation that survivors of suicide face as early as possible. LOSS (Local Outreach to Suicide Survivors) is the Center's pioneering program, now being used as a model throughout the country, that works with the local police and coroner's offices immediately after a suicide occurs. Survivor volunteers as well as staff from the Center are part of a first-response team that goes directly to the location where the suicide has occurred. There, LOSS team members offer resources, support, and sources of hope to the newly bereaved person or family.

"Our goal is to bring immediate support to survivors as close to the time of death as possible," says Dr. Campbell. "We are currently working on a plan to include a team of trained child-trauma specialists from the Center to work with children survivors from the instant we arrive at the scene of the suicide. By providing an initial, intensive intervention with children as well as adults, we hope to reduce the long-term effects of their sudden and traumatic loss."

A woman whose father shot himself describes how talking with other survivors of suicide within 15 minutes of finding her father's body meant more to her than anything else.

"My family and I knew from the start that we were not alone," she says. "The members of the LOSS teams let us know that they were there for us twenty-four hours a day. Their support has helped us through the most difficult thing a person could ever have to face."

Kay Redfield Jamison writes in *Night Falls Fast: Understanding Suicide* that the last line from Douglas Dunn's poem "Disenchantments" continues to draw her to life: *"Look to the living, love them, hold on."* By reaching out for support and, when ready, offering it to others in return, you will not only begin to heal but also honor and commemorate the memory of the person you love and have lost.

Connecting with Other Survivors

Carla:

I am comforted and reassured by the stories of other survivors. At conferences and lectures, through e-mails and telephone calls, I listen to the descriptions of beautiful and loving children and spouses, siblings and parents, relatives and friends, all of whom have inexplicably ended their lives. These recollections help me reconnect with Harry, to remember our 21 years together, to think of him when he was happy and proud. This lifeline of connection also assures me, once again, that I am not alone, and gives me the courage and language to reach out to others for support.

Survivors share a special bond that is based on trust, not secrecy or shame. We are a community of resilient and empathetic men and women, passing on our insights of hope and endurance to each other along with whatever wisdom we may have picked up along the way.

FINDING A SUPPORT GROUP

To find a support group in your area throughout the United States and Canada for people who have lost a family member or friend to suicide, contact the American Association of Suicidology at 1-202-237-2280 (www.suicidology.org) or the American Foundation for Suicide Prevention at 1-888-333-AFSP (2377) (www.afsp.org).

"As strangers, we entered the room of the support group," writes Gloria Vanderbilt in *A Mother's Story*, her moving book about the suicide of her 20-year-old son, Carter Cooper. "But later, sitting in a circle, we were not strangers, not even friends. We were a family, one that does not judge, for pain had stripped us bare. Ah, yes, we knew each other well."

When someone you love dies by suicide, your world as you once knew it is wrenched from you. At sea, you begin a passage of transformation and look for some anchor or ballast to support yourself. Meeting with fellow travelers can be almost magnetic. Sharing your stories speeds intimacy, and you find yourself feeling less helpless and alone. As you get to know other people with similar experiences, you begin to feel like family: You are all there to protect, defend, and lean on each other, and be leaned on in return. Like a solo traveler in a foreign country who hears a familiar language being spoken, survivors feel automatically connected to each other. Some say it is like coming home.

"At first, I thought it was going to be a circle of losers, and I told my wife no way," says Rafael, a 48-year-old salesman whose mother killed herself after being diagnosed with Alzheimer's disease. "But my wife gave me an ultimatum—if I didn't do something fast, she was going to move out. It's true, I was turning into a basket case since I found my mother hanging in her bedroom closet. I had driven over to her house to take her to a new doctor, and when I went in to get her, I found her note on the kitchen table. My mother didn't want me to be shocked when I found her body, I guess, but I totally freaked out. It's been almost a year, but I can still see her image hanging there when I close my eyes. I can't get it out of my head.

"My health insurance doesn't pay for mental conditions, so my wife suggested I try a support group. She went online and found one around forty-five minutes from where we live. I'm not known for talking about my feelings, so I really resisted. But I have to admit, meeting other people who understand suicide has really helped. They don't ask more than they should, and no one pushes me to speak. I'm usually silent at most of the meetings, but never feel that I'm being judged or criticized.

"When I went back to work after my mother's suicide, the other people there seemed to view me differently. I don't know if they were afraid I would go postal on them, but I felt so uncomfortable that I asked to be transferred to another office. Right now, the only place where I feel better is at the suicide support meetings. I guess I had assumed that people who need help to get through their problems must be losers because that's how I was feeling about myself. But maybe if I'm wrong about them, then I'm also wrong about myself."

One of the key factors in what makes or breaks a support group is the facilitator. Although everyone in a group is an adult with equal rights, a facilitator is the one who sets the tone of the meeting. He or she respects a member's right to remain silent but also invites and encourages participation in a nonthreatening way. This calls for intuition and sharp perception.

A good facilitator has his or her finger on the pulse of the group, and keeps everyone's best interests at heart. For example, if one individual seems to be dominating the group or is controlling and seems to be upsetting others, an astute facilitator will pick this up early and redirect the discussion so that the person doesn't lose face and another group member can also speak. In a good support group, members respect each other and feel that they're getting something out of attending as well as helping others in some small way.

It's important to keep in mind that not all facilitators are survivors themselves. Some are professionals trained in counseling and working with groups. The education and life experience of facilitators can vary enormously, but the bottom line is their comfort level with people and their ability to make a group of human beings want to be together.

If you have been to a support group for a few visits and found yourself feeling worse, not better, you might consider looking for another available group in your area. It's possible that a different group may function more to your liking by having a more experienced facilitator, people you have more in common with, more anonymity, a different philosophy, and so on.

Can you ever talk too much about your loss? Yes, but this is rare. If a year or more has passed since your loved one's suicide and you still feel stuck, this could be a problem. You may not be able to discuss anything else but the suicide, and people may stop calling or visiting you. If you have been attending a support group, you can ask the other members for their feedback and benefit from their impressions and experience when they were at your stage of healing. You may also want to consider getting the perspective of a mental health professional.

NOTE: For some people, support groups may not be that helpful or comforting. If the idea of people coming together to talk about a family member or friend who has died by suicide is not appealing to you, remember that attending a regular support meeting is only one item on your menu of options.

"Listening to the specific details of the different suicides was too painful for me," explains Tess, a secretary from New Jersey. "I also found myself coming home feeling even worse than before. Not only was my heart broken about losing my sister, but I would also grieve for everyone else at the meeting. It would take me hours to fall asleep after attending a group. It felt like I was pouring salt into an open wound, and I knew that if I continued to go I would never heal. I couldn't relive the pain over and over again. People kept talking about how they were feeling, but moving on worked best for me."

Some individuals heal best by meeting the demands of everyday life and even taking on additional responsibilities. You may choose to devote your time to your work, family, friends, recreation, hobbies, and community. By keeping busy and serving others, you may regain a sense of purpose and meaning.

"I don't want to be reminded of my wife's suicide because it hurts too much," says Philip, an obstetrician in Des Moines. "By trying to be a good doctor and helping others, I help myself. When I coach my son's soccer team, I feel I'm moving forward. The kids are there to have fun, not to be sad. I'm the master of my grieving, and that's what I prefer."

How Can Friends Help?

Suicide is a topic that is defined by silence—we hide it, we deny it, we're afraid to talk about it. Many people are at a loss about what to do when their friend or relative has lost a loved one to suicide; when this happens, their lack of support can be both painful and distressing.

"The message seems to be the same from everyone," writes Dr. Edward Rynearson, describing the lonely journey of a suicide survivor. " 'We are over this, and you should be too.' "

Yet, there will always be others who will come through for you— sometimes unexpectedly. "I kept asking myself how I could help," says Natalie, a hair colorist and the mother of two girls. "My friend's fifteen-year-old daughter shot herself last month, and I had no idea what to do. What do you say to a parent who has lost her child to suicide? How do you express sympathy without sounding intrusive? I didn't know what I should do or what I shouldn't do. Then, I started wondering if maybe I was using my fear of being insensitive as an excuse to stay away from my friend and to avoid the entire situation.

"I thought it over, and decided to give my friend a blank journal, one of these nice ones you get at the bookstore. My children and I have been journaling for a while, and what we do is write down what we are thinking, then read our entries out loud to each other. We sometimes find it easier to first write how we're feeling before we say it. I wrote a note to my friend and her surviving daughter that said, 'Here's a journal to share,' and dropped it off at her house.

"My friend called me that evening to thank me for the gift. I was almost going to ask her if she needed anything, but said instead that I was doing some grocery shopping the next day and would pick up food for her. I didn't ask her if she needed anything or what she needed. I just announced what I was doing, and she started to cry.

"Since then, I've been helping my friend with her errands and taking her daughter to our house several times a week for an overnight. I keep on thinking, *What if it were me, what would I want?* Not words but action. I can't bring my friend's daughter back to her, but if I can make this time any easier for her, I will try."

Friendship is in the details. Cutting the grass, deciphering insurance policies, babysitting, talking over endless cups of tea, and

WHAT SHOULD A FRIEND DO?

1. Listen without judgment, criticism, or prejudice.
2. Educate yourself about suicide in order to overcome any preconceptions you may have or discomfort you may feel talking about the subject.
3. Ask the person if and how you can help.
4. Let the person talk at his or her own pace, and share the details of the suicide when ready to do so.
5. Be patient. Repetition is part of the healing process and people need to tell their stories as many times as is necessary.
6. Use the loved one's name instead of "he" or "she." This humanizes the person who died, as well as comforts the survivor.
7. Don't worry if you don't know what to say. Your presence and unconditional listening is most important.
8. Don't try to lead people through their grief. Don't tell them how they should act, what they should feel, or that they should feel better "by now."
9. Avoid statements like "I know how you feel." Unless you are a survivor, you can only empathize with how a survivor feels.
10. Suggest going to a support group for suicide survivors. Help locate a group in your area, and offer to go to the first meeting together.

Reprinted with permission from the American Association of Suicidology (2005).

warm embraces can go a long way to ease your feeling of being overwhelmed and forgotten.

Don't be concerned, however, if you find that you are unable to respond to certain people who may be reaching out to you. Perhaps it's their manner—they don't seem sincere, they're too nosy, they're doing what makes them feel better, not what's right for you. Don't waste your energy on the *why* of your turning away from their help; you already have enough on your plate. Your good friends will understand your reticence and not feel rejected if you decline their offers of support: It's never too late to return their calls or take them up on their goodwill. Each of us heals at our own pace, and accepts help when we are ready.

"For four months after my brother died, I just sat in front of the television and watched mindless videos," says Hank, a 26-year-old freelance graphic artist from Seattle. "I stopped working and cut myself off from everyone. No one in my network had a clue about suicide, and my parents refused to talk about my brother's death. It was over for them, and because my brother lived in another state, they just told everyone that he died in a car crash. It was as if he never existed.

"People tried to help me, or at least some did. One of my friends called and offered me a job, but I turned him down. Another friend called and told me that it was time to get on with my life, and that we should go out drinking and partying together. I know he meant well, but the worst thing you can do is tell someone to drink when they're feeling depressed. You just want to numb out anyway, and you end up using the booze as a crutch.

"One day, my old girlfriend called and said she wanted to fly in for the weekend. I'll never forget how she put her suitcase down in the kitchen without unpacking it, then announced she wanted me to talk for as long as I needed to, and to give her all the details, no matter how grisly they were. She was there to listen, she explained, and that's all she wanted to do.

"It was as if a dam had opened up. I talked and talked, almost nonstop. I never felt judged or stupid or wrong. After she left, I started to go back to the gym. I had gained all this weight from the junk food I was existing on, and was out of shape. I had a goal to look presentable again. After several weeks, I called my friend who had offered me a job to ask if he knew of any other openings. He was so happy when I phoned him that I realized how hard it must have been for him to feel so shut out and useless around me. He quickly found me some freelance work, and I later found out it was a job he had already accepted for himself. It's amazing who comes through for you when something horrible like this happens."

Concrete gestures of friendship make you feel connected and valued, and lighten your very heavy load. Many survivors find solace from members of their religious or spiritual community, as well as from their neighbors, coworkers, and professional colleagues. This friendship and community is what holds us together.

Carla:

Reaching out for support is more difficult than you may think. You can barely function after a suicide, let alone make a deliberate, thought-out decision to ask friends and family for their help. Hopefully, support will come to you from people who take the time to break through your barriers and remind you of their humanity as well as your own. I will always remember and cherish those who stood by me; they are in my heart forever.

Michael:

My patients have taught me a lot about friendship. As they meander through adversity—the turmoil of divorce, a son diagnosed with schizophrenia, a wife's battle with postpartum depression, or the long recovery from a psychotic illness—I am privy to what they think of their friends. Sometimes it's melancholic: "Well, I sure know who my friends are now." But more often, it's positive: "I wouldn't be alive today if it wasn't for my friends. They've been there for me and my family day and night."

Research has demonstrated that people with friends tend to enjoy better physical as well as mental health. Friendships positively affect your ability to fight disease, and individuals who have a solid and steady base of outside support have been shown to have stronger and more resilient immune systems.

Let your friends, family, and other survivors be allies in your healing. They will help you to feel whole again as you begin to reclaim your body, mind, and spirit in a new and ever-evolving way.

EIGHT

Getting Help from
Mental Health Professionals

"Postvention is prevention for the next generation."
—Dr. Edwin Shneidman

Carla:

Survivors are people who need help—who desperately want help—and we look to mental health professionals to assist us in sorting out and making sense of our complicated feelings after the suicide of someone we love. If we go to a therapist or counselor who is uncomfortable with the subject of death or suicide or both, we know it right away. Our radar is finely tuned. A mental health professional's uneasiness with our grief only serves to reinforce the guilt that we are already feeling and confirms our worst fear that we are somehow to blame for our loved one's death.

Suicide is very dramatic: A person crosses a forbidden boundary and creates a mystery that can never be solved. Those of us touched by suicide are left behind as witnesses, and when our emotional responses are defined primarily in the context and circumstances of our loved one's death, we feel even more isolated and unsettled.

Luckily, there are many of us who have been able to make it through with the help of a sensitive and sympathetic mental health professional. My therapist was not afraid of the subject of death, nor death by suicide, and her insights and wisdom helped me through the darkest of times. She created a sanctuary where I could speak openly and without shame about Harry's suicide, and also encouraged me to join a survivor group for additional support. My therapy was an essential part of my healing process, and one that I know I can always call on for reinforcement and help at any time.

Michael:

Mental health professionals are people who have been trained to help individuals who are suffering with various emotional symptoms or changes in their behavior. This includes survivors of suicide. The relationship that you form with a *therapist*—the general term for a mental health professional—is one based on trust. He or she has a responsibility to be of assistance to you and to have your best interests at heart; you, in turn, should have confidence that you will be able to get the help you need.

Because your therapist has the education and experience, and your relationship with him or her is a professional one, you should feel free to talk about anything you want—especially thoughts or feelings that you wouldn't necessarily bring up with family or friends. Above all, you should always feel listened to and respected. I can't emphasize this enough—concentrating with care and showing empathic consideration for my patients are the guiding principles in my work.

When Do I Need Professional Help?

"I thought I could handle this on my own, but it's just getting worse," says Mitch, a television producer in Los Angeles. "I've always been able to take care of my problems by myself, but I'm still a basket case six months after my wife's suicide. My concentration is off at work, I can't sleep and am losing weight, and all I do is wonder if I was too self-involved or blinded by denial to see what was happening."

When should you consult with a professional after the suicide of a loved one? If you have already had a positive firsthand experience with a therapist in the past, your first instinct may be to go for help immediately. If you know a family member or friend who was helped by professional advice, or you are familiar with and respect the mental health field and its practitioners, you may also decide that some kind of therapy or counseling will be sound and beneficial for you at this time.

On the other hand, you may find the whole notion of therapy to be somewhat foreign, and may never have consulted with a mental health professional before. You may also find it awkward to open up to someone you don't know about your personal and private matters, or have a negative impression of mental health professionals as people who are full of problems themselves and just sit there and listen without saying anything. You may also be aching so much that you tell yourself: "What good can therapists do? They can't bring back my son, and that's the only thing I need." Or, you may reason that therapists charge a lot of money for their services, money you don't have.

Do all survivors need professional help? No. Do some survivors need professional help? Yes—it is more than helpful; it is lifesaving. Could all survivors benefit from some professional help? Probably.

The bottom line? Go see a mental health professional if you're feeling stuck and time is passing but you're still not feeling any better. You may even be feeling worse, scarily worse, despite talking to your friends and family and receiving their love and support. Losing your loved one to suicide can be very damaging to your mental and physical health, so you may have to try to accept that you just can't do it all by yourself.

Here are some signs to keep in mind to alert you when it's time to go for professional help:

1. You can't stop thinking about the suicide, no matter how hard you try to get your mind free for brief intervals.

2 You get visual flashbacks of your loved one's face or body, especially if you found him or her. These images keep coming back to you over and over.

3. You can't eat and you're losing weight.

4. You can't sleep properly: You can't fall asleep; you keep waking up; or you wake up very early and can't get back to sleep.

5. You're very tense, nervous, and jumpy.

6. You feel guilty and blame yourself for your loved one's suicide.

7. You can't stop crying.

8. You can't get things done around the house or at work.

9. You can't concentrate on reading or watching television.

10. You don't want to see anyone.

11. You wish you were dead.

12. You have thoughts of killing yourself.

Surviving the suicide of a loved one transports you into a world filled with confusion, shock, and chaos. Guilt and blame and second-guessing consume you: You didn't take care of your mother properly; you should have had the foresight to see what was happening with your daughter; you could have acted differently to save your brother. As you try to find sense and rationality in a death by suicide, you may find that it's easier to tolerate your own failings than to accept that your loved one has died by his or her own will.

Asking for help is not easy. In addition, the taboo against suicide makes it difficult to talk openly about what has happened, and it's not uncommon for survivors to cover up, lie, or avoid the subject all together. This barrier of silence only serves to increase your feelings of isolation and dislocation, and may make it difficult for you to consult a therapist for help with your problems. You may also be nervous about revealing your family secrets to an outsider, or find that the legal and religious issues surrounding suicide are complicated and intimidating, and stand in the way of seeking out professional advice.

Some survivors may also be reluctant to go to a mental health professional if their loved one had been in any kind of therapy, counseling, or analysis at the time of his or her suicide. You may be upset that the psychiatrist, psychologist, social worker, or counselor did not see the impending signs of anguish or despair, or did not try to intervene more actively or tell you what was going on. You may also reason that if mental health professionals were unable to help your partner or brother or mother, how can they possibly help you?

The goal of therapy is to reduce suffering and instill hope so that you can survive what at times does not feel survivable. Here's how speaking with a mental health professional may be able to help you at this time:

- You will get an assessment from a trained professional about the current state of your health—simply put, how well or ill you are. This will give you a perspective on yourself that you do not have at the moment.
- Your therapist will acknowledge the stigma associated with seeking professional help, and will understand your reticence or ambivalence as well as honor your decision to seek help.
- You will get an opportunity to talk without interruption, nonstop if you like. Therapists are there to listen.
- You can cry without anyone trying to shut you down. Or if you can't cry but want to, your therapist is trained to gently facilitate this.
- You can express your anger, rage, and resentment, again without anyone trying to judge you or shut you down.
- Your therapist will be able to explain things that don't

make any sense to you. He or she will help you to ask questions and live with unanswered questions.

- You will not be pushed to talk about subjects that are too painful or that you are not ready to discuss.
- Even though you are speaking with a mental health professional, you can feel free to talk about the care—or lack of care—your loved one received, and your anger and disappointment at the mental health professionals who treated him or her. If you are struggling with indecision about suing or not, you should be able to discuss the conflict you're having about this with your own therapist.
- You can talk about feeling suicidal yourself. Your therapist will want to examine this in great detail with you, to understand your reasons, and to monitor and protect you.
- You will know that everything you discuss is private and confidential.
- Unlike talking to your friends and members of your family, you do not have to worry about "wearing out" your therapist.

Most important, when you see a mental health professional for help and support, you will feel safe and in good hands. You will know that your therapist cares about you and is watching out for you, especially now, when it's so difficult for you to be your own protector.

Whom Should I See?

"After my daughter killed herself, I decided to go to a psychiatrist right away," explains Yvette, an interior designer from New Orleans. "She was recommended by a social worker who thought it was best that I go to a medical doctor in case I needed prescription medication for depression or anxiety.

"I was so nervous, but the psychiatrist was lovely—very sympathetic and caring. In our first session, she told me that she had lost a son when he was young. She said that she usually didn't reveal personal information to patients, but she thought this may help me. She was right. Her son's death was a bridge, and I knew I could trust her from the very beginning."

How do you know whom you should consult after the suicide of a loved one? To begin, it's important to understand the differences among mental health professionals.

- *Psychiatrist*—Psychiatrists are medical doctors who specialize in the diagnosis, treatment, and prevention of mental illnesses, including substance abuse and addiction. They are trained to assess both the mental and physical aspects of psychological troubles.
- *Psychologist*—Psychologists are specialists in the study of the mind, human experience, and behavior. Psychologists have master's or doctorate degrees in psychology, and are trained to help people cope more effectively with life problems based on research as well as their clinical skills and experience.
- *Social worker*—Social workers have master's degrees in social work and at least two years of supervised clinical experience in a social agency or organized setting such as a hospital, clinic, or school. They are trained to help individuals in emotional distress due to personal, family, or social problems.
- *Grief counselor*—Grief counselors are professionals who have done supervised training in grief studies and bereavement counseling. They may be physicians, nurses, social workers, psychologists, or clergy. They may or may not be certified by the American Academy of Grief Counseling.

- *Family therapist*—Family therapists come from a range of backgrounds: psychiatry, psychology, social work, nursing, education, and pastoral counseling. They treat a range of individuals, couples, and families struggling with conflict and communication difficulties. They may or may not be certified by the American Association for Marriage and Family Therapy.
- *Pastoral counselor*—Pastoral counselors are trained in both psychology and theology. They are helpful for individuals who want to address their emotional difficulties in a context of religion and spirituality.

Knowing something about the qualifications of the various groups of mental health professionals and their similarities and differences may help you choose a therapist: A psychiatrist is helpful when you are feeling both mentally and physically ill and may need medication plus therapy. A psychologist is good for listening carefully and applying whatever form of therapy may be best for you. A social worker may be helpful in the same way as a psychologist, plus assist you with employment, social assistance, and housing issues if these are additional stressors for you. A grief counselor will address specific issues dealing with your loss and will help you with all dimensions of bereavement. A family therapist is beneficial if the suicide is not only affecting you, but also affecting other family members as well. A pastoral counselor can be very helpful if you are religiously oriented.

NOTE: Rigorous academic or clinical training in suicide and its aftermath is not mandatory in any of these disciplines except psychiatry. Even then, psychiatrists in clinical practice can vary enormously in their level of experience with suicide. You may also want to ask individuals in any of the above disciplines if they have completed advanced studies in suicide sponsored by the American Association of Suicidology or the American Foundation for Suicide

Prevention (or other organizations researching suicide), or if they have attended any conferences or workshops on the topic of suicide.

Often, your choice of a therapist may be limited to a mental health professional who is covered by your health insurance plan. In addition, if you are paying entirely out-of-pocket, you may be able to afford only certain individuals and categories of help.

You can also ask your primary care physician to recommend a therapist who is known to be effective with people dealing with suicide or sudden death. In addition, a friend, family member, or an-

WHERE CAN I GET HELP?

The following organizations can help you locate available mental health professionals throughout the U.S. and Canada.

- ◆ American Psychiatric Association. 1-888-35-PSYCH (77924). www.healthyminds.org
- ◆ Canadian Psychiatric Association. www.cpa-apc.org
- ◆ American Psychological Association. www.apahelpcenter.org
- ◆ Canadian Psychological Association. www.cpa.ca
- ◆ National Association of Social Workers. www.naswdc.org Look for "Find a clincal social worker."
- ◆ American Academy of Grief Counseling. www.aihcp.org
- ◆ American Association for Marriage and Family Therapy. www.aamft.org
- ◆ American Association for Pastoral Counselors. www.aapc.org

For a complete listing, see Resource Directory, page 275.

other survivor may suggest therapists who are highly regarded by their patients or former patients.

What Should I Expect from a Mental Health Professional?

"I left after three sessions," says Bonnie, whose mother took an overdose of sleeping pills one week after her seventy-fifth birthday party. "I found a grief counselor in my small town, but I think I was the first patient she had ever treated who suffered the loss of someone to suicide. She wanted to know all about my mother, but every time I brought the subject back to how I was feeling, she would seem embarrassed. I honestly believe that the counselor felt worse than I did, and I made it my responsibility to reassure her that I was going to be okay. I would tell her not to worry about me, that I was tough, and that I was a survivor. She almost seemed relieved when I told her that I was ending counseling."

Keep in mind that mental health professionals are human beings first, mental health professionals second. You already know only too well the continuum of comfort and discomfort when discussing the topic of suicide with different family members and friends. Suicide affects every person in one way or another; some mental health professionals are uncomfortable with the subject, others not at all, and most are somewhere in between.

Mental health professionals can be survivors themselves, and their loss of a family member, friend, colleague, or patient may be recent or long ago. Some may have family members who are living with a serious psychiatric illness and others may have lost one or more patients to suicide. These therapists, much like their patients, will be at varying stages of healing, grief, and resolution about their loss as well as about the care they provided to their patients.

In a very real sense, suicide can be threatening to the therapist who is treating you. Your story may set off old memories about the suicide death of a family member, a classmate, a colleague, or the mother of a friend. Therefore, what you have to say to your therapist about your loved one's suicide may hit very close to home, both personally and professionally. As your therapist listens to your anguish and heartache about your father's suicide, she may be thinking of one of her own patients who killed himself while in her care. As you speak, she may feel guilty by association. If you describe your thoughts about how you believe that your father's psychiatrist misread how self-destructive your father really was and how he should have been put in the hospital, your therapist may be identifying with you. Would her deceased patient be alive today if she had done more for him?

While it's important to understand the humanness of therapists, in no way should inadequate treatment or unprofessional behavior ever be excused or defended. It is always the responsibility of mental health professionals to recognize uncomfortable feelings in themselves and not let such inner turmoil affect their professionalism. If this happens, they should seek supervision or therapy for themselves. As the patient, you have a right to expect thorough, sensitive, and helpful care from any therapist you decide to see.

Mental health professionals gather information—called *history taking*—in order to get a better picture of what their patients are experiencing. By understanding how your husband or grandmother lived and died, your therapist is trying to help you gather insights that may shed some understanding on the suicide. This focus on the death is intentional and in the service of assisting you.

If you feel that your therapist is overly preoccupied with your loved one's suicide, however, and is not concentrating enough on your welfare, there may be a problem. You may wonder if your therapist has gotten caught up in the "spectacle" of suicide, and is intent on solving the mystery or puzzle of such a death more as a detective or voyeur than as a person there to help you. Not only will you feel dismissed or not attended to, but your therapist's questions or musings may also serve to reinforce your feelings of guilt and self-blame at not having done more to protect your loved one. At worst, you may feel shunned or stigmatized by your therapist.

If this is happening, you must tell your therapist immediately. His response is key. If he listens to you, accepts your criticism, apologizes, and changes course, good treatment should ensue. If he gets defensive and continues on as before, you will need to go elsewhere.

"When I told my psychiatrist that I thought I was crazy, he suggested hospitalization," says Kendall, a 59-year-old financial analyst from New Mexico whose 24-year-old son killed himself. "I panicked, and practically walked out of his office. My son was my best friend, and I thought I knew him better than anyone else in the world. He confided in me, he trusted me, and he always did the right thing. He wrote me a note before he shot himself, asking me to forgive him. How could I have let my son die? And let him die all alone?

"My life had been pretty orderly up until my son's suicide. I've always prided myself on being in control and determining what happened to me. But now everything is turned upside down. It's as if I have entered an alternate universe.

"Several weeks after my son's death, I sought out a very highly recommended psychiatrist—it was the first time in my life that I ever even considered any kind of counseling—and I told the doctor how surreal and insane I was feeling. That's when he suggested medication and possible hospitalization. I didn't know what he was talking about. Was he saying I had become unhinged? I left before the session was over. I'm now in a suicide support group, although part of me would like to find another psychiatrist to sort out this incessant chatter in my brain."

If your therapist tells you something that you find upsetting or that makes no sense to you, feel free to speak up. You should be able to enter into a dialogue or discussion with her about what she thinks about your condition and what she recommends you should do about it. Granted, she is the expert, but you should be able to ask questions, disagree, and have time to consider what is being said.

It's possible, for example, that the psychiatrist whom Kendall saw was actually well-intentioned but moved into treatment too quickly or inappropriately. He might have been worried about Kendall's symptoms, felt that medication was essential to treat him, and suggested hospitalization thinking that Kendall might feel relieved or safe. What matters most is that the psychiatrist's words backfired and Kendall bolted in terror.

What Kendall needed was to be reassured that it's normal to feel surreal and insane when you lose your son to suicide. Kendall also needed to know that his psychiatrist would be comfortable exploring and discussing these frightening ideas with him. Kendall might have been helped by a statement from his therapist such as: "I'd like to see you again. I'd like to learn more about your son and the special bond that the two of you had—and the terrible tragedy of losing him like this. I'll keep an eye on these thoughts and feelings that you're having, and should they get worse, I'll help you with them."

If you've been seeing a therapist for a few visits and you don't feel that it's helping, bring that up. How your therapist responds to you should make you feel a little better. Sample dialogues might include

1. *You*: "This is my fourth visit and I don't feel any better. I don't think it makes any sense to continue coming here." *Therapist*: "I'm sorry to hear you're not feeling better. I was wondering about that myself. As you know, we're talking about very painful stuff here. Would you feel a bit better if we switched gears for the next couple of visits? Maybe it's just too much to keep talking about your mom week after week, and you're becoming overwhelmed."
2. *You*: "I'm ready to stop therapy. This isn't really working, and I'm feeling worse than when I started."

Therapist: "I've also been kind of worried that despite the hard work we're doing here together, you still can't sleep, your appetite is still off, and you're continuing to lose weight. I'd like to ask you some other questions to make sure that your grieving, which is normal, is not moving into a clinical depression. Would that be okay with you?"

If you're not reassured by your therapist, you may need to consult with someone else. You should feel no obligation to continue. Use the following checklist for trusting your radar when seeking out a mental health professional who is comfortable with the topic of death by suicide:

1. The therapist never forgets that you are the patient, not the person who died by suicide.
2. She allows you to tell your story and fully express your thoughts and feelings.
3. She is compassionate and nonjudgmental.
4. She is sensitive to language.
5. She respects your wish *not* to talk about your loved one's suicide if you are not ready. This is your journey of healing, not hers.
6. Your therapist will not challenge you if you cannot accept that your loved one died by suicide, or, if you're not sure about how your loved one died, she will listen and guide you with your thoughts.
7. You should receive an honest answer if you ask your therapist if she has ever treated a survivor before.
8. Your therapist answers any questions that you might have with truth and respect.

"When I was in my sophomore year in high school, my best friend killed herself," says Courtney, now 30. "Neither of us had dates for the prom, so we decided to go together. We thought it would be fun, and everyone in our class thought we were odd anyway. When I went to pick up my friend, her parents said she was still in her room dressing and I should go get her. I walked into her bedroom and she was hanging from the light fixture. At first, I thought it was some kind of joke. It was as if my mind couldn't absorb what my eyes were seeing.

"I became hysterical and my friend's parents ran upstairs. After that it was all a blur—screaming, crying, the police, my mother coming over. The next day, I got a card from my friend in the mail. It was postmarked the day before she died. It was a thank-you note and on it she had written, 'I'll miss you forever.' On the front of the card was a little bear holding flowers.

"My parents didn't want to talk about my friend's suicide with me. They told me that she was sick mentally and that things like this happen. But I was totally freaked. I didn't know where else to turn, so I went to the school counselor for help. I know it sounds stupid, but he had me write a letter to my friend explaining how I was feeling. I thought it was ridiculous, but it really helped me. It made me see how angry I was at her, and what my feelings were. After I wrote the letter, I was able to cry for the first time.

"It's been fifteen years, and I still have a hard time talking about my friend's suicide. I can't even reach out to people who have lost someone to suicide. A neighbor's friend killed himself, and I never said a word to her. I felt paralyzed.

"Now, I'm thinking of finding a therapist to talk to. I still remember how helpful it was to discuss my friend's suicide with my school counselor. Suicide isn't something you can get over without some outside help. Your whole world shatters—what was is no longer and you can't put it back together. People kept telling me to be myself, but I was devastated after my friend killed herself. I didn't know who I was, so how could I be myself? I still need to figure out who I am and who I will be."

It's never too late to seek professional help. Pay attention to signals or thoughts that something inside you is not right, that you're not at peace, and that you haven't really healed from or come to some resolution about your loved one's suicide. Here are some ways in which you reach that goal by therapy:

1. The act of talking in the presence of another person can be very helpful. You may hear yourself saying things that you have not been able to say before.

> **Michael:**
> A patient of mine who lost her sister to suicide stumbled and blocked when trying to say the word "killed." I sat quietly as she stuttered, "When my sister kil . . . , when she kill . . ." Then she said, "Isn't that weird? I can say the 'k' word to myself, but I can't say it out loud. If I'm talking to my friends about my sister, I always say she committed suicide. I say it in a very matter-of-fact way. But I want to express what I believe inside, that my sister was tormented, that it was a violent thing to do, that she murdered herself." By the end of the visit, speaking slowly and through a lot of tears, she was able to say to me that her sister had killed herself.

2. You may get in touch with emotions that have been buried inside you for a long time. After some months, you may be able to feel anger at your wife for the first time since she drowned herself and left you to raise your children alone. Up until this point, you may have only been able to express your sorrow and guilt about what happened. You might actually identify the anger yourself in a session. Or, your therapist, noting how your voice is changing or your face is grimacing, may say something

to you like: "What are you feeling right now as you talk about your wife?"

3. Revisiting your past and talking about your loved one's suicide might bring memories to your consciousness that you didn't even know were there. This can clarify things, maybe even explain or answer a question. In addition, sometimes the questions that your therapist asks will get you on a train of thinking that is new to you.

4. It's not unusual for people in therapy to remember their dreams more than usual. Analyzing your dreams with your therapist can be very helpful in explaining some of the ways you're feeling, the conflicts you're facing, and the *why*s of your loved one's suicide.

A good therapist is a guide, an anchor, and a companion on the journey. These qualities allow you to join with him or her on an adventure of healing that can be rough and even frightening at times. You need to feel that you will emerge stronger and more in control of your life. And you will.

How Do I Know If I'm Getting Better?

"How do I know when I'm done with treatment?" asks Angelo, 46, whose brother killed himself two years ago. "I've been seeing a social worker for a couple of months now, and he tells me that understanding suicide is a 'process.' I still don't understand what that means. I'm feeling better, but my social worker says we still have work to do. My health insurance doesn't cover any more visits, and my wife is hinting that enough is enough. Can you ever really resolve a suicide?"

Unfortunately, the word *process* has evolved into a meaningless buzzword. When it is used by a mental health professional, he or she probably means that a *course of action* is underway; more specifically, that you have started to accept how your loved one has died and have begun the actual healing from your loss even though you still need more time to deal with your situation.

Remember, you certainly don't have to remain in therapy any longer than you would like. If you are feeling somewhat better, it may be appropriate for you to tell your therapist that you would like to stop coming to see him. Even if he thinks that you could benefit from continuing in treatment, a good therapist will honor your decision and will feel pleased about your independence. "I'm here if you would like to return at any time" is a professional response that should reinforce your decision to leave therapy and reassure you that you made the right choice.

NOTE: If you are stopping therapy because it is too difficult or painful for you, your therapist may ask you to reconsider your decision. Her response may be something like: "I can understand why you would like to stop therapy. It's tough, isn't it, to focus on such sad thoughts and to talk about your loneliness? But there are some other options. We could meet less often. We could take a break and meet again in a month or six weeks. We could talk about some of those other things that you mentioned in your first visit with me, like your unhappiness with your job or the tension with your husband. Do you want to think about these things and we'll start here next session?"

If you're not sure you want to continue therapy after only the first visit, you should consider a second meeting unless you have an intense gut feeling that you and the therapist are simply not connecting. If you've seen your therapist several times and still don't think that you are deriving any benefit from your time together, ask a trusted friend who knows you well for some feedback. Maybe he or she can see a change in you that you don't notice and will encourage you to continue in therapy for a while longer. If you are still very clear that therapy is a waste of time and money, by all means, stop going. If you have mixed feelings—you're pleased in some ways but not others—tell your therapist how you're feeling. If his response doesn't help you or leaves you frustrated, it may be time for you to go elsewhere.

What about a family member who is in therapy with someone? If neither you nor your family member is happy with the care, that might be sufficient reason to decide to stop treatment. If you're not happy but your loved one is, then the two of you need to talk about how your expectations of therapy may differ from one another's.

Carla:

I went to my therapist, a psychologist, for five years after Harry killed himself. My health insurance covered the bulk of my payments. Although I tried to prepare myself for ending therapy, it was much more difficult than I imagined. I knew that I was feeling more whole, less guilty, and almost eager to begin a life that Harry would be part of, but not the entire focus. Yet I was afraid that my connection to Harry would mysteriously vanish the instant that I stopped talking about him for one designated hour every week. I also knew that I would miss my therapist; she had become such a big part of my life and I was worried I would be unable to sustain her absence.

But I also recognized that it was time for me to try it on my own. With the help of family, friends, and other survivors, I trusted that my years of professional help had prepared me to live as best I could with the not knowing and the unanswerable *why*s. Over the years, I have come to understand that my therapist's guiding hand and compassionate wisdom did not end with our last session, but continues to exist in the foundation that we constructed so carefully together.

Should I Contact the Therapist Who Was Treating My Loved One at the Time of the Suicide?

"My daughter's therapist called me after her suicide to ask if I wanted to see him," says Vera, an elementary school principal from Baltimore. "I went to his office the next day, and he answered all my questions in an open and nondefensive way. Our talk helped give me a context for my daughter's death, and it also made me feel better to know that she was getting help from such a caring person at the end of her life. He never charged me for the session, and I appreciated his sensitivity about that."

The official position of the American Psychiatric Association is in support of psychiatrists communicating with family members if a patient dies by suicide. These guidelines may apply to other mental health professionals as well. Even if you do not hear directly from your loved one's therapist, you can call him or her yourself and request a meeting. This may help to lessen your shock and confusion about the suicide, and will also give you the opportunity to ask questions about the person you lost.

What can you expect from such a meeting? Therapist-patient confidentiality continues after death, so very few details can actually be disclosed by the mental health professional who was treating your loved one. However, even if your mother's social worker or your husband's psychiatrist answers your questions only in very general terms, your speaking together can still be very helpful. The therapist may express her sadness and sympathy for you, as well as her own personal feelings of loss. Her sense of humanity may comfort you, and you will also see firsthand that your loved one was in the care of a compassionate human being.

"Talking to your loved one's therapist after a suicide takes a big burden off your shoulders," advises Skip Simpson, a lawyer specializing in suicide cases. "It helps you to know as many details as possible when trying to figure out what happened, and it also helps you understand that you're not to blame for the death."

Don't be surprised if you find your loved one's therapist to be tense or on guard during your time together. Losing a patient to suicide is among the most difficult experiences of a mental health professional. In addition, the most frequent lawsuits against mental health professionals are for patients' suicides. As a result, there may be some initial discomfort because of the therapist's internal unrest and uncertainty about your intentions.

"My wife suffered from horrible depression her entire life," says Ed, a San Francisco chef. "She also made me promise her that I would never let her be hospitalized. But it got so bad at the end that I was afraid that our children were being traumatized to see their mother so sick. I put my wife in one of the finest psychiatric facilities in the area, and the first night she was there she used the bedsheets to strangle herself. So much for suicide watch. Ironically, the night my wife killed herself was the only time I had felt relief in months because I assumed that she was safe and being looked after. I feel so guilty that I broke my promise and committed my wife against her will."

It is always heartbreakingly tragic when patients kill themselves in a psychiatric facility. It is rare, but that is small comfort. Despite state-of-the-art attention to patient safety and exemplary training of the psychiatric staff, some people still kill themselves even when on the highest level of observation. What must be remembered is that involuntary admission to hospitals saves the lives of many desperately ill people. Their testimonials when well again are usually ones of gratitude to their families and to those who treated them. As they recover, many come to understand that they were too ill to comprehend that they could be helped and restored to good health.

NOTE: Although it's better to err on the side of action than the other way around, it is extremely difficult to hospitalize or force individuals into a psychiatric facility against their will. If you're worried about family members or friends and think that they are seriously considering suicide, call their doctor or 911. If they resist your help, tell yourself that you have tried your best and your best is all you can do. If they eventually harm themselves, terrible as that is, *it is not your fault*. You are not responsible or to blame.

If your loved one is admitted to a hospital and you have questions about the treatment, request a meeting with the psychiatrist and the rest of the team. Ask your questions. Express your disagreements. If you are an immediate family member such as a spouse or parent of a child who is not yet an adult, you have rights to a second opinion or an unbiased assessment by a third party. You may or may not need legal assistance.

What is a therapist's obligation to communicate with you while your loved one is in treatment? Confidentiality is the bedrock of trust between a patient and his or her therapist, and for psychiatrists, at least, this covenant can be broken only if their patients are at high risk of harming themselves or others. Psychiatrists do not disclose private information easily; their decision to talk to a family member during treatment is based on a careful and recent suicide risk assessment of their patient, sound clinical judgment, and an ethical obligation to do so.

If you are currently worried about your daughter's safety or your mother's state of mind and think that she is in danger of self-harm, do not hesitate to call her therapist as soon as possible. He can listen to you, and note and record all of your concerns. This information will help him revise any ongoing treatment plan and take immediate action if necessary. Because he will not be revealing anything to you, he is not violating the trust that your daughter or mother has placed in him.

Michael:

Almost 25 years ago, I was left a note by a 30-year-old patient of mine with bipolar illness. It came in the mail the day after he hanged himself. The details are confidential, but there was a request: "Please watch out for my mom and dad." And I did. I hope that I eased their grief in some small way through the few meetings that I had with them for more than a year after their son's death.

Being a physician, I have always known that my relationship with my patients does not end with their death. Their passing has an impact on their loved ones, and if I have earned the respect of those who survive them, they may want to consult with me. I have been told more than once that I represent a connection, a link to the person who died. Sometimes it is both concrete and mystical at the same time. One woman asked me to point out the chair her husband sat in when he met with me. "I want to sit in the same chair," she told me. "I want to be close to him while I'm here with you."

If you are a survivor, don't hesitate to contact your loved one's therapist. You may meet once, twice, or even more. You may find that some of your questions may be answered and some of your confusion may be lessened. If your loved one was not in treatment at the time of his or her suicide, you might consider seeking help yourself. Hopefully, you will forge a mutually respectful bond with a therapist who is kind and compassionate, who is comfortable with you, and who commits to the therapeutic journey that you are embarking upon.

If you are a therapist, open up your door and your heart to survivors. You may or may not have met them when their loved one was alive. Help them and they will help you. As they confront their anguish and raise those very big and often unanswerable questions about life and death, you will feel privileged to walk with them. Survivors are undoubtedly some of the best teachers that a therapist could ever hope for.

The Therapist as Survivor

"Six years ago, one of my patients shot herself in the chest when she was on the phone with me," recalls an Ohio psychologist. "She called to tell me that she was feeling desperate, and then I heard what sounded like a cough, then monosyllables, then silence. I used my cell phone to call her husband at work, and he said that she was probably faking. I then called the police, who went over to my patient's house and found her there. When the police called me back, my first reaction was denial. 'This couldn't be,' I said, and my whole body lurched forward. I wanted to throw up. It was a nightmare in slow motion and still is when I think about it.

"I had been seeing my patient for five years. She was a very intelligent but manipulative person, and had been threatening suicide for a long time. Near the end, I wanted to say to her, 'Go ahead and do it already.' That night, she did. I still feel guilty for those thoughts. I went to the funeral home for the wake but didn't introduce myself or tell anyone in her family who I was. I'm sure they suspected.

"For several years, my patient's suicide haunted me day and night. I relived the last thirty seconds of our phone call over and over. I thought I understood the fragility of life, but then I would remember that I had this woman's life in my hands and I blew it. I kept going over and over what I might have missed. I felt defeated and hopeless and went back into therapy myself.

"I still have a lot of guilt, and try to analyze what happened in my professional relationship with my patient. Through my own therapy, I am finally beginning to understand the powerlessness of trying to help someone whom you can't help. I cared for my patient immensely, but all my experience and understanding couldn't keep her going. I consider my failure professional as well as personal."

Suicides can and do occur in the professional lives of mental health professionals. And their patients can kill themselves despite their best efforts at assessing suicide risk and applying the appropriate treatment. Research shows that therapists who lose a patient to suicide can develop symptoms of post-traumatic stress disorder such as shock, anger, grief, guilt, isolation, shame, diminished self-esteem, altered confidence in their effectiveness as therapists, and heightened sensitivity to the reactions of their colleagues.

In one study of psychiatrists who had lost patients to suicide, 50 percent were found to have experienced levels of stress similar to individuals who were recovering from a parent's death. It is recommended, therefore, that therapists receive training in what to expect after losing a patient to suicide. Mental health professionals are also encouraged to seek out the support of colleagues following a patient's suicide, as well as to consider supervision of certain cases in their practice and going for personal therapy.

Are therapists survivors? One of the definitions of *survivor* is an individual who loses someone he or she deeply cares for to suicide. Another definition is the loss of someone you have known on a first-name basis. These criteria apply to many therapists who have lost a patient to suicide. There are some mental health professionals, however, who may technically be survivors but who do not refer to themselves in this way; they may not understand the full meaning of the term or they may feel differently because their loss was in a professional context and not in their personal lives.

NOTE: Some therapists attend their patients' funerals and others do not. The therapist, like all of the mourners, is there to say good-bye and to pay his respects to the family and close friends. Being present at the funeral, and its ritualistic aspects also helps the therapist with his own grief and loss. Many families are pleased if their loved one's therapist comes to the funeral, but some are not. If you hold your father's therapist responsible for his death, you will not want that person there. The therapist may sense—if you have not already communicated your feelings to him directly—that he is not welcome and will probably decide that attending his patient's funeral would be perceived as insensitive and inappropriate. He may have also sought a legal opinion on this decision or consulted with his malpractice insurance company.

> ## HELP FOR THERAPISTS WHO HAVE LOST A PATIENT TO SUICIDE
>
> *For a complete listing of resources for therapists who have lost a patient to suicide, contact the Clinician Survivor Task Force of the American Association of Suicidology at www.suicidology.org or 1-202-237-2280. The American Foundation for Suicide Prevention also has a Suicide Data Bank project underway for therapists, offering both research and support. Information is available at www.afsp.org or 1-888-333-AFSP (2377).*

"Being a therapist in your family is like being a lifeguard in a hurricane," says New York psychologist and suicidologist Dr. Edward Dunne, whose 16-year-old brother Tim killed himself in 1973. "My mother and sister were both nurses, with specialties in mental health counseling. At the time of Tim's death, there was an institutional belief that suicides did not occur in a therapist's family. Nobody in the mental health community talked about the subject openly."

Since 1973, there has been much more openness and understanding if a suicide occurs in the family of a mental health professional, even though some "Dark Age" horror stories of denial, shame, and shunning still continue to exist. Mental health professionals are human beings first and trained professionals second. They are subject to the same illnesses and outcomes of those illnesses as the rest of humankind. In fact, it is believed that at least some individuals train as mental health professionals because their lives have been touched by mental illness while growing up. They may have a father or mother with a psychiatric illness, a sister with cocaine dependence, or an alcoholic grandfather. Or they may have had an eating disorder while a teenager or a bout of depression in college. This firsthand experience often contributes to the insight and compassion for others that is present in so many mental health professionals.

NOTE: It is very difficult for mental health professionals when one of their colleagues dies by suicide. They are not only coping with the loss of someone whom they've known and liked, but also confronting the stigma associated with the suicide death of a member of the healing profession. Patients and the general public are also threatened by the suicide of a trained professional or expert in mental health: If they give up, what is the message they're sending to the rest of us? But if we accept that it's usually an illness that kills them, like cancer taking the life of an oncologist or coronary artery disease felling a cardiologist, then, hopefully, we can accept the suicide deaths of mental health professionals with less fear and judgment.

Michael:

Therapy means treatment, care, and healing. The idea of seeing a mental health professional may not appeal to you and may not be something you can afford. But there are other avenues of therapy all around you. You may find therapy in gardening. Greeting the morning sunrise. Preparing afternoon tea. Walking in the rain without an umbrella. Listening to a Bach fugue. Reciting aloud a poem by Robert Frost. Praying in your house of worship. Volunteering at a food bank. You will know what embraces you, what cloaks you in warmth, and what restores meaning and hope.

Suicide is a death like no other. It leaves a lot of people in its wake, including professionals who are dedicated to trying their best to prevent their patients from killing themselves. Although we know that even our most advanced diagnostic tools and interventions cannot stop all individuals from ending their lives, mental

health professionals agonize when a patient takes that lethal overdose or leaps from a bridge. We apply the salve of the realization
that they have suffered plenty and are now at peace. This helps a
bit, but not entirely. I tell myself, as well as my students, to pay attention to grief and to use those wrenching emotions to self-
examine, learn, and join hands with the researchers and survivors
on the front lines of suicide prevention.

Carla:

My mourning was about Harry; my therapy was about me. I gained
insights from exploring my grief, guilt, anger, terrors, and love for
my husband. Although many survivors do very well without seeking out help from a mental health professional, I needed a guide to
lead me through territory that was unfamiliar and unknown. I came
to understand that help is where you find it, and most of the time
you must look for it and accept it when it's offered. Unlike our
loved ones who were unable or unwilling to find the help they
craved, we know we must find strength from others to help us re-
build and carry on.

PART THREE

How Can I Go On?
Finding Meaning after Suicide

NINE

Suicide, Religion, and Spirituality

Carla:

We've lived through it. We've accepted it. We've incorporated our loved one's death by suicide into our lives as best we are able. Our family compliments us for "moving on"; our friends admire our courage in adversity; our coworkers respect our determination and strength. Through daily, intimate, and extremely personal acts, we honor and remember our parents, our children, our spouses, our siblings, and our friends. Yet, our heartache remains, and we continue to search for ways to come to terms with our eternally senseless loss.

My husband's decision to take his life shook my faith in him, in myself, and in the order of the universe, which I had never questioned until the instant of his self-inflicted death. With no other choice, I was forced to acknowledge the absence of control that each of us ultimately has; this realization humbled and terrified me at the same time.

Like many survivors, I was mystified at how deep my resolve was to carry on and restore my world after such an unimaginable loss. I found myself calling on inner resources I never knew I had in order to help myself redefine what I once held so important and dear. I also had a great desire to find some kind of meaning in Harry's death, to discover insights that would not only provide me with some relief but also comfort others as well.

Over the years, I have come to understand that each survivor's search for spiritual peace is different, and that our private framework of strength is created and sustained by our own individual values and beliefs. In accepting the unknown, there is an acknowledgment that certain things cannot be changed. My faith lies, therefore, in the permanence of infinite hope and the continuous renewal of connection and love.

Faith and Suicide

Many people find great strength from their religious and spiritual values and beliefs after the suicide of a person dear to them. Their loved one's death becomes part of the overwhelming mystery—and glory—of life itself. This faith shapes an acceptance of what can and cannot be controlled or changed, and creates a structure for living as well as thriving in the aftermath of suicide.

"I guess you could say that I suffered a crisis of faith after my husband's suicide," says 88-year-old Annette, a Holocaust survivor whose husband killed himself after more than 50 years of marriage, two children, and five grandchildren. "Morris survived Auschwitz, as did I, but then he turned away from God and religion. I went in the opposite direction, and embraced my faith as a tribute to my survival and also to bear witness to the millions of people, including most of my family, who were murdered so brutally.

"Although my husband loved us to the limits of his ability, he was a melancholy man. Even so, in a million years I would never have believed that he would take his life. A gentle soul, Morris somehow got hold of a gun and shot himself in the basement of our house. After all this time, after all we had gone through together, how could he have done this? His sudden and unexpected death has been the greatest tragedy of my life. How could he have left me? Why did he leave me alone? He knew what I went through. Initially, his act shattered my beliefs along with his body. But I eventually found comfort from the faith that had sustained me in the past."

Is it possible to reconcile our faith with the reality and consequences of the suicide of a person we love and trust? Reverend Elizabeth Maxwell, associate rector of the Episcopal Church of the Holy Apostles in New York City, says that clergy are used to counseling people like Annette, who suffer a crisis of faith after a suicide or other seemingly senseless death.

"Faith is a mystery," Rev. Maxwell explains. "It gives you time to wonder about things bigger than yourself. 'Mystery' is the ancient name for God, and God doesn't give up on you even if you give up on yourself. When individuals come to me with their faith shaken by an event like suicide, I tell them to try to look for love and beauty in the middle of their darkness. I remind them that asking questions and having doubts is normal, and that I hope the love and prayers of the community will help sustain them during this terrible time.

"If they then ask me how God can let such a horrible thing as suicide happen, I say that we all want the best for those we love and it's sometimes a mystery where God is during all of this. But I also have very deep faith in a loving God, and offer them the wisdom of the Reverend William Sloan Coffin, who said after the death of his young son: 'I believe that when my son died, God's heart was the first to be broken.' "

Some people embrace their faith after the suicide of a loved one while others may turn away, either temporarily or permanently. Yet all survivors need whatever reinforcements they can find to regain their footing after such a devastating and puzzling loss, and many look for spiritual and religious guidance to help them sort out how they are feeling.

"My definition of faith changed after my friend's suicide," says

Alex, a writer from New York. "I saw how limited our individual power is, no matter how much we would like to change the outcome of what happens or influence the events in our life. I now believe that faith means giving up control and accepting that there will always be mystery and the unknown. I also had to make peace with destiny or God or whatever I care to name it, and accept that my anger and defiance would not bring my friend back or explain his decision to kill himself. For me, faith is believing in—and ultimately accepting—something you can't know and are unable to prove."

For the past decade, scientists have been conducting hundreds of studies to try to measure the effects of faith and spirituality on a person's physical well-being. The results are mixed, and health professionals themselves are polarized about the role that religious and spiritual beliefs play in medicine. The relationship between faith and healing continues to be explored, however, and is taken into consideration by all of the health sciences.

FAITH-BASED RESOURCES CONCERNED WITH SUICIDE

For a wide range of faith-based programs, publications, Web sites, and organizations throughout the U.S. and Canada for people who have lost a loved one to suicide or are concerned with suicide in any way, contact OASSIS (Organization for Attempters and Survivors of Suicide in Interfaith Services) at www.oassis.org or 1-240-632-0335, or Fierce Goodbye, a faith-based perspective on suicide, at www.fiercegoodbye.com. For a complete listing of additional resources and programs, see Resource Directory, page 275.

Religion and Suicide

Suicide has a long and complicated relationship with religion. Taking your own life was considered a sin by all of the major faiths until not so long ago. This was very painful for survivors because their loved ones could not receive a religious funeral with the traditional rituals of death, nor could they be buried inside the cemetery or on consecrated ground. Although today's clergy are more enlightened about current thinking on suicide, there still remains a residue of discomfort, puzzlement, and shame about the topic. For example, the clergyperson may not name the cause of death at the funeral, and may encourage eulogists to omit any reference to suicide. There may be a hushed silence in the chapel or whispered huddling at the reception. Some surviving family members may worry that their loved one is in hell or may be stuck in purgatory. Some may rage at God.

But this is the dark side. There are theologians and religious leaders at the national and international forefront who are educating men and women of the cloth about suicide, forgiveness, and compassion. They want the most up-to-date information—that suicide is most often brought about by a mental illness and is not a sin—to be espoused from the pulpit so that congregants from all faiths will understand the message and reach out to survivors during their difficult times.

"The word *sin* in Greek literally means 'missing the mark,' " explains Rev. Maxwell. "We all do that in our lives. We also experience alienation in large and small ways, and when you kill yourself, you are alienated from your own being. When people ask me if suicide is a sin, I tell them the the love of God is beyond our imagination, and religion is about compassion and forgiveness."

Dr. James T. Clemons, president and founder of OASSIS (Organization for Attempters and Survivors of Suicide in Interfaith Services) is one of the major forces in teaching religious leaders from every denomination to recognize suicide as the finality of an illness and not as a sin.

"A very wise priest once replied, when asked by a grieving mother if her son would go to hell because of his suicide, 'Your son has suffered enough,' " relates Dr. Clemons. "There are no limits to God's compassion; His mercy and wisdom are infinite. How can a human being have the ability to move beyond God's compassion? There must be trust and belief—or what we call 'faith.' And faith cannot be proven scientifically."

Dr. Clemons, a United Methodist minister, is the author of the book *What Does the Bible Say about Suicide?* "There is *no* explicit condemnation of suicide in either the Old or the New Testament," he emphasizes. "It was only in the fourth century that the commandment 'Thou shall not kill' was interpreted to mean killing yourself as well as others. Suicide then became an unforgivable sin, and if you killed yourself you would go to hell. Now, as a result of compassion, understanding, and education, suicide is no longer considered an unforgivable sin by most major religions. In addition, the clinical pastoral movement within the religious community is growing, and many clergy are now being trained in understanding mental illness, suicide, and depression to assist in their counseling."

The role of the church in the African-American community has always been an important one, and black pastors throughout the United States are taking on a growing role in reaching out to people who have lost loved ones to suicide, as well as those with suicidal thoughts.

"Historically, there has been a gulf between mainstream psychology, which was negative toward religion's role in one's mental well-being, and African-American pastors and congregants, who were suspect about psychology and psychotherapy," explains Dr. Sherry Davis Molock, who is both an ordained minister and a professor of psychology at George Washington University in Washington, D.C.

Dr. Molock, a pioneer in bridging the understanding about suicide between the clergy and mental health professionals, teaches that God understands hopeless situations—such as what happens with people who are suicidal—even though God does this with sadness. "There is a moment between mortality and eternity when I think the spirit of God can still speak," she says.

A religious advisor's guidance can also define a survivor's healing. "My minister got me through my mother's suicide," says Lorraine, a librarian from Vermont. "He was the first person to come over after her death, and he spoke to me about how kind and gracious my mother was. He told me stories about her good work at the church as well as her acts of charity. We talked about my mother's life, not her death, and there was no judgment, only love. I called upon our conversations many times to help me during those first excruciating months after my mother died."

On the other hand, a religious advisor's lack of acceptance and tolerance can have a devastating effect. "After my daughter's suicide, I went to my pastor, who told me that my eleven-year-old daughter was in limbo because she killed herself," sobs Jane, 35. "My daughter used my husband's gun—she had managed to cut the padlock off—and shot herself in her bedroom. I found her when I came home from work. I cry all the time now, thinking that my baby is alone in the cold and the dark, and I can't comfort her. I have to believe that she is with God, no matter what my minister says."

According to Rev. Maxwell, if you go to your clergy for help after the suicide of a loved one and they cannot accept that suicide is driven by an illness, not a sin, *go somewhere else*. And Dr. Clemons agrees: "If you make suicide so bad and evil, people will be nervous and afraid to turn to religion for help. In addition, some survivors may be extremely angry at God after a suicide, and feel abandoned and let down. This is normal. Besides, you can get as angry at God as you want—God can take it."

Many survivors find comfort from prayers after the suicide of a loved one, although most define their prayers in deeply personal ways. "Sometimes I think of praying as just pleading, and I envy those people with more assured concepts of faith than mine," says Sally, a college student from Indiana. "My brother suffered from schizophrenia and bipolar illness, and he had multiple suicide attempts before he killed himself last year at the age of twenty-one.

I prayed for God to protect him, and I guess my prayers weren't answered in the way I would have liked. Now, I don't pray to God to make things happen—after my brother's suicide I no longer believe that you can change your destiny—but to give me the strength to cope with whatever occurs in my life. I also pray that the people I love will be able to bear the circumstances of whatever will happen to them."

The almost complete turnaround in the way the religious and faith communities currently view suicide is reflected in the funeral and memorial services conducted for people who die by suicide. According to the widely respected Suicide Prevention Resource

RECOMMENDATIONS FOR MEMORIAL SERVICES FOR A PERSON WHO DIES BY SUICIDE

These recommendations are edited from a larger publication by the Suicide Prevention Resource Center to aid community and faith leaders as they care for those who have survived the loss of a loved one due to suicide, and to assist them in planning memorial observances. The complete version is available for download from the Suicide Prevention Resource Center at www.sprc.org.

1. Comfort the grieving.
2. Help survivors deal with their guilt.
3. Help survivors face their anger.
4. Attack stigmas and take the opportunity to make as much sense as possible of what happened. Dispel the common myths about moral weakness or character flaws as a cause of suicide.
5. Use appropriate language. Avoid the phrases "committed suicide," "successful suicide," and "failed at-

tempt," and instead use such phrases as "died by suicide," "took his life," "ended her life."

6. Prevent imitation and modeling. Don't glamorize the
current state of "peace" that the deceased may have
found after death, and avoid normalizing the suicide
by interpreting it as a reasonable response to particularly distressful life circumstances. Instead, make a
clear distinction, and even separation, between the
positive accomplishments and qualities of the deceased and his or her final act.

7. Consider the special needs of youth. Address the young
people in attendance very directly, since they are most
prone to imitate or model their behavior after a suicide.
Focus attention on the hope of a brighter future and dis-
covering constructive solutions to life's problems.

8. Consider appropriate public memorials. Dedicating
memorials in such public settings as park benches,
flagpoles, or trophy cases is discouraged as it may facilitate the suicidal acts of others, particularly young
people. Offer examples of expressing grief in tangible
ways, such as personal expressions that can be given
to the family to keep privately—letters, poetry, recollections captured on video, or works of art. Also suggest
activities such as fundraising for suicide prevention organizations, purchasing library books addressing the
topic of suicide, sponsoring mental health awareness
programs, and honoring the deceased by giving back
to the community in different ways.

Reprinted with permission from the Suicide Prevention Resource
Center.

Center (SPRC) in Newton, Massachusetts, members of the clergy now have an opportunity to "bring comfort to survivors by framing their informed responses with sensitivity, compassion, grace, and love." SPRC believes that the ultimate goal of a memorial service is to foster an atmosphere that will help survivors understand, heal, and move forward in as healthy a manner as possible.

"A community will be able to bring healing to its members if it has a better awareness and more accurate understanding of suicide," writes David Litts of SPRC. "A better-informed community is also better equipped to recognize and respond to signs that someone they know and love is at risk of taking his or her own life."

Survivors are all individuals with unique personal experiences with religion. You may be helped by one particular religion and house of worship, or you may stay with your religion but leave your congregation for another that better meets your needs. You may also "experiment" with different religions until you find a belief system or religion where you feel most comfortable and at ease.

NOTE: There is no evidence that not being religious is bad for your health. If you feel judged or pressured by family members who urge you to seek some form of religious direction, don't hesitate to speak up: Your route to healing is yours alone, and how you do that is your business.

Suicide is an act that severs the normal structure of a community and affects each of its members. If you are lucky, you will be able to turn to your religious or faith community, or find one that may better fit your spiritual needs. There, you can search for some kind of peace and understanding in a safe and sympathetic place.

Spirituality and Suicide

"After my wife killed herself and left me and our daughter, I went to my minister for comfort," explains Jude, a 40-year-old mechanic from Little Rock, Arkansas. "He was very uncomfortable with what

REAL VOICES:

My son's death helped me value life in a way that I never did before. It shocked me out of my complacency, and made me realize how fragile life is. I also came to accept that there were things I could not change.

Over the years, I have found ways through alternative approaches to enhance, expand, and enliven my healing. I guess it could be called "working on the soul"! My spirituality is basically a belief in a greater or higher power, and a trust that there is more to life than just the material world and one prescribed set of beliefs to guide me.

Many people find comfort in their religion after the suicide of someone they love: They will look for guidance and find it. Some get angry at God and stay angry, while others get angry and then come back.

I recently went on a vision quest with the Lakota Indians in Canada. My purpose was to see if I could connect to some kind of spirit or higher power, and make sense of what I had been going through since the suicide of my son. Here is what I learned:

1. *Stand tall.*
2. *Stay deeply rooted in the ground.*
3. *Trust the process.*
4. *You have more to do.*

Adventuring has also helped me greatly—climbing mountains, exploring, swimming with dolphins, drumming. I want to experience life and do different things. Meeting these physical and spiritual challenges makes you feel that anything is possible and gives you hope—and proof—that you will be able to survive.

—Iris Bolton

had happened, and gave me passages to read from the Bible. I needed more—I wanted human contact—and came back to see him. I couldn't stop crying and was of no use to my daughter. My minister actually seemed annoyed, like I was complaining and was resisting accepting God's will. Who can I turn to now that I feel my minister doesn't want me to bother him anymore?"

Many survivors find themselves looking for a deeper meaning to their loved one's suicide, a spiritual explanation that may not be available by conventional or familiar means. The hurt is so bad, the burn is so raw, the pain is so excruciating, that any kind of balm, no matter how experimental or unlike any previous experiences, is sought for comfort.

Spirituality and faith are extremely intimate and personal. "Faith is a gift, and theology is our attempt to understand the giver," says Dr. Clemons. "Our spirituality is our response to the acceptance of the gift of faith that we are given."

Exploring your spiritual side can also help you discover resources and pathways to help with your healing and recovery. Mahatma Gandhi said, "You must be the change you wish to see in the world." You may find yourself surprised not only by what treasures are inside you, but also by how much you may touch the hearts of others.

"Two springs after my mother killed herself, I was walking through a park near my house and I noticed that the grass had started to grow," says Margo, a paralegal from Pittsburgh. "It was a very poignant moment for me—this connection with nature made me feel as if I was coming out of a coma. I had been experiencing almost paralyzing grief and despair since my mother's death, and when I saw I could still relate to the world around me, I felt my first spark of hope. I started to cry when I realized that my ability to appreciate the beauty and mystery of nature had not been extinguished by my mother's suicide. I also felt an almost physical awe that although my life had been on hold for so long, nature had continued on.

"In the fourteen years since my mother's death, I have come to appreciate the present, the here and now. Above all, I'm keenly aware of how much I value my connection to the people I love. It may sound funny, but I'm grateful to my mother for helping me open up this spiritual side of myself, and consider this new dimension to my life as her gift to me."

Michael:

I have struggled for years to find meaning in my college roommate's death by suicide. I was 19 years old when he died. All I could conclude for a long time was, "What a waste."

I know now that Gord's death fueled a lot of questions for me. Did his suicide influence my career path into psychiatry, and in particular, reaching out to ailing physicians and their loved ones? Did facing suicide at such a young age make me a better psychiatrist, more sensitive to my patients' anguish, less afraid to probe dark caverns with them? Am I more attuned to hidden signals of despair and better able to prevent some patients from harming themselves? Did Gord's death give me some wisdom to pass on to my students, something that he didn't live long enough to do himself?

I will never know the answers, but my questions give me some peace.

TEN

Life-Preserving Insights into Suicide and Attempted Suicide

Carla:

Even though it's been more than 16 years since Harry killed himself, I still can't figure it out. True, I no longer think about his suicide day and night like I used to, and there are actually fairly large chunks of time when I miss him the way I imagine a "normal" widow misses her husband. I see a movie and wish I could share it with him. I wonder how he would look with gray hair. I read about a new medical advancement or surgical technique in his field and regret that he'll never know about it. I try to remember if there even was e-mail in 1989, and fantasize about how much Harry would have loved to use all the latest computer programs to share his research and ideas with his colleagues throughout the world.

And then—once again—I remember: It was Harry's decision to stop living. There is no cancer or heart attack I can rail against, no drunken driver or thief in the night at whom I can direct my anger. There isn't even a murky image of terrorists I can picture, like the ones who killed thousands of people in New York City on September 11, 2001, or a natural disaster like the hurricanes in 2005 that destroyed and uprooted the lives of tens of thousands of Americans.

I have reluctantly come to accept that I will never really know why the color in Harry's life faded into black and white, then gray, then nothingness. Yet, in my ongoing search to make sense of my husband's death, I have unexpectedly found a renewed sense of purpose from connecting with survivors throughout the world as well as with others who are dedicated to erasing the stigma of suicide through education and prevention. These powerful and essential bonds validate and give meaning to my own life as well.

Suicide transforms those of us who are left behind. To the existential question of "Why?", our loved ones answered "Why not?" and chose to leave. Even though we may spend the rest of our lives trying to make sense of what they have done, we honor their memories by sharing our insights into their deaths with others who are touched by suicide in so many different ways.

Michael:
Whether we are survivors or clinicians or both, wrestling with suicide and its ultimate meaning changes us. On an intimate and personal level, we must try to understand why someone we knew took his or her own life. At first, our questions may be self-serving. Our lives have been upended and we need to feel better. By knowing the reasons as best we can, we hope to comprehend the incomprehensible and regain some stability and resolution. As time goes on, however, we find ourselves reaching out to help others who, like us, are also struggling to solve the enigma of suicide. We are messengers speaking for those who can no longer speak for themselves. Or perhaps they never could.

Why Does Life Lose Its Meaning for Some People?

"Nothing seems to matter anymore since my sister killed herself," says Sofia, an accomplished portrait artist from Oklahoma City. "My work feels flat, my connection to my husband and children is shaky, and my physical state of well-being is shot. I can't get my enthusiasm back. It's not that I feel hopeless or desperate; it's more as if I've lost my sense of purpose and I'm drifting away from everything that used to anchor me."

Losing meaning in your life is different from losing hope. Meaning is associated with belonging, and if you don't feel connected to another person, a family, a group, a community, or a cause, you can feel very alone and isolated. You may experience a sense of not mattering, a sense that whether you live or die is not important to anyone else in the world. These feelings may not be enough to make you want to end your life, but they can be a contributing factor.

"Because part of being human is being aware of our mortality, we focus on making sense or ascribing meaning to our lives," says Dr. James Rogers of the University of Akron, a prominent suicidologist and pioneer in studying the interplay of suicide and how people value themselves. "This includes defining who we are in the world through our work, our leisure activities, our families, and our relationships with others. When these worlds that we have created for ourselves are somehow shattered for whatever reason, we can be left with overwhelming feelings of isolation or loneliness and lose sight of the threads that hold us to life."

Feeling and being needed gives meaning to your life. If you don't believe you have a purpose for existing, you can feel forsaken and forlorn. For example, many elderly people struggle with redefining their role in society as the circumstances in their lives begin to change. "My husband died, my children have their own lives, and my grandsons live far away," says Esther, 86, a retired guidance counselor. "It feels as if I'm the last of my generation to still be alive. You tell me why I should go on living—nobody needs me anymore."

Meaning can also lessen or evaporate when people are struggling with mental illness, especially depression, the most common illness associated with suicide. Severe and unrelenting depression can rob its sufferers of so much—vitality, energy, the ability to love and be loved, appreciation of family, sexual pleasure, the beauty of music, the joy of laughter. Life as they once knew it becomes meaningless, bleak, and painful: *It's difficult to go on living if you can no longer trust that you will ever feel normal again.*

NOTE: If you are worried about a family member, a friend, or yourself, call 1-800-273-TALK(8255), the National Suicide Prevention Lifeline. A trained counselor is available to speak with you 24 hours every day.

What Are the Differences between Thinking about Suicide, Attempting Suicide, and Completing Suicide?

The following terms are used to distinguish between thinking about suicide, attempting suicide, and completing suicide:

1. *Suicidal thinking*: This term refers to having self-destructive thoughts about ending your life.
2. *Suicide attempt*: This means that an individual has tried to kill himself or herself. Although suicide attempts vary in lethality, they all need to be treated seriously.
3. *Suicide*: This is defined as taking one's own life. There is evidence that the person intended to die and that the death was not an accident or a result of natural causes.

When Should I Become Concerned that Suicidal Thinking May Turn into a Suicide Attempt?

Thinking about suicide is always serious. Although many people who have had thoughts of suicide never act on them, others do. When should you become concerned about someone you care about?

- If your sister tells you that she is having thoughts of killing herself, but refuses to talk to you about them, this could mean that she has a plan to harm herself and is at risk for attempting suicide.
- If your boyfriend says that he's thinking about killing himself every day, most of the day, or all day, he is at high risk of attempting or completing suicide.
- If your daughter is having thoughts of suicide but isn't frightened or dismayed about them, this is worrisome. She may be planning a way to kill herself and has no fear of dying or being dead.
- If your father is hearing a voice or voices that are telling—or ordering—him to kill himself, he is at very high risk of attempting suicide.

NOTE: People who have thoughts of suicide plus a very severe physical depression may long to be dead but are usually so weak, so tired, and so slowed in their movements and thinking that they are often unable to put their self-destructive plans into action. If they do express thoughts of killing themselves, however, it is critical that they receive immediate attention and treatment. They must also be monitored very closely if they have been prescribed an antidepressant medication, because energy is often the first function to return as the medicine begins to work and their spirits start to lift. During this window, they are at risk of putting their suicide plan into action.

COMMON MISCONCEPTIONS ABOUT SUICIDE

1. People who talk about suicide won't really do it. <u>False</u>: Almost everyone who dies by suicide or attempts suicide gives some clue or warning. Do not ignore suicidal threats. Statements like "You'll be sorry I'm dead," "I can't see any way out," or "I wish I were dead" indicate serious suicidal feelings, no matter how casually or jokingly said.

2. Anyone who tries to kill him/herself must be crazy. <u>False</u>: Most suicidal people are not psychotic or insane. They may be upset, grief-stricken, depressed, or despairing, but extreme distress and emotional pain are not necessarily signs of mental illness.

3. If a person is determined to kill himself or herself, nothing is going to stop him or her. <u>False</u>: Even the most severely depressed person has mixed feelings about death, wavering until the very last minute between wanting to live and wanting to die. Most suicidal people do not want death; they want the pain to stop. The impulse to end it all, however overpowering, does not last forever.

4. People who die by suicide are unwilling to seek help. <u>False</u>: Studies of people who die by suicide show that more than half have sought medical help within six months before their death.

5. Talking about suicide may give someone the idea. <u>False</u>: You don't create self-destructive feelings in another person by talking about suicide. The opposite is true—bringing up the subject of suicide and discussing it openly is one of the most helpful things you can do.

Used with permission from SAVE (Suicide Awareness Voices of Education), Minneapolis, Minnesota.

Losing meaning in your life can be absolute ("my life never did have any meaning") or relative ("my life used to have meaning but it doesn't any longer"). You may begin to feel that things are never going to change or improve. You may ask yourself: Will I ever get better? Will I laugh again? Will this black cloud lift and will I be able to see the sun shine once more?

Keep in mind that although you may have these feelings, you may not necessarily be suicidal; the memories of your children, your good deeds, your faith, your accomplishments, your beauty, and so on may be enough to sustain you and give you a sense of purpose. You may also be comforted by your anticipated legacy—your unborn grandchildren, the knowledge and insights you have passed down to family members, your philanthropy. You may tell yourself that although you know life is finite and you will be gone one day, a piece of you will live on. This realization may help you think of your life as more worthwhile and meaningful.

Young people who feel alienated from society, or their particular microcosm of society, may also have a difficult struggle with finding meaning in their lives. They may be upset that they have not achieved much at school or sports, that they don't have many friends, or lack a boyfriend or girlfriend. Most young people take little comfort from such well-meaning advice as "You're a late bloomer," or "You march to the tune of a different drummer." Killing yourself can be very compelling if you are unable to see that your life will change somewhere down the road.

NOTE: It's impossible (and probably folly) to try to separate existential reasons for feeling suicidal from psychiatric illness. The same holds true for the many social reasons that may contribute to suicidal thinking. Each of us experiences many different types of losses in our lifetime, and **loss is one of the biggest determinants in a person's decision to end his or her life.** What is important, however, is our view of ourselves as well as the world. Negative thoughts are one of the most dangerous features of a suicidal mind and interfere with your ability to clearly see yourself, your family, and your friends. This situation can be made even worse if you believe that having such negative thoughts is the way you have always been, and you are unable to see how deeply pessimistic your state of mind has become.

"Hold a good thought for me," Marilyn Monroe wrote shortly before killing herself. This beautiful actress's high-visibility suicide continues to intrigue and perplex scholars and artists as well as the general public: How could a person who seemed to have everything come to feel that her life no longer had meaning?

Some investigators have suggested that Marilyn Monroe may have had mixed feelings or regrets after taking the pills that killed her. There was also some evidence that she tried to call her psychiatrist before she died. Like Marilyn Monroe, most people who attempt suicide or die by suicide are ambivalent and have contradictory emotions and thoughts about living and dying. Although Marilyn Monroe did not live to explain what she did, many people who have survived very serious suicide attempts are able to give us invaluable insights into the suicidal mind.

"After waking up in the intensive care unit of the hospital and seeing the pain in my husband's face, I vowed that I would never try to kill myself again, no matter how desperate I felt," says Rose, 57, a librarian from Portland, Oregon. "My husband was so pale, and looked as if he had aged ten years in the thirty-six hours I had been unconscious. There was so much hurt in his eyes, and sorrow oozed from every pore of his skin. I realized that you can't do this to someone you love. Even though I was still terribly depressed and couldn't imagine ever being happy again, I decided that I had to soldier on no matter what. Before the overdose, my life had no meaning. When I regained consciousness, I felt restored and happy to be alive. I was spared—there has to be meaning in that alone."

Why do some people carry on day after day in the midst of unbelievable heaviness and adversity? Why do some of these individuals not only persevere but also help others who are struggling? Why do other people give up and passively await death, or actively embrace it by killing themselves? Each person's definition of meaning speaks to the diversity of humankind and the unidentified nature of what inspires us to value and appreciate life.

What About Assisted Suicide?

Carla:

Both my 90-year-old mother, in intractable physical pain, and my 43-year-old husband, in relentless emotional pain, died by intravenous drip. Both decided they wanted to end their lives this way. When my mother nodded to start the morphine that would end her suffering, she was at peace and so was I. When Harry inserted the needle into his vein that would unleash a lethal amount of the anesthesic thiopental, he was alone, and I will never know if he was tormented or calm.

I supported my mother's choice to cease living with her increasingly debilitating and terrifying death-by-drowning congestive heart failure. I railed against my husband's act, and am still angry and heartbroken at what he did.

How can we judge another person's anguish? Why does my mother's death feel "right" and Harry's death seem "wrong"? As our world becomes more complex and medical science more exact, most of us will probably be confronted at some time with decisions of life and death—ours or those of the people we love. The most we can do is hope that we're correct, and pray they—and we—will be all right.

In the ongoing debate about assisted suicide, it's important to define the terms associated with this controversial subject:

1. *Assisted suicide* is when a person requests and engages another person or persons to help participate in a deliberate and well-thought-out plan to end his or her life. The person is provided with

the means and/or assistance to carry out his or her suicide plan. **NOTE**: If a person stockpiles pills to use in a suicide and does not ask anyone to help him or her die, this is not assisted suicide.

2. *Physician-assisted suicide* is when a physician provides the means to complete the suicide and/or participates directly in the suicide. Physician-assisted suicide remains controversial, both within the general population and in the medical community. According to Dr. Herbert Hendin, former medical director of the American Foundation for Suicide Prevention (AFSP) and a world authority on this subject, many suffering individuals who request help with dying from their physicians are primarily concerned with pain, loss of dignity, and being a burden on others. They may have undiagnosed depression or inadequate treatment for their depression, and what may seem like a rational decision to die is not rational at all.

Physician-assisted suicide is not widely condoned by members of the medical community, although that may change over time. Physicians fall into the traditional position of healer, and although they may have enormous empathy for their patients, the great majority probably feel that actively and openly assisting with a death by suicide goes against their medical ethics.

Even so, most compassionate physicians agree that tending to a dying patient is not the same as living with a close family member who is suffering and in intractable pain. Do merciful physicians quietly and privately practice some form of euthanasia from time to time? Yes. They are simply responding to unspoken or obliquely spoken directives from their dying patients. It is the essence of the physician-patient covenant.

Issues surrounding physician-assisted suicide, the medicalization of death, life-extending technology, and the role of the courts in the rights of individuals and their treatment options continue to spark discussion and debate throughout the world. For additional literature and references on these subjects, see the Resource Directory, page 275.

3. *Rational suicide* is the decision to complete suicide by a person who is considered mentally competent and who has realistically assessed his or her situation. In addition, the individual's peer group understands his or her motives to die.

4. *Euthanasia* is a practice in which an individual who is suffering from an incurable or terminal illness is helped to die painlessly, usually as an act of compassion. It is the same as *mercy killing*.

Different forms of euthanasia include *active*, involving the administration of treatment or some act that causes death; *passive*, or the withholding or withdrawal of life-sustaining treatment or nourishment; *voluntary*, meaning that the person has made the decision to stop treatment to end his or her life; and *involuntary*, which is the merciful killing of a person without his or her consent.

5. *Hastened death* is another term that is sometimes used as an alternative for assisted suicide or physician-assisted suicide. Dr. James Werth, the noted suicidologist and psychologist from the University of Akron, writes that he uses this term to describe end-of-life decisions that shorten the lifespan because "as long as we use the term 'suicide' to describe or define something, then that act will be stigmatized and assumed to be the result of irrational decision-making."

Hastened death can be requested by people whose disease is progressing or worsening. Their decision may be based on fears of a loss of independence, dignity, self-worth, or social support. They may also worry about being a burden to their families. It's critical to keep in mind that a request for hastened death may also be sparked by conditions that can be treated or corrected such as uncontrolled pain, shortness of breath, or medical information that is frightening or makes a person feel hopeless.

Participating or declining to participate in another person's death is extremely personal and wrenching. You may believe that your help is a demonstration of love or a final gift to someone you cherish to help end his or her unbearable suffering. Or you may be convinced that your loved one is asking to die for reasons that can be medically remedied and refuse such a request.

Whatever you decide, you will probably find yourself agonizing about what you should do, what you should have done, or what you already did. You may ask yourself: Are all the necessary resources being utilized to ease my father's discomfort and control his pain? Am I abandoning my best friend and denying the enormity of his suffering? Is it possible that I may be harboring some dark, deep ulterior motives that I'm not even aware of in considering helping my wife end her life? Could some other medication have been administered to improve my sister's quality of life? Did I turn away from my grandmother in her hour of need? The catch-22 is that you may be filled with some degree of guilt, regardless of your ultimate decision.

Michael:

Being a psychiatrist has given me a window into the thoughts, feelings, actions, and memories of many people who want to talk about assisted suicide. Patients of mine who are health professionals describe a mix of feelings regarding taking part in an assisted suicide: Some have participated in such a death; others have refused to participate; and still others have not yet had to face the matter but know they probably will sometime in their career. Each of them, however, welcomes the opportunity to talk aloud, and to have someone listen to them and guide them on their path.

I also have patients who are living with chronic or progressively deteriorating health and function, and have deliberately acquired a stash of stockpiled medications that they know can kill them. They are buoyed up and reassured that they have the means to end their lives if and when it ever becomes necessary, and are relieved that they have an increased sense of autonomy about their illness and imminent death. Other patients have an abiding belief that their suffering will be eased by their doctors and nurses, their home-care aides, their families, or prayer. They feel no need to take death into their own hands.

Each of us will eventually face and ponder these very big questions about living and dying. Our answers will be deeply personal, and our actions will reflect who we are and what we believe in.

What About People Who Attempt Suicide?

REAL VOICES:

I lost complete consciousness the moment I jumped—I was jumping into oblivion. I was in the intensive care unit for almost two months—it took me one month to regain consciousness. I had no recollection of what happened. I remember asking, "Did I commit suicide?"

This happened three years ago when I was in my first year of medical residency. I was beginning to feel overwhelmed, and became consumed with feelings of worthlessness and inadequacy. I started to think about suicide all the time. I didn't have a concrete plan to kill myself; my feelings of wanting to die were more passive, like wishing that I would disappear or no longer exist. I read a story about an elderly woman who had been hit by a bus and died instantly, and I remember feeling guilty about wanting that for myself. I also had thoughts of a knife stabbing me, although I never went to the drawer and looked at the knives.

One morning, a short while after I had returned from being on call overnight, I was in my apartment and realized that I did have a way out—I could jump off my balcony. I started telling myself that I wasn't meant for this life, that the world would be better without me. The rational part of me was not working—I never would have chosen such a public death as jumping into the street. At that moment it did not occur to me that I might be unsuccessful at dying.

I went to the ledge of the balcony at least two times, looked down, then returned to the couch. I was very ambivalent, and then suddenly the telephone rang and it was my program director. I couldn't disguise the fact that I was crying, or what I was contemplating. He asked for my address, saying that he would send the chief resident over immediately.

I had this thought that I was insulted. How could my director send over a complete stranger and not come himself? I had just confided something so intimate, so personal to another human being and I did not expect the response that I got. Suddenly, my ambivalence became a resolution. I didn't want anyone to think that what I was doing was manipulation. I told my program director that this is something I had to do and jumped off the balcony.

I thought it was cruel that I was allowed to survive. My apartment was on the sixth floor—I should have realized that there was a chance I wouldn't die. My injuries included pulmonary hemorrhages, rib fractures, ruptured spleen, abdominal hemorrhages, fractured jaw, a fractured wrist, fractured vertebrae, and spinal cord transection at T4, which means that I'm paralyzed from the chest down.

My future? I am now planning to return to residency, but the specifics will depend on further assessment of my psychological abilities. I still have feelings of hopelessness and worthlessness, but I'm looking forward to practicing medicine again. I have always had a feeling of warmth and love for humanity, and see medicine as a way for me to express that love.

When I was in the rehabilitation center, one of my psychiatrists, who had known me during medical school, told me, "You do belong in medicine." His faith in me had a very powerful effect—he said this to me when I was being so hard on myself. But he believed in me, and now I also will try to believe in myself.

—Dr. Amole Khadilkar

Unlike Dr. Khadilkar, most people are ashamed to speak openly about their past suicide attempts. Since suicide is still considered in certain sectors of society to be a stigma, a mark of disgrace, a blemish, or a flaw, many individuals with a history of suicide attempts decide to keep their actions a secret for their entire lives. Some will tell only very dear friends or family members, while others find themselves whispering from embarrassment when relating their story.

SUPPORT IF YOU HAVE ATTEMPTED SUICIDE

The Organization for Attempters and Survivors of Suicide in Interfaith Services (OASSIS) is a national organization for people who have made suicide attempts as well as those who have lost loved ones to suicide. For further information, go to www.oassis.org or call 1-240-632-0335.

Individuals who sustain physical injuries from their suicide attempts often live with a great deal of regret and shame, at least in the early months and years; their bodies are a reminder of that terrible time when they considered death as their only way out. Other people express sorrow that they didn't die, and judge themselves harshly as pathetic failures who can't even kill themselves properly—they are often filled with both self-hatred and disappointment, and are deeply remorseful for what they have done and the pain they have caused others. In addition, some individuals may suffer from a form of "survivor guilt" for being rescued while others have died from similar actions.

Do some people try to kill themselves again? Yes, but many do not. The risk of a second attempt is highest during the first and second year after the initial attempt. Individuals who rarely try again include those who attempt suicide in the face of overwhelming stress, who are young, who cannot see other options at the time, and who do not have a problem with alcohol, drugs, or an underlying psychiatric illness. They have learned from what they have done, and they can see that there are many other ways of dealing with their desperate feelings, such as contacting a close friend, calling a crisis center hotline, calming down and letting their anxious feelings pass, or seeking professional help.

The risk of a second attempt at suicide is highest in individuals who are living with untreated depression, alcohol abuse, a longstanding medical illness, or are socially isolated. If their first suicide attempt was very serious—they truly intended to die, they took measures to avoid being discovered, they used a more lethal method and were physically injured—they are at risk of attempting again if they do not receive good follow-up treatment.

Multiple suicide attempts almost always involve the same symptoms as the original incident—agitation, impulsive feelings, pressing thoughts of suicide, extensive planning, withdrawal from family and friends, trouble sleeping, and so forth. These feelings are a "wake-up call" that the person's underlying illness is returning, and that he or she is in trouble. This can be a very dangerous time, and immediate help and intervention is recommended.

NOTE: If a person has a serious illness such as a major depressive disorder or bipolar illness and the treatment is working well, the risk of attempting suicide again is greatly lessened and may even be gone forever. The key to avoiding future suicide attempts is accepting the illness, understanding its recurrent nature, and embracing the treatment that is helping.

How can you help a friend or family member immediately after an attempted suicide?

1. If your daughter has taken an overdose, first make sure that she isn't in any immediate danger, then call 911 or get her to the hospital immediately. Even if she says that

SUICIDE ATTEMPT STATISTICS

An estimated 800,000 people try but fail to kill themselves each year in the United States—10 to 20 million people worldwide. For every suicide in the U.S. there are 25 attempts, five hospitalizations, and 22 hospital emergency department visits (over 670,000) for suicidal behavior. Approximately 5 million living Americans have attempted to kill themselves, with the rate three times greater for women than for men.

What about young people? According to the Substance Abuse and Mental Health Services Administration (SAMHSA), in 2004, an estimated 712,000 young people in the U.S. ages 12 to 17 attempted suicide, representing 2.9 percent of this country's youths. SAMHSA also found that 3.6 percent of the nation's youths, or 900,000 young people, had formulated some kind of suicide plan, and more than 7 percent—an estimated 1.8 million young people—had thoughts about killing themselves at some time.

NOTE: Eighty percent of all suicide attempts in human beings occur in teens ages 15 to 19.

she has taken only a few pills and seems alert to you, the pills may not yet have begun to act or she may not be telling you the truth. Even if your daughter doesn't want you to call or tell anyone else, do it anyway. Let the emergency health professionals sort out the next steps.

2. Try to be understanding and nonjudgmental. If you are angry or upset that your boyfriend tried to kill himself, keep that to yourself until you know he will be okay. You may have thoughts like "He's just trying to get my atten-

tion," or "He's trying to manipulate me to move back in with him," or "I refuse to feel guilty." Again, wait to express these thoughts until he is no longer at risk. Your boyfriend may be trying to communicate something by what he's done, and there will be time later on for you to deal with it.

3. Do more listening than talking. Your brother may need to get things off his chest. Try to avoid giving advice, as it may be misinterpreted as inappropriate or invading his privacy.

4. If you are sad that your mother has tried to end her life, tell her so. If you should become tearful or begin to cry, that's also okay—you are showing her that you care about her and what she has done.

5. Don't try to make your friend promise that she will never do anything like this again. Yes, you may be worried about a second attempt, but it's better to ensure that she gets good care as soon as possible.

6. When a person attempts suicide, it can be a shock for family and friends. If you should blurt out something like "Why did you do such a stupid thing?" or "How could you do this to me?" or "Let's get to the bottom of all this silliness," try to apologize. Your loved one needs your unconditional support and affection in the immediate aftermath of his or her attempt.

NOTE: Once your family member or friend is out of danger and is feeling stable again, you may want to talk about the factors that seemed to trigger the suicide attempt. That may be helpful for both of you, especially if there was some misunderstanding or miscommunication in your relationship. If the two of you can't discuss the subject, or talking doesn't seem to help, consider meeting together with your loved one's physician or therapist.

How should you respond if your friend or family member has attempted suicide in the past? If he has tried once or twice before, this means that his illness has returned and he may be in very grave trouble, even if the way he tried to kill himself did not seem serious. He is at high risk of attempting suicide again, and this time he may be even more determined to die. He needs help and he needs your support.

But what do you do if this is the fourth or fifth suicide attempt? What do you do with your feelings of frustration or anger or being manipulated? Again, wait until the crisis has passed before you say anything. Because many people who attempt suicide over and over again eventually do kill themselves, you must take them seriously. To be on the safe side, it's best if you wait to talk about your feelings until you are in the presence of your loved one's therapist or physician.

Talking About Suicide Attempts

Revealing your past suicide attempts is a personal choice. You may want to be open with those people you trust who will respect your confidence, or you may be more reserved or guarded about what happened and choose not to tell anyone, which is also your right. If you are ashamed of what you did, however, you might feel better if you tell one or two people whom you love and respect. Their acceptance will lessen your feelings of humiliation and shame.

There are also other reasons for telling your story. If you are worried that your son or daughter may be developing a depressive illness or suicidal feelings, letting them know about your past struggle with depression and suicide may reassure them that you understand them, are not judging them, and will do everything possible to make sure that they get good care. In addition, you can help other family members and friends by explaining that having thoughts of suicide or attempting suicide are symptoms of an un-

REAL VOICES:

When I was 16, one of my most intimate secrets was feeling suicidal and being suicidal. I couldn't even disclose how I was feeling and what I was thinking to my psychiatrist. I was the middle of three boys, and was very creative and intellectual. I did karate classes to become more masculine, but I never really fit in anyway. I was very geeky, and tried hard to conform to a male sex role.

I started developing a suicide plan, which included combining speed with the epinephrine I took for my asthma and injecting myself with it. I knew this would give me a major cardiac dysrhythmia because I had looked up the information in a poison control book. I stockpiled the epinephrine by faking asthma attacks, and when I had enough syringes, I injected the medication into myself. I expected to feel a sharp pain in my chest and a shortness of breath. Instead, I felt manic. So, I went on to my next plan, which was to use downers—Quaaludes, phenobarbitals, and Seconals—and take a shot of vodka with each pill.

I swallowed all the drugs and had a near-death experience. I saw my grandmother, who died when I was 12, along with other family members. I remember a voice—plus a pure whiteness—saying, "It's not your time yet." The voice also stated three principles that I should follow in my life: to make a difference in the world for the better; to earn the admiration of someone or a group; and to be a good man, a good person.

Everything reversed itself. I reentered my body. Then I heard my younger brother trying to wake me up and I thought, "I'm alive—why am I still here?" I still felt that darkness and despair. How could no one notice?

My next and last suicide plan involved driving my car into a wall at a shopping mall. As I raced up the street, I heard the same voice from my last attempt say, "It's not your time." After that, I felt a certain peace.

> *I continued going for help and, over time, started coming out of my despair. In my third year of medical school, I began transitioning from male to female. I went to a psychotherapist who helped me with this. I also learned that 100 percent of transgendered youth are suicidal at one time or another.*
>
> *I have never been suicidal or attempted suicide again since that time when I was 16 years old. Yet, I make it a point of self-disclosing my suicidality to my medical residents. I feel strongly that students look for concrete examples to help them understand and expand their knowledge. The fact that I can resonate with suicidal patients as a psychiatrist and explain the feeling of despair to my residents feels like a gift. My pain can now help others.*
>
> —Dr. Melanie Spritz

derlying problem, and that although these symptoms are serious, so are chest pains associated with heart attacks or blurred vision signaling the onset of glaucoma. Your honesty lets them know that there is no need to feel ashamed.

Like Dr. Spritz, some people talk about a previous attempt at suicide to educate others about the illness of depression or other types of mental illness. These testimonials help remove the stigma associated with suicide.

Michael:

How can you communicate your inner pain without harming yourself? Or, if you already have hurt yourself, how can you learn new ways of letting others know what you're planning so you can get help?

If you can tell anyone about what you're feeling, do it! This alone will lessen the darkness and the intensity of your anguish. Call a friend. Call a family member. Call a crisis center. Get to the nearest emergency room. For some people, going from thinking about suicide to actually trying to kill themselves can happen in a nanosecond. If you are very low, you may not be able to express yourself coherently. That's okay—all you need to say is, "I'm in trouble, please help," and even complete strangers will understand. They will see the pain in your eyes and most will respond to your request for assistance.

If you have attempted suicide before, you can learn ways to protect yourself in the future. Try to remember how you were feeling before your self-harming thoughts began. At what point did you make a specific plan to kill yourself? What was it like when the idea of being dead felt more gripping than living? Should you ever find yourself that low again, you now know you have options other than acting on your thoughts. You may have already made an agreement with your spouse or partner or other close person to let him or her know immediately when you are feeling suicidal. If so, tell him or her right away, before you change your mind. And call your doctor—or have someone else call on your behalf if you cannot make that call yourself. **NOTE**: Do not drink any alcohol.

Why Is Language Important in Understanding Suicide?

Suicide is a sensitive and often misunderstood subject; therefore, the language associated with it is constantly being adjusted to reflect the clinical advances in the field as well as the concerns of survivors. The following terms are used most frequently in the discussion and study of suicide:

1. *Commit suicide*: Many survivors, as well as others involved with studying and preventing suicide, are opposed to using the verb "commit" to describe the act of suicide. "It sounds like my son perpetrated a crime," explains a Michigan mother. Other individuals recoil because "commit" is associated with sin. Some people,

however, feel that suicide is literally self-murder and "commit" is an appropriate term to describe such an act.

The phrase "commit suicide" has been used for decades by mental health professionals and in professional publications. Only now is this beginning to change. Another common term that should be replaced is "successful," as in, "The person's attempt at suicide was successful this time." For similar reasons, "failed suicide attempt" should be replaced with "previous suicide attempt."

Alternative and preferred terms for "commit suicide" currently used in literature and spoken communication include "Died by suicide." "Completed suicide." "Suicided." "Killed himself/herself." "Took his/her life." "Ended his/her life."

2. *Decide or choose to die*: There are some survivors who object to the terms "decide to die" or "make a choice" when describing suicide. They feel that this language sounds judgmental, and that their loved ones were unable to think or reason clearly when they ended their lives. Most survivors, however, are comfortable with the idea that the person they lost did make a decision to end his or her life—for whatever reason. Furthermore, this concept often gives survivors comfort during their healing.

3. *Survivor*: This term refers to a person who loses a family member or close friend to suicide. A person who attempts suicide but does not die is referred to as a *survivor of a suicide attempt* or an *attempter*.

4. *Suicide bomber*: The intent of a "suicide bomber" is to kill others by using his or her body as a weapon. A more accurate description for a person who commits this act of murder may be "homicide bomber" or "homicide/suicide bomber."

5. *Mass or group suicide:* These suicides are different from individual suicides in that they tend to be driven by a powerful and charismatic figure or a conviction that a person is going to a better place. In mass suicides, the individual no longer has free will and is influenced to cross the line into self-destruction by adopting the beliefs of the group's leader. Internet suicide, in which people kill themselves individually or in groups after meeting through online chat rooms, is an emerging phenomenon in some cultures.

Words have power as labels and reflect our changing values. As we learn more about suicide—its causes, its consequences, and its effects on those it leaves behind—the language surrounding it should remain fluid and change accordingly.

How Can I Find Meaning in My Loved One's Suicide? In My Own Life?

Many survivors look to create something meaningful from their loss: They work to prevent suicide in young people, lobby for more funding for mental health programs, organize suicide support groups in their communities, or reach out to comfort a friend who has also *been there*.

"Current data suggest that many bereaved people find new and sustaining meaning in their lives and losses," write Drs. Robert Neimeyer and James Werth in *The Cambridge Handbook of Age and Ageing*. "This 'post-traumatic growth' can be experienced with or without professional help."

Michael:
People who have been plagued with suicidal thinking, or who have tried to kill themselves and are now well, believe that they have been given a second chance. They are grateful to be alive, and feel that their lives have more significance and purpose. Many emerge from their ordeals with special insights; having been in that awful place, they know both the terror and the allure of wanting to end your own life.

We have much to learn from survivors of suicide attempts,

whether we are survivors of a loved one's suicide, clinicians, re-searchers, or everyday citizens. Individuals who have attempted to take their lives can help us make sense of the life and death of a family member, a friend, a colleague, and show us ways to seek clarity and definition after suicide has touched our lives. By fight-ing to eradicate the stigma of self-inflicted death, we can start to bring about wholesome dialogue as well as more effective preven-tion. Above all, we will be able to save lives.

Carla:

Writing about suicide is very important and cathartic for me. It re-minds me that I didn't lose my capacity to express myself after Harry killed himself, and am still able to communicate to others with my words. Through my work, I have also had the privilege to come to know thousands of other survivors, as well as to meet many mental health professionals, crisis care workers, and re-searchers who are devoting their careers to understanding suicide. Being part of this international community of dedicated and com-passionate women and men helps me restore and retain purpose in my life.

Survivors look to find meaning in suicide by honoring and cele-brating the lives of those they have loved and lost. Our survival is a testimony to a resilience we wish they'd had, a hope we wish they'd shared, a future we wish they'd believed in, and a love that we hope and pray they realized we had for them when they de-cided to end their lives.

ELEVEN

Erasing the Stigma of Suicide

*S*uicidology, or the study of suicide, is a relatively new field. Yet, over the past decade, there has been a remarkable shift in the way the medical, scientific, and survivor communities have come to regard this once-taboo and misunderstood topic.

"It's important for us to be honest and forthright about Garrett's suicide because our son was honest and forthright during his life," says U.S. Senator Gordon Smith of Oregon. "There's no owner's manual for the death of a child, especially a death by suicide. I consider the Garrett Lee Smith Memorial Act, which funds suicide prevention programs throughout the country, to be my most worthwhile accomplishment in the Senate. By bringing suicide out of the shadows, we can begin to erase the stigma associated with it and, most importantly, help save the lives of many people."

Why Is It Important to Erase the Stigma of Suicide?

"Telling the truth about my husband's suicide makes his life—and death—seem more real," says Carissa, a 28-year-old magazine editor. "I changed jobs six months after Andy shot himself, and at first, I told everyone at work that my husband had died of cancer. The lies made me feel disconnected and detached from my own life; it was almost as if Andy had never existed and I was making up my entire marriage. If you ask me why I felt the need to hide what had happened, I can't really answer. Maybe I was afraid my coworkers would think that I had been a bad wife, or my husband had been crazy, or both.

"I decided to 'come out,' and started with my boss. I asked her to shut her office door, then blurted out about Andy's suicide. I was stunned by her reaction—it turns out that her brother had killed himself two years before. She then went on to tell me about other people at the magazine who had lost a family member or friend to suicide. 'It's nothing to be ashamed of,' she said. 'There are more of us out there than you would ever believe.'

"I felt a great weight lift. Why should the fact that my husband killed himself be such a stigma, for him or for me? From that moment, I made it my business to educate myself about suicide. I enrolled in a graduate course online and also joined a local support group that my boss recommended. I have a great desire to learn as much as I can about suicide so that one day I can help other people cope with this type of loss. I am committed to make something constructive emerge from Andy's death."

Eradicating the stigma attached to suicide—and its most common antecedent, mental illness—is a pressing public health imperative. The World Health Organization estimates that 121 million people worldwide suffer from depression, and underscores that depression's worst outcome is suicide, which kills 850,000 individuals every year. Yet, fewer than 25 percent of people with depression receive effective treatment, and social stigma is cited as one of the major obstacles to care. The impact of reducing this stigma is no less important than implementing pap smears to detect cervical cancer, mammograms to look for breast cancer, and colonoscopies to diagnose bowel cancer.

Penetrating the silence and shame surrounding suicide will have far-reaching and continuous benefits: Survivors will be able to get on with their healing from the moment of their loved one's death and not be derailed into deception or disgrace. Researchers will be able to compete for grant money without discrimination because psychiatric illness will be regarded as no less important than cancer or heart disease. The lack of parity in health insurance coverage for the treatment of physical and mental illnesses will be rectified. And individuals struggling with depression, anxiety, stress, or substance-abuse disorders will feel less hesitant to seek out much-needed help, and will go for and receive treatment earlier.

Stigma is like a chokehold—it grips us by the throat and weakens our voices, sometimes literally, sometimes metaphorically. As we continue to reduce the stigma associated with suicide, fewer people will kill themselves and fewer will suffer needlessly.

"Men and women are happy in a multitude of ways, but in sorrow's deepest moments, all are one," writes the philosopher Terrence Des Pres in his book *The Survivor*. We are all in this together.

What Is Being Done for Suicide Prevention and Education?

The number and strength of the many individuals and organizations working to promote awareness about suicide continue to grow. *Suicide is now considered a public health problem, not just an individual problem*, and strategies to prevent suicide are being offered at the local, state, and national levels. In addition, the combined voices and perspectives of survivors, mental health professionals, crisis care workers, and researchers are creating a powerful force that is helping to advance the understanding of suicide throughout the world.

"Preventing suicide is no small task," says Dr. Lanny Berman, executive director of the American Association of Suicidology. "Our work demands an integration between science and practice, as well as a broad collaboration among all sectors of society. By bringing together different points of view, we are increasingly successful in saving more lives."

Survivors put a face to suicide, and are especially effective in reaching the public as well as members of the media and legislators, according to Jerry Reed, executive director of the Suicide Prevention Action Network USA (SPAN USA), a national advocacy group.

"Survivors are changing the landscape of suicide awareness," he explains. "By sharing their personal stories, they are able to turn their grief into action and communicate the urgent need to take concrete steps to prevent more deaths by suicide. Their openness also sends a message of hope that there is always a tomorrow after suicide."

There is a wide range of organizations dedicated to suicide prevention and education, and their work is critical in helping to destigmatize this once secret and hidden topic. For a complete listing, see the Resource Directory, page 275.

How Can I Help?

"Organizing a local support group for suicide survivors helped me to find some meaning in my son's suicide," says Joan Fine (no relation to the coauthor), chairperson of the American Foundation for Suicide Prevention (AFSP) Florida Southeast chapter. "I started our group twelve years ago, and I am still facilitating the meetings twice a month. My husband, Norman, is also very active in AFSP, both on a local and national level. Guilt is something that survivors embrace with both arms, so it's very important to avoid becoming isolated in your grief. We honor our loved ones by trying to understand what they went through and using this knowledge to reach out to others who need it."

Like Joan and Norman Fine and many other survivors, you may find great comfort and fulfillment from becoming involved with your local support group or from volunteering for a national or-

RECOMMENDATIONS FROM THE SURGEON GENERAL'S CALL TO ACTION TO PREVENT SUICIDE

A comprehensive blueprint on ways to prevent suicide and promote public awareness of this national health problem was issued by former U.S. Surgeon General Dr. David Satcher in 1999. This historic call to action catapulted the topic of suicide onto the front pages, bringing the once-hidden subject out of the darkness and into the light.

The report's recommendations include

1. Awareness: Broaden the public's awareness of suicide and its risk factors:
   - Promote public awareness that suicide is a public health problem and, as such, that many suicides are preventable. Use information technology to make facts about suicide and suicide prevention widely and appropriately available to the general public and health care providers.
   - Expand awareness of and enhance access to resources for suicide prevention programs in communities.
   - Develop and implement strategies to reduce the stigma associated with mental illness, substance abuse, and suicide, and with seeking help for such problems.
2. Intervention: Enhance services and programs, both population-based and clinical care.
   - Extend collaboration with and between public and private sectors to complete a National Strategy for Suicide Prevention.

- Improve ability of primary care providers to recognize and treat depression, substance abuse, and other major mental illnesses associated with suicide risk. Increase the referral to specialty care when appropriate.

- Eliminate barriers in public and private insurance programs for provision of quality mental health treatments and create incentives to treat patients with co-existing mental and substance-abuse disorders.

- Institute training for all health, mental health, and human services professionals—such as clergy, teachers, correctional workers, and social workers—concerning suicide risk assessment and recognition, treatment, management, and aftercare interventions.

- Develop and implement effective training programs for family members of those at risk and for natural community helpers on how to recognize, respond to, and refer people showing signs of suicide risk. Natural community helpers are people such as educators, coaches, hairdressers, and faith leaders, among others.

- Develop and implement safe and effective programs in educational settings for youth that address adolescent distress and crisis intervention, and incorporate peer support for seeking help.

- Enhance community care resources by increasing the use of schools and workplaces as access points for mental and physical health services and providing comprehensive support programs for persons who survive the suicide of someone close to them.

- Promote a public/private collaboration with the media to ensure that entertainment and news coverage represent balanced and informed portrayals of suicide and its prevention, mental illness, and mental health care.
3. Methodology: Advance the science of suicide prevention.
   - Enhance research to understand risk and protective factors, their interaction, and their effects on suicide and suicidal behaviors.
   - Develop additional scientific strategies for evaluating suicide prevention interventions and ensure that evaluation components are included in all suicide prevention programs.
   - Establish mechanisms for federal, regional, and state interagency public health collaboration toward improving monitoring systems for suicide and suicidal behaviors, and develop and promote standard terminology in these systems.
   - Encourage the development and evaluation of new prevention technologies to reduce easy access to lethal means of suicide.

Department of Health and Human Services, U.S. Public Health Service, 1999.

ganization dedicated to suicide research and prevention. By channeling your pain and loss in a positive direction, you will see that you are still capable of being useful and making a difference. A Japanese proverb says, "A kind word can warm three months of winter"; knowing that you are helping others can be very freeing and will allow some light back into your life.

REAL VOICES:

My 20-year-old son, Jamal, killed himself in 1990, and at that time there was hardly any information about suicide in the African-American community. Eight years later, as a result of grassroots efforts with other people of color throughout the United States who had lost a loved one to suicide, the National Organization for People of Color Against Suicide (NOPCAS) was founded. Up until then, the problem of suicide in minority communities was not being addressed: Although the suicide rate among African-American women was the lowest for all racial and gender groups, the suicide rate among all African-Americans had more than doubled between 1980 and 1995, increasing at a rate more than twice that of white Americans. In addition, the suicide rate for Native American youths was twice as high as any other group, and three times higher for all children ages 5 to 14.

NOPCAS's mission is to increase the awareness of the cultural differences in the ways African-Americans and other people of color express symptoms of depression and suicidal thinking. We are also trying to eliminate the stigma about getting help that still exists in our communities, and are reaching out to churches and other faith groups to help us with this goal.

I feel that my research and teaching about suicide keeps me close to my son. I also run support groups in the Washington, D.C., area, which help me to remember that I am part of a survivor family and am not alone. Survivors never stop asking "why," and I find it comforting and reassuring to hear how other people also find meaning in their life after the suicide of someone they love.

—Donna Barnes, Ph.D., president of NOPCAS and
faculty member, Howard University

For survivors, the avenues available to help eliminate the stigma of suicide are many. "Suicide is how my sister died," says Theresa, 25, of Vancouver, "but her brutal rape by a complete stranger two years before she died is what really killed her. I don't want anyone else to suffer the way my sister did, and I feel that I am able to honor her memory by volunteering at a local rape crisis center. My work there keeps me connected to my sister in a more hopeful way."

Other survivors become involved with volunteer or charitable activities that speak to specific factors they believe may have contributed to their loved one's suicide. For example, they may tutor adults with severe learning disabilities, walk for schizophrenia research, train as alcohol or drug counselors, make sandwiches for homeless youth, speak to elementary school students about the emotional hazards of bullying, and so on.

How can you become involved and make a difference in preventing suicide and erasing the stigma associated with it?

1. Contact your local representative regarding passing and funding legislation for suicide awareness, education, and prevention.
2. Lobby for more money for mental health programs.
3. Speak out to your local press and the national media about responsible and accurate reporting on suicide deaths and attempts.
4. Encourage more spending to be allocated for scientific research in the study of suicidology.
5. If your loved one lived with a mental illness, volunteer for organizations and advocacy groups that promote awareness and research in this field.
6. Create a quilt panel in your loved one's memory through the Lifekeeper Memory Quilt project (www.lifekeeper.org).
7. Work to prevent suicide in young people, on college cam-

puses, among the elderly, in the gay and lesbian community, among people of color, and in other specific groups. (For a complete listing of organizations, see Resource Directory on page 275.)

8. Be honest. Every time you tell other people that your loved one died by suicide, you help them to be more comfortable with the subject and to overcome remnants of stigma within themselves.

NOTE: Each of us has a different time frame for healing, as well as our own individual way of working through our grief. Although many survivors find great satisfaction in devoting their energies to the prevention and understanding of suicide, others prefer not to become involved with the subject on a public level. Some survivors find that what is most important to them is sharing their story with a friend or stranger who has also lost a loved one to suicide. Only you will know what works for you; there is no right or wrong course for you to take in your healing process.

Can We Make a Difference?

Michael:

I have been working in psychiatry, a stigmatized branch of medicine, since 1969. Although we still have "miles to go before we sleep," to paraphrase the poet Robert Frost, over the years I have witnessed phenomenal progress being made toward reducing the stigma associated with suicide. When I was a resident in the early 1970s, attempting suicide was considered a crime. Did we call the police to our emergency room and turn our patients in? Of course not. Even back then, I was impressed by the sensitivity of my mentors, my colleagues, and our mental health teams, and by the regard they showed to their anguished and distraught patients— individuals who already had plenty to worry about.

ADVOCACY: TURNING GRIEF INTO ACTION

1. What is advocacy?
   - *Advocacy* is the work of *advocating*—supporting or speaking in favor of something.
2. Why do people advocate?
   - To raise awareness.
   - To educate.
   - To change laws.
   - To obtain funding.
   - To improve services.
3. How can I be a successful advocate?
   - Know your issue.
   - Know what you want.
   - Know your representatives' positions.
   - Know your facts, figures, and statistics.
   - Know what others are saying about this issue.
   - Know who supports and who opposes.
4. How can I communicate with my elected officials?
   - Sign petitions.
   - Write a letter to your legislator.
   - Phone/fax your legislator's office.
   - Write a letter to the editor (contact local editors).
   - Visit your legislator's office.

Reprinted with permission from the Suicide Prevention Action Network USA (SPAN USA).

I am convinced that we are winning the war against stigma, and my belief is crystallized when I see the many talented and bright young women and men currently pursuing careers in the health sciences. Some are drawn to neuroscience and brain research, or to laboratories in the psychological sciences investigating treatments for anxiety and depressive disorders. Others are studying medicine, nursing, occupational therapy, or social work with a goal of treating mentally ill children and adults. Still others have been jolted by suicide in their personal or professional lives, and want to focus their research and clinical skills on preventing more tragic deaths. But what is most impressive is that these young people are not judgmental, and are able to stand up to peers who may question their decision to help an often marginalized group of citizens.

My hope soars and my eyes glisten when I attend meetings of the National Alliance on Mental Illness (NAMI) and listen to the personal testimonials from folks of all walks of life who speak openly about their struggles with suicidal thinking, attempts, and injuries. At national conferences and public forums on suicide, I am also moved by the stories of people who tell about the life and death of a gifted daughter, a son who was a star athlete, a father who was the mayor of his hometown, a mother who loved and embraced life more than anyone could imagine. The experiences of these survivors not only touch us deeply but also help us to come to terms with our own grief and loss.

The more we learn about the mysteries of suicide, the less confused and frightened we will be. It has been said that if you can change people's thinking, their hearts will follow. Yes, we can make a difference. A big difference.

Carla:

Some of the finest people I have ever known devote their energy and time to doing everything they can to try to eradicate the stigma associated with suicide. Many work on the grassroots level: They organize support groups in their communities; they give talks to raise public consciousness about suicide at schools, houses of worship, and local businesses; they take the time to reach out to others who have lost a loved one to suicide on an intimate and one-to-one basis. Others are involved with national and international organizations that are committed to suicide prevention through the support and funding of innovative programs, scientific research, and educational outreach.

As a survivor, I know personally that the stigma of suicide is often deep within ourselves. During the months that I covered up the truth about Harry's suicide, I carried around a secret that I found both shameful and surreal. Telling the truth and accepting the manner in which my husband died gave me the freedom to begin to accept what had happened and reflect on how it would shape me and define my future.

I am so proud to meet other survivors and to learn about their loved ones, to ask them for directions and help, and to offer, in return, whatever insights I have gathered throughout my journey. I learn something new from every survivor I meet, and am guided by every story I hear. Stigmas are marks imposed on us by misinformation and ignorance; once we cast them off, we can begin to protect ourselves from the misperceptions and prejudgments of others, and be proud of who we have become.

Conclusion

Breaking the Silence, Easing the Pain

Suicide touches people's lives across generations, creating an unparalleled legacy of unanswered questions, sadness, and loss. Millions of us are affected by suicide each year, and we are changed forever. As the taboo surrounding death by suicide begins to fade and enlightened understanding of this topic replaces misconceptions and myths, we will not only begin to save more lives but also ease the heartache of those who have been left behind.

Whether you have lost a loved one to suicide or have experienced self-destructive thoughts yourself, it's important to keep in mind that you are not alone: Every 18 minutes, someone in the United States kills himself or herself—every 40 seconds worldwide—setting off a ripple effect of guilt and uncertainty that touches family, friends, and colleagues. As suicide becomes increasingly identified—and treated—as a public health problem instead of an unexplained mystery or mortal sin, new means of preventing it and understanding its impact are constantly being discovered.

Healing after suicide is all about the day-by-day, minute-by-minute. You may never understand the reason for your loved one's death or actions; you may now doubt all that you once held to be true; your faith may be shaken, and your life upended. Yet, there are roads you can travel, paths you can navigate, shoulders you can lean on, and actions you can take to make your journey one of hope and not of despair.

Our mission in writing this book is to speak candidly about suicide, a subject that for too long has been disregarded and unmentioned in our society. The real voices of people whom we interviewed, and others whose identities we have disguised, are gifts to all of us. Each one of their stories is both unique and universal, and creates a kinship and bond that helps ease our feelings of separateness and isolation.

Throughout the book, we pose many questions—some without answers—with the goal of clarifying confusion about suicidal behavior and thinking. Having someone's actions explained is not the same as defending those actions, and approval or acceptance is not a prerequisite for forgiveness and rebuilding your life. We do hope, however, that the information and insights we offer—from our combined and different perspectives of survivor and mental health professional—will help you with your hurt, your sorrow, and your continuing steps to healing.

Our book has another purpose that goes beyond its content. It is confirmation that you are not alone and never need to feel alone with your loss. You may even find some calm in the physicality of the book itself, and think of it as a conduit and link to other members of our global community. It is our hope that *Touched by Suicide* continues to speak to you throughout the years, and that you gain comfort from our efforts long after you have put the book away. We are all family now, including those who are no longer with us.

Appendix A: Resource Directory

Most of these organizations and Web sites have links to other relevant resources and information.

For Immediate Help

National Suicide Prevention Lifeline
1-800-273-TALK (8255)
www.suicidepreventionlifeline.org

Organizations

American Association of Suicidology (AAS)
5221 Wisconsin Avenue, NW
Washington, DC 20015
202-237-2280
www.suicidology.org

American Foundation for Suicide Prevention (AFSP)
120 Wall Street
New York, NY 10005
888-333-AFSP (2377)
www.afsp.org
Both AAS and AFSP have a complete listing of survivor support groups throughout the United States and Canada.

American Psychiatric Association
1000 Wilson Boulevard, Suite 1825
Arlington, VA 22209-3901
703-907-7300
www.psych.org

Baton Rouge Crisis Intervention Center
4837 Revere Avenue
Baton Rouge, LA 70806
225-924-1431
www.brcic.org

National Alliance on Mental Illness (NAMI)
Colonial Place Three
2107 Wilson Blvd., Suite 300
Arlington, VA 22201-3042
703-524-7600
www.nami.org

National Organization for People of Color Against Suicide (NOPCAS)
4715 Sargent Road, NE
Washington, DC 20017
202-549-6039
www.nopcas.com

Organization for Attempters and Survivors of Suicide in Interfaith
Services (OASSIS)
101 King Farm Blvd., #D401
Rockville, MD 20850
240-632-0335
www.oassis.org

Suicide Awareness Voices of Education (SAVE)
9001 E. Bloomington Fwy., Suite 150
Bloomington, MN 55420
952-946-7998
www.save.org

Suicide Prevention Action Network USA (SPAN USA)
1025 Vermont Avenue, NW, Suite 1066
Washington, DC 20005
202-449-3600
www.spanusa.org

The Link Counseling Center
348 Mt. Vernon Highway
Atlanta, GA 30328-4139
404-256-9797
www.thelink.org

Web Sites

American Psychiatric Association and the American Academy of Child and Adolescent Psychiatry, "Guide for parents regarding medication for depression in children and adolescents."
www.parentsmedguide.org

American Psychological Association
www.apa.org

Befrienders Worldwide
www.befrienders.org

Canadian Association for Suicide Prevention (CASP)
www.suicideprevention.ca

Canadian Psychiatric Association
www.cpa-apc.org

Canadian Psychological Association
www.cpa.ca

Centre for Suicide Prevention
www.suicideinfo.ca

Clinician Survivor Task Force of AAS
www.suicidology.org

Columbia University TeenScreen Program
www.teenscreen.org

Compassionate Friends
www.compassionatefriends.org

Depression After Delivery
www.depressionafterdelivery.com

ePrevent: Suicide
www.eprevent.com

Fierce Goodbye: A Faith-Based Perspective on Suicide
www.fiercegoodbye.com

Gay/Lesbian/Bisexual/Transgender Suicide
www.lambda.org

Geriatric Mental Health Foundation
www.gmhfonline.org

Health, Mental Health, and Safety Guidelines for Schools
www.nationalguidelines.org

Jed Foundation
www.jedfoundation.org

Kristin Brooks Hope Center National Hopeline Network
www.hopeline.com

Lifekeeper Memory Quilt
www.lifekeeper.org

National Center for Injury Prevention and Control
Centers for Disease Control and Prevention (CDC)
U.S. Department of Health and Human Services
www.cdc.gov/ncipc

National Institute of Mental Health (NIMH)
www.nimh.nih.gov

National Mental Health Association
www.nmha.org

National Women's Health Information Center
U.S. Department of Health and Human Services
www.womenshealth.gov

Office on Women's Health
www.4women.gov/owh/about/index.htm

Postpartum Support International
www.postpartum.net

Preventing Suicide Network
www.preventingsuicide.com

Provincial Suicide Prevention Resource Center
www.suicideinformation.ca

Samaritans
www.samaritansnyc.org

Substance Abuse and Mental Health Services Administration
(SAMHSA)
U.S. Department of Health and Human Services
www.samhsa.gov

Suicide Prevention Resource Center (SPRC)
www.sprc.org

Tears of a Cop
www.tearsofacop.com

Yellow Ribbon Suicide Prevention Program
www.yellowribbon.org

Suggested Reading

AFSP. *Surviving a Suicide Loss: A Financial Guide*. 2004. www.afsp.org

Allen, Jon G. *Coping with Trauma: Hope Through Understanding*. Second Edition. American Psychiatric Publishing, 2005.

Bolton, Iris with Curtis Mitchell. *My Son, My Son: A Guide to Healing after Death, Loss, or Suicide*. Bolton Press, Atlanta, 1983.

Calgary Health Region. *Hope and Healing Guide*. 2002. www.hope-andhealingguide.com

Cammarata, Doreen. *Someone I Love Died by Suicide: A Story for Child Survivors and Those Who Care for Them*. Grief Guidance, Inc., 2000.

Casey, Nell. *Unholy Ghost: Writers on Depression*. William Morrow, 2001.

Churn, Rev. Arlene. *The End Is Just the Beginning: Lessons in Grieving for African Americans*. Harlem Moon/Broadway Books, 2003.

Clemons, James T. *Children of Jonah: Personal Stories by Survivors of Suicide Attempts*. Capital Books, 2001.

———*What Does the Bible Say about Suicide?* Parthenon Press, 1990.

Coleman, Penny. *PTSD, Sucide and the Lessons of War*. Beacon Press, 2006.

Collins, Judy. *Sanity and Grace: A Journey of Suicide, Survival, and Strength*. Tarcher/Penguin, 2003.

Des Pres, Terrence. *The Survivor: An Anatomy of Life in the Death Camps*. Oxford University Press, 1976.

Didion, Joan. *The Year of Magical Thinking*. Knopf, 2005.

Dougy Center for Grieving Children. *After a Suicide: A Workbook for Grieving Kids.* Dougy Center, 2001.

Dunne, Edward J., John L. McIntosh, and Karen Dunne-Maxim. *Suicide and Its Aftermath: Understanding and Counseling the Survivors.* W.W. Norton & Company, 1987.

Etkind, Marc. *. . . Or Not to Be: A Collection of Suicide Notes.* Riverhead Trade, 1997.

Farr, Moira. *After Daniel: A Suicide Survivor's Tale.* HarperCollins, 1999.

Fine, Carla. *No Time to Say Goodbye: Surviving the Suicide of a Loved One.* Main Street Books, 1999.

Gray, Spalding. *Life Interrupted: The Unfinished Monologue.* Crown Publishers, 2005.

Griffith Gail. *Will's Choice: A Suicidal Teen, a Desperate Mother, and a Chronicle of Recovery.* HarperCollins, 2005.

Groopman, Jerome. *The Anatomy of Hope: How People Prevail in the Face of Illness.* Random House, 2004.

Hartley, Mariette and Anne Commire. *Breaking the Silence.* G. P. Putnam's Sons, 1988.

Hendin, Herbert. *Suicide in America.* W. W. Norton & Company, 1995.

Jamison, Kay Redfield. *An Unquiet Mind: A Memoir of Moods and Madness.* Vintage Books, 1997.

————*Night Falls Fast: Understanding Suicide.* Vintage Books, 2000.

Joiner, Thomas. *Why People Die by Suicide.* Harvard University Press, 2006.

Lipsyte, Robert. *In the Country of Illness: Comfort and Advice for the Journey*. Knopf, 1998.

Livingston, Gordon. *Too Soon Old, Too Late Smart: Thirty True Things You Need to Know*. Marlowe & Company, 2004.

McIntosh, John. "The Suicide of Older Men and Women: How You Can Help Prevent Tragedy." American Association of Suicidology, 2001.

Poussaint, Alvin F. and Amy Alexander. *Lay My Burden Down: Suicide and the Mental Health Crisis among African-Americans*. Beacon Press, 2000.

Risenhoover, C. C. *The Suicide Lawyers: Exposing Lethal Secrets*. Kiamichi House, 2004.

Rivers, Joan. *Bouncing Back: I've Survived Everything . . . and I Mean Everything . . . and You Can Too!* HarperCollins, 1997.

Rynearson, Edward K. *Retelling Violent Death*. Brunner-Routledge, 2001.

Shneidman, Edwin S. *Autopsy of a Suicidal Mind*. Oxford University Press, 2004.

———*The Suicidal Mind*. Oxford University Press, 1996.

Solomon, Andrew. *The Noonday Demon: An Atlas of Depression*. Scribner, 2001.

Steel, Danielle. *His Bright Light: The Story of Nick Traina*. Delacorte Press, 1998.

Styron, William. *Darkness Visible: A Memoir of Madness*. Random House, 1990.

Vanderbilt, Gloria. *A Mother's Story*. Knopf, 1996.

Weiner, Kayla Miriyam, editor. *Therapeutic and Legal Issues for Therapists Who Have Survived a Client Suicide*. The Haworth Press, 2004.

Werth, J. L., Jr. and D. Blevins. *Psychological Issues Near the End of Life: A Resource for Professional Care Providers*. American Psychological Association, 2006.

Wrobleski, A., and D. Reidenberg. *Suicide: Why? 85 Questions and Answers*, Third Edition. SAVE (Suicide Awareness Voices of Education), 2005.

Appendix B: Bibliography

Books

American Psychiatric Association. *Diagnostic and Statistical Manual of Mental Disorders*. Fourth Edition. American Psychiatric Publishing, 1994.

————*Practice Guideline for the Assessment and Treatment of Patients with Suicidal Behaviors*. American Psychiatric Publishing, 2003.

Barnes, Donna Holland and Gray Ekwenzi. *Crossroads: Suicide Stories of Two Black Males*. Work in progress.

Campbell, Frank. *The Canyon of Why: Healing Metaphors for Survivors of Suicide*. Work in progress.

Clemons, James T. *What Does the Bible Say about Suicide?* Parthenon Press, 1990.

Des Pres, Terrence. *The Survivor: An Anatomy of Life in the Death Camps*. Oxford University Press, 1976.

Dunne, Edward J., John L. McIntosh, and Karen Dunne-Maxim. *Suicide and Its Aftermath: Understanding and Counseling the Survivors*. W. W. Norton & Company, 1987.

Etkind, Marc. *. . . Or Not to Be: A Collection of Suicide Notes*. Riverhead Trade, 1997.

Fine, Carla. *No Time to Say Goodbye: Surviving the Suicide of a Loved One*. Main Street Books, 1999.

Foley, Kathleen and Herbert Hendin. *The Case Against Assisted Suicide: For the Right to End-of-Life Care*. Johns Hopkins Press, 2002.

Hendin, Herbert. *Seduced by Death: Doctors, Patients, and the Dutch Cure*. W. W. Norton & Company, 1997.

———*Suicide in America*. W.W. Norton & Company, 1995.

Hendin, Herbert and J. John Mann, editors. *The Clinical Science of Suicide Prevention*. Annals of the New York Academy of Sciences, Volume 932. 2001.

Jamison, Kay Redfield. *An Unquiet Mind: A Memoir of Moods and Madness*. Vintage Books, 1997.

———*Night Falls Fast: Understanding Suicide*. Vintage Books, 2000.

Johnson, M., et al., editors. *The Cambridge Handbook of Age and Ageing*. Chapter, "The Psychology of Death," by Robert Neimeyer and James Werth. Cambridge University Press, 2004.

Livingston, Gordon. *Too Soon Old, Too Late Smart: Thirty True Things You Need to Know*. Marlowe & Company, 2004.

Risenhoover, C. C. *The Suicide Lawyers: Exposing Lethal Secrets*. Kiamichi House, 2004.

Rynearson, Edward K. *Retelling Violent Death*. Brunner-Routledge, 2001.

Rynearson, Edward, ed. *Violent Death: Resilience and Intervention Beyond the Crisis*. Routledge, 2006.

Shahrokh, Narriman and Robert Hales. *American Psychiatric Glossary*. Eighth Edition. American Psychiatric Publishing, 2003.

Shneidman, Edwin S. *Autopsy of a Suicidal Mind*. Oxford University Press, 2004.

Simeon, Daphne and Eric Hollander. *Self-Injurious Behaviors: Assessment and Treatment*. American Psychiatric Publishing, 2001.

Simon, Robert I. *Assessing and Managing Suicide Risk: Guidelines for Clinically Based Risk Management*. American Psychiatric Publishing, 2004.

Solomon, Andrew. *The Noonday Demon: An Atlas of Depression*. Scribner, 2001.

Periodicals

"After-the-Baby-Blues." MetroPlus Health Plan, New York, NY, 2005.

Alexander, David A., Susan Klein, and Nicola Gray. "Suicide by Patients: Questionnaire Study of Its Effect on Consultant Psychiatrists." *British Medical Journal*. June 10, 2000.

Barber, Catherine. "Fatal Connection: The Link Between Guns and Suicide." *Advancing Suicide Prevention*. July/August 2005.

Bridge, Jeffrey, Barbe Remy, and David Brent. Datapoints: "Recent Trends in Suicide among U.S. Adolescent Males, 1992–2001." *Psychiatric Services*. May 2005.

Curwen, Thomas, "His Work is Still Full of Life." *Los Angeles Times*. June 5, 2004.

Dervic, Kanita, Maria Oquendo, Michael Grunebaum, et al. "Religious Affiliation and Suicide Attempt." *American Journal of Psychiatry*. December 2004.

"Ending Their Lives, in Control." Letters to the Editor. *The New York Times*. January 15, 2002.

Foster, T. "Suicide Note Themes and Suicide Prevention." *International Journal of Psychiatry in Medicine*. April 2003.

Glass, Richard. "Is Grief a Disease? Sometimes." *Journal of the American Medical Association*. June 1, 2005.

Goode, Erica. "And Still, Echoes of a Death Long Past: Doctors Now Focus on the Families Left Behind by Suicide." *The New York Times*. October 28, 2003.

———"Patient Suicide Brings Therapists Lasting Pain." *The New York Times*. January 16, 2001.

"Grief After Suicide: Notes from the Literature on Qualitative Differences and Stigma." SIEC Current Awareness Bulletin, ISSN: 08340-8340. 2002.

Grossman, David, et al. "Gun Storage Practices and Risk of Youth Suicide and Unintentional Firearm Injuries." *Journal of the American Medical Association*. February 9, 2005.

Hendin, Herbert, Ann Haas, John Maltsberger, et al. "Factors Contributing to Therapists' Distress after the Suicide of a Patient." *American Journal of Psychiatry*. August 2004.

Hendin, Herbert, Alan Lipschitz, John Maltsberger, et al. "Therapists' Reactions to Patients' Suicides." *American Journal of Psychiatry*. December 2000.

Ho, T.P., P.S. Yip, C.W. Chiu, et al. "Suicide Notes: What Do They Tell Us?" *Acta Psychiatr Scand*. December 1998.

Hubert, Cynthia. "Farewell Gesture: Suicide Notes Rarely Yield Adequate Answers." *The Sacramento Bee*. January 24, 2004.

Joe, Sean and Mark Kaplan. "Firearm-Related Suicide among Young African-American Males." *Psychiatric Services*. March 2002.

Kellermann, Arthur, et al. "Suicide in the Home in Relation to Gun Ownership." *New England Journal of Medicine*. August 13, 1992.

Kenyon, Sue and Marsha Norton. "Hard Issues Faced by Child Survivors." Baton Rouge Crisis Intervention Center. 2005.

Kessler, Ronald C., et al. "Trends in Suicide Ideation, Plans, Gestures, and Attempts in the United States, 1990–1992 to 2001–2003." *Journal of the American Medical Association*. May 25, 2005.

Ketter, William B. "Death and Self-censorship." *The Eagle-Tribune*. Andover, MA. August 15, 2004.

Lehmann, Christine. "Military Ratchets Up Effort to Prevent Suicide." *Psychiatric News*. American Psychiatric Association. December 17, 2004.

Litts, David and Suicide Prevention Resource Center. "After a Suicide: Recommendations for Religious Services and Other Public Memorial Observances." Newton, MA: Education Development Center, Inc., 2004.

Mann, J. John, Alan Apter, and Jose Bertolote, et al. "Suicide Prevention Strategies: A Systematic Review." *Journal of the American Medical Association*. October 26, 2005.

Mann, J. John, Christine Waternaux, and Gretchen Haas, et al. "Toward a Clinical Model of Suicidal Behavior in Psychiatric Patients." *American Journal of Psychiatry*. February 1999.

Maris, Ronald. "Suicide." *The Lancet*. July 27, 2002.

Marzuk, Peter, Kenneth Tardiff, and Charles Hirsch. "The Epidemiology of Murder-Suicide." *Journal of the American Medical Association*. June 17, 1992.

"More Global Death through Suicide than War and Murder: WHO." AFP News Agency. September 8, 2004.

Murphy, SL. "Deaths: Final Data for 1998." *National Vital Statistics Reports*. 2000.

Rimer, Sara. "With Suicide, an Admiral Keeps Command Until the End." *The New York Times*. January 12, 2002.

Rogers, James. "Theoretical Grounding: The 'Missing Link' in Suicide Research." *Journal of Counseling and Development*. Winter, 2001.

Rogers, James and Carla Fine. "The Search for Meaning of Suicide— A Scientist and Survivor Seek Common Ground." AAS Newslink. Spring, 2003.

Rosack, Jim. "FDA Tones Down Warning on Use of Antidepressants in Children." *Psychiatric News*. March 4, 2005.

Shear Katherine, Ellen Frank, Patricia Houck, et al. "Treatment of Complicated Grief." *Journal of the American Medical Association*. June 1, 2005.

Smith, Dinitia. "Evolving Answers to the Why of Suicide; Is It a Medical Problem? A Moral or Social Failure? An Assertion of Freedom?" *The New York Times*. July 31, 1999.

"Suicidal Thoughts Among Youths Aged 12 to 17 with Major Depressive Episode." The National Survey on Drug Use and Health Report. SAMHSA. September 9, 2005.

"The Surgeon General's Call to Action to Prevent Suicide." U.S. Public Health Service. Washington, DC. 1999.

"The Surgeon General's National Strategy for Suicide Prevention: Goals and Objectives for Action." U.S. Public Health Service. Rockville, Maryland. 2001.

Web Site Articles

Fawcett, Jan. "Suicide and bipolar disorder." Medscape. August 12, 2005. www.medscape.com

Fine, Carla and Michael Myers. "Suicide Survivors: Tips for Health Professionals." Medscape. September 17, 2003. www.medscape.com

Hendin, Herbert. "Suicide, Assisted Suicide, and Euthanasia: The Netherlands and Oregon." www.afsp.org

Kennedy, Robert. "Familial suicidal behavior: A newsmaker interview with Maria Oquendo, M.D.," Medscape. February 12, 2004. www.medscape.com

Myers, Michael and Carla Fine. "Suicide in Physicians: Toward Prevention." Medscape. October 21, 2003. www.medscape.com

"Recognizing Postpartum Depression." National Mental Health Association. 2003. www.nmha.org

Tondo, Leonardo and Ross Baldessarini. "Suicide: Historical, Descriptive, and Epidemiological Considerations." Medscape. March 15, 2001. www.medscape.com

Index

abnormal grief, 24
acceptance of death, 24
adolescents. *See* youth
adventuring, 229
advice in suicide notes, 67
advocacy organizations. *See also specific organizations*
  described, 269
  and family relations, 105
  participation in, 156, 262, 265
  and stigma of suicide, 267
African-American community, 224, 266
aggressive behavior, 141
agitation
  and impulsivity, 59
  and repeated suicide attempts, 248
  as warning sign, 42, 44, 54
alcohol. *See also* substance abuse
  and depression, 50, 51
  and family relations, 110, 122
  and gender differences in grieving, 107
  and genetic components of suicide, 49
  and impulsivity, 58
  and mental illness, 144
  and police suicides, 156
  and reasons behind suicides, 50–53
  and repeated suicide attempts, 248

  as risk factor, 41, 42, 248, 254
  and stress responses, 84–85
  and suicidal thinking, 254
  as warning sign, 44
  and youth, 140
alienation, 18, 175. *See also* isolation
American Academy of Child and Adolescent Psychiatry, 277
American Academy of Grief Counseling, 195, 197
American Association for Marriage and Family Therapy, 196, 197
American Association for Pastoral Counseling, 197
American Association of Suicidology (AAS)
  contact information, 275
  credentialing, 196
  on depression, 41
  hotline for therapist survivors, 214
  on prevention of suicide, 261–62
  on responding to threats of suicide, 86
  on support groups, 180
  on warning signs, 42, 44
American Foundation for Suicide Prevention (AFSP)
  contact information, 275
  credentialing, 196–97

prevalence of suicide, 175, 249, 260, 273
Preventing Suicide Network, 279
prevention of suicide, 261–62, 263–65.
  See also advocacy organizations
privacy
  and high-profile suicides, 160
  and planning a suicide, 64
  and public nature of suicides, 77,
    148–49
  and reactions from friends, 166
  and secrecy, 21–22
  and seeking support, 177
  of therapy, 194
productivity, 192
professional and work relationships,
  89–90
protecting the deceased, 21
Provincial Suicide Prevention Resource
  Center, 279
psychache, 26
psychiatric facilities, 209–10
psychiatry and psychiatrists. *See also*
  therapy and therapists
  and fears of going crazy, 15
  and hospitalization, 210
  and medications, 196
  role of, 195
psychology and psychologists. *See also*
  therapy and therapists
    psychological components of depres-
      sion, 45
    and religion, 224
    role of, 195, 196
psychosis, 14–15
psychotherapy. *See* therapy and therapists
public awareness about suicide, 261–62,
  263
public nature of suicides, 77, 148–49,
  160–64

questions of survivors, 10
quilt panels, 267

rational suicides, 37, 243
reasons for suicides
  anger and revenge, 60–62
  assigning blame, 39–41
  bipolar illness, 47–48
  depression, 41–47
  existential distress, 62–63
  genetic components of suicide, 48–49
  impulsivity, 58–60
  medical conditions, 55–57

and methods of suicide, 63–65
  Real Voices, 36, 46, 49, 61, 70
  resolution after suicides, 69–71
  searching for understanding, 36–39
  substance abuse, 50–53
  suicide notes, 65–69
  unknown reasons for suicides, 54–55
recklessness, 44
Reed, Jerry, 262
Reiss, Harry, 2, 9–12
relationships. *See also* family; friends and
  acquaintances; marriage
    and alcoholism, 50–51
    breakups, 37–38, 58, 159
    dating, 32, 37–38, 107
    loss of, 51
    people affected by suicides, 97, 175
    professional and work relationships,
      89–90
    unhealthy relationships, 88–91
religion and religious survivors
  and afterlife of deceased, 92, 223, 225
  and anger at God, 223, 225, 229
  and child survivors, 128, 139
  and explanations for suicides, 230
  and faith of survivors, 220–22, 224
  and funerals, 223, 226, 228
  and grieving process, 28
  and healing rituals, 116–17, 228
  and pastoral counselors, 196, 221, 225
  prayer, 225–26
  Real Voices, 229
  religious needs of survivors, 87
  and seeking support, 187
  "sin" of suicide, 223, 225
remembering deceased in families, 115
research, 261, 265, 267
resentment, 193. *See also* anger
resolution after suicides, 69–71
restlessness, 60, 151
Retelling Violent Death (Rynearson), 14
revenge, 44, 60–62
risk factors for suicide. *See also specific
  risk factors, such as* subtance abuse
    identifying, 42, 237
    public awareness of, 263
    and suicide prevention, 264
Rogers, Cynthia, 65
Rogers, James, 235
role-play, 68
romanticizing suicide, 162–63
Russo, Kathie, 49, 130
Rynearson, Edward
  on change, 14